UNDER THE SAME MOON

D1615359

Edna Longley

UNDER THE SAME MOON

Edward Thomas and the
English Lyric

ENITHARMON PRESS

First published in 2017
by Enitharmon Press
10 Bury Place
London WC1A 2JL

www.enitharmon.co.uk

Distributed in the UK by
Central Books
50 Freshwater Road
Chadwell Heath, RM8 1RX

Distributed in the USA and Canada
by Independent Publishers Group
814 North Franklin Street
Chicago, IL 60610
USA
www.ipgbooks.com

ISBN: 978-1-911253-14-3

British Library Cataloguing-in-Publication Data.
A catalogue record for this book is available
from the British Library.

Designed in Albertina by Libanus Press
and printed in Wales by
Gomer Press

CONTENTS

ACKNOWLEDGEMENTS

I am grateful to Stephen Stuart-Smith for suggesting that I should write this book, and to Daniel Roberts for help with Chapter 2. I am also grateful to Alison Harvey, Special Collections and Archives, Cardiff University Library. Chapter 3 began as a lecture to the English Association conference, 'British Poetry of the First World War', at Wadham College, Oxford, in September 2014. An earlier version of Chapter 4 appeared in *Literary Imagination* 16, 2 (2014), and of Chapter 5 in *Letter Writing Among Poets*, edited by Jonathan Ellis (Edinburgh: Edinburgh University Press, 2015). Poems and extracts from poems by Robert Frost are reprinted by permission of Henry Holt and Company, LLC. Extracts from Robert Graves, *The Complete Poems* (2000), are reprinted by permission of The Trustees of the Robert Graves Copyright Trust and Carcanet Press Ltd. 'Wants' by Philip Larkin is reprinted by permission of the Estate of Philip Larkin, Faber and Faber Ltd, and Farrar, Straus and Giroux, LLC.

———

Note: Bracketed numbers in the text are the page numbers of poems in Edward Thomas, *The Annotated Collected Poems*, ed. Edna Longley (Tarset: Bloodaxe Books, 2008).

Preface

On 9 April 1917 Edward Thomas was killed in the Battle of Arras. A hundred years after his death, Thomas's reputation has never been higher. That says something about the power and complexity of his poetry, its long reach into the century ahead. 'The English lyric' can mean (and sometimes does in this book) the entire body of poetry in the English language. But, for Thomas, 'lyrical impulse' is the heart of that body. Thomas wrote lyric poems; he thought deeply about the traditions and future of poetry in English; and 'a few most English poems' defined his sense of what was culturally at stake in the Great War. He also saw that 'the myriad-minded lyric' is a slippery genre.[1] Like Thomas himself, it resists being pinned down. In each chapter I will approach the relation between Thomas and lyric from a different angle, sometimes an angle that involves other poets. I will start with the extraordinary fact that Thomas was a prose-writer and poetry critic who, in December 1914, aged thirty-six, began to write poems. The war (he enlisted in July 1915) and the influence of Robert Frost played incalculable parts in his metamorphosis.

Over the years, poets and poetry-lovers have done more than academic criticism to advance Thomas's reputation. His poetry often falls outside literary-historical narratives and critical categories. Elusiveness may be intrinsic to its nature, but timing has been a factor too. Thomas's two collections, *Poems* (1917) and *Last Poems* (1918), were published after his death, when his pre-war literary context was also dead, when there was no critical backup to launch his poetry into the post-war era. It then took years for Thomas to be considered a 'war poet': not that attempts at classification should stop there. In Chapter 3, I argue that his poetry obliges us to rethink that category; and also to rethink the contribution of Great War poetry to modern poetry. Further, like Frost, Thomas was sidelined by the 'modernist' paradigm, which came to dominate academic study of twentieth-century literature. Thus, despite belonging profoundly to its historical moment and prophetically to our own, Thomas's poetry never quite caught up with itself. He remained an oddly isolated figure, if always important to poets and common readers. Of course, paradigms shift. For instance, Thomas has latterly been embraced by eco-criticism (although he got there first). But perhaps all critics of Thomas's poetry, as of poetry in general, should heed his warning in *Maurice Maeterlinck* (1911):

> Whatever be the subject, the poem must not depend for its main effect upon anything outside itself except the humanity of the reader. It may please for the moment by the aid of some irrelevant and transitory interest – political interest, for example; but, sooner or later, it will be left naked and solitary, and will so be judged, and if it does not create about itself a world of its own it is condemned to endure the death which is its element … Anything, however small, may make a poem; nothing, however great, is certain to.[2]

Alongside the welcome Selected Edition of his *Prose Writings*,[3] recent studies have opened up Thomas's literary context. Matthew Hollis's *Now All Roads Lead to France* (2011) illuminates his last years, with reference to the poetry circles of that day; and Jean Moorcroft Wilson has published an indispensable biography: *Edward Thomas: From Adlestrop to Arras* (2015). Every student of Thomas is in her debt. Yet context can clutter, if Thomas's poetry does not lead the way. Hollis almost seems to lack confidence in Thomas since he surrounds him with so many other figures: not only Frost, but also the poets usually lumped together as 'Georgian' or sub-grouped as 'Dymock poets' owing to their ties with Gloucestershire: poets like Wilfrid Gibson and John Masefield. Hollis even tells us about T. S. Eliot

(whom Thomas never met) coming to London. Thomas's posterity
sometimes gets cluttered too. His status as a 'poets' poet' proves his
quality; but not when tribute-poems bury him beneath inadequate
wreaths or when he is turned into a sentimental icon, praised for
'his affectionate perception of little-regarded things', 'artless simplic-
ity of utterance'. This is not what Thomas means by 'Anything,
however small, may make a poem'. Thankfully, such attitudes have
become rarer. Poet-contributors to *Branch-Lines: Edward Thomas and
Contemporary Poetry* (2007) salute the 'almost epic scale of Thomas's
small poems'; 'the extraordinarily developed technique of his verse';
'a great critical, as well as poetic, intelligence of the twentieth
century'.[4] Among the poets who have admired Thomas, and learned
from him, are W. H. Auden, Ted Hughes and Seamus Heaney. In
Chapter 5, I discuss some lyric parallels between Thomas and Philip
Larkin; and my Afterword argues that Thomas occupies a special
position in the network of modern 'Anglo-Celtic' poetic relations.
Here again 'English' means English-language. To quote Heaney:
'Ulster was British, but with no rights on/ The English lyric'.[5]

Like (or with) the English lyric, Thomas slips across national
borders. In *Edward Thomas and World Literary Studies* (2013) Andrew
Webb criticises the stress often placed on Thomas's 'Englishness'. He
contends that 'an historical and continuing Anglocentrism within
British literary studies' has repressed Thomas's 'Welshness', thereby
obscuring the 'transnational' significance of his work.[6] Webb's
argument adjusts an imbalance and may position Thomas globally,
but does not strictly centre on poetry. As regards aesthetic politics,
the US has done more than British literary studies to repress Thomas.
My chapter on Thomas and Frost argues that American poetic
nationalism, in 'modernist' and other guises, has marginalised their
conjoined legacy (picked up, nonetheless, by poets). It's relevant that
critical modernism usually fails to accommodate W. B. Yeats's
formal differences from Eliot and Ezra Pound. In my book *Yeats and
Modern Poetry* (2013) I align Thomas with Yeats and Wallace Stevens
as poets who, by way of Symbolism, remade Romantic aesthetics for

the modern world. Thomas's definition of poetry, quoted above, is essentially Symbolist in excluding everything that is not poetry. Because his poems are so multi-layered, some will turn up in more than one chapter here.

Thomas supported himself and his family by constantly writing reviews (over a hundred in some years); also by writing country books, such as *The Heart of England* (1906), and literary studies like *Maurice Maeterlinck*. He lived in the countryside – from 1906, he rented houses in or near the Hampshire village of Steep – but could never escape contemporary Grub Street. He was often exhausted, sometimes clinically depressed and even suicidal, always artistically dissatisfied with his serious prose-works. Reviewing, in particular, ground him down. Yet Thomas's critical as well as creative prose underlies his poetry – because of his commitment to poetry. He reviewed other kinds of book too, but was mainly a poetry reviewer, and mainly for two newspapers: the *Daily Chronicle* and *Morning Post*. His opportunity to review poetry so copiously (the *Chronicle* had a daily literary page) shames the sparse newspaper coverage of poetry today. Even so, Thomas lamented the lack of good poetry criticism: both in the emergent literary academy, on which he kept a wary eye, and in the belles-lettres sector of literary journalism. Perhaps this is to say that, between 1900 and 1914, Thomas was an unwitting poet-critic as well as unwitting poet. Indeed, he distinguishes between criticism based on 'pure intelligence' and the insights generated by enthusiasm: 'The difference is as the difference between a man going about with a lantern in a dark wood, and a man sitting afar off and seeing it in the glimpses of the moon.'[7] This book draws on reviews that show Thomas thinking intensively about poetry in ways that few poets have done – certainly not before the event. His critical 'glimpses of the moon' include reviews of editions and reprints, from *Beowulf* onwards. Chapter 2 connects Thomas's writings on the Romantic poets with how his poetry 'remixes' their work. It's odd that Eliot and Pound are supposed to have extended poetry's reading-list: Thomas had read everything, although he distrusted bookishness. He was an astute judge of translations from classical poetry. He reviewed works translated from oriental and European languages. Thomas's criticism helps us to see that, far from being isolated, his poetry is a kind of hub, with many roads running to and from it. For Robert Crawford, it 'sends out a ripple that never stops, a resonance that quietly crosses oceans and continents'.[8]

Other poets too, and other readers, seem curiously haunted by Thomas's poetry. One reason may be its own haunting by earlier poetry; another, its unobtrusive aesthetic force. This is art that conceals art, form that conceals form. Like poems by Yeats and Stevens, Thomas's poems often involve reflexive self-commentary. They are Symbolist in their tendency to be (partly) about poetry itself. One such poem is 'The sun used to shine', from which my book takes its title:

> The sun used to shine while we two walked
> Slowly together, paused and started
> Again, and sometimes mused, sometimes talked
> As either pleased, and cheerfully parted
>
> Each night. We never disagreed
> Which gate to rest on. The to be
> And the late past we gave small heed.
> We turned from men or poetry
>
> To rumours of the war remote … (122)

'We two' are Thomas and Frost. Written in May 1916, the poem recalls August 1914 when the poets spent time together in rural Gloucestershire.

All poems of love or friendship are ultimately elegiac. But here, given Thomas's chances of dying in a war now less 'remote', elegy enters the poetic foreground. 'Used' already tinges retrospect with valediction. Later, the sun itself vanishes when 'Pale purple' crocuses call up 'sunless Hades fields'. This provisional elegy covers literary as well as personal friendship. Talk about 'poetry' encodes the larger conversation between Frost and Thomas, without which the poem might not exist. 'Talk' itself encodes their common aesthetic ground, phrased by Thomas as 'absolute fidelity to the postures which the voice assumes in the most expressive intimate speech'.[9] 'The sun used to shine', in which talking and walking kinetically combine, in which sentence over-rides line and stanza, affirms as well as manifests 'fidelity' to speech. The poem's movement also seems bound up with the movement of history from 1914 to 1916. Its last three quatrains add to the temporal and rhythmic complexity by undergoing a shift of tense and consciousness, a shift from sun to moon:

> Everything
> To faintness like those rumours fades –
> Like the brook's water glittering
>
> Under the moonlight – like those walks
> Now – like us two that took them, and
> The fallen apples, all the talks
> And silences – like memory's sand
>
> When the tide covers it late or soon,
> And other men through other flowers
> In those fields under the same moon
> Go talking and have easy hours.

Past and present dissolve into symbol. 'Those fields under the same moon' counters 'Hades fields' and stabilises 'memory's sand' by turning a few summer weeks into the perennial domain of poetry, a lyric microcosm, a legacy to 'other' poets.

The moon is a traditional but ambiguous symbol for poetry. In 'The sun used to shine' it presides over Thomas's possible death as well as his poetic birth: 'The war/ Came back to mind with the moon-rise'. In one of his first poems, 'The Penny Whistle', the 'crescent' moon figures his crescent poetry: 'The new moon hangs like an ivory bugle/ In the naked frosty blue' (50). Since 'ivory' suggests aesthetic purity, 'ivory bugle' is a near-oxymoron akin to 'war poetry'. It exposes lyric to rhetoric and history. Nonetheless (or all the more) 'under the same moon' signifies poets talking to each other across the centuries – and Edward Thomas's role in that conversation.

CHAPTER 1

'The myriad-minded lyric'

1. LYRICAL IMPULSE

In his early reviews for the *Daily Chronicle* Edward Thomas liked to
speculate about the poetry of the new century. In 1901 he placed a
bet on the lyric poem:

> [T]he lyric will prosper, at least so long as individualism
> makes way in literature. Increasing complexity of thought
> and emotion will find no such outlet as the myriad-minded
> lyric, with its intricacies of form as numerous and as exquisite
> as those of a birch-tree in the wind.[1]

Thomas is already noting that 'the best lyrics seem to be the poet's
natural speech'. Then, having called the lyric 'self-expression', he
offers a second simile, now for the poet rather than the poem:
'Everyone must have noticed, standing on the shore, when the sun
or the moon is over the sea, how the highway of light on the water
comes right to his feet, and how those on the right and on the left
seem not to be sharing his pleasure, but to be in darkness.' In
December 1914 this image shaped Thomas's poem 'An Old Song II',
where a moonlit 'footbridge' on the sea points to the discovery of
poetic vocation: 'And no one else in the whole world/ Saw that
same sight' (47). The image's recurrence as a self-image suggests that
lyric continued to govern Thomas's thinking about poetry. In 1913,
reviewing *The English Lyric* by the American critic Felix Schelling, he

argued: 'Unless a lyric is any short poem in stanzas the name should not be used for what is mainly narrative or dramatic. It should be possible to see in the modern lyric a core like that in an old ode.' He also says that a lyric 'by music and suggestion … must, incalculably and at once, sow in us a seed of emotion'; that its 'appeal is to the central part of our nature, not to intelligence or experience merely'; and that it 'should convert us by ecstasy'.[2]

In both reviews Thomas seemingly promotes an idea of 'lyric', which has become subject to historical, theoretical and aesthetic question. Critics argue that lyric is not one of Aristotle's foundational genres; that 'expressive' definitions go back no further than the Romantic poets; and that 'twentieth-century critical thought' controlled expectations of what a poem is by 'producing an increasingly capacious sense of poetry as lyric'.[3] So Thomas was proved right: the lyric did 'prosper'. But in the 1970s the rise of literary theory threw the lyric, along with much else, into question; as did the associated rise of 'language poetry' or 'conceptual poetry'. This paradigm rejects such notions as individual expressiveness, the autonomous poem, syntactical coherence, thematic or formal 'closure'. Certainly 'ecstasy' (which Thomas elsewhere defines as a man being 'exalted out of himself, out of the street, out of mortality')[4] plays no part in its vocabulary. Virginia Jackson and Yopie Prins, editors of *The Lyric Theory Reader* (2014), include a section on 'Avant-garde Anti-lyricism'. They point out, however, that anti-lyricism is more an attack on the mid-century literary academy than a longer view of this ancient genre; and that the term 'lyric' 'is the product of so many confused histories and discourses that any resistance to it inherits that confusion'. Indeed, modern pro- and anti-lyricism may be equally partial. If some critics have simplified lyric in overegging its hegemony; so anti-lyricists narrow the scope of this 'mummified ethos', this 'Romantic fossil', to present an easier target for caricature. The lyric, perceived as a self-centred autocracy on every structural level, is set against an allegedly more collective 'textual' poetics.[5]

Yet theory, of whatever stripe, is not practice. Few essays by poets are anthologised in the *Lyric Theory Reader*. The lyric poem in itself might indeed be thought 'capacious': not as a portmanteau for 'vague idealisations and insufficiently examined psychological constructs',[6] but in the sense of flexibility and versatility: 'myriad-minded' (Thomas borrowed Coleridge's adjective for Shakespeare). Although Aristotle failed to theorise lyric (possibly a good thing), the metre-based genres of classical poetry hybridised to establish the univocal poem that is neither drama nor narrative nor discourse, although it may subsume all three. Sub-genres like elegy, love poetry, praise poetry, religious poetry, pastoral, parable, have been remade, combined and recombined over the centuries, not to mention the lyric's (continuing) intersections with song: in his Schelling review, Thomas says: 'the nearer a poem is to a song, or to what would have been a song in a singing age, the more lyrical is it'. 'Songs and Sonnets' covers a multitude. If, to quote Ralph Cohen, genres are 'open systems',[7] the classifying critic tends to be less open than the practising poet or actual poem. Recalling the 1890s, a historical moment when 'intensity' (and hence 'the short lyric') was at an aesthetic premium, Yeats describes how poets then had 'looked back' for lyrical models: 'We tried to write like the poets of the Greek anthology, or like Catullus, or like the Jacobean Lyrists, men who wrote while poetry was still pure.' In his influential essay 'The Symbolism of Poetry' (1900) Yeats attacks poetry which 'loses itself in externalities'; and claims that a poem does not contain symbols but *is* a symbol: manifested by 'sound, and colour, and form ... in a musical relation ... to one another'.[8] Or, as Thomas, more or less on the same intense wavelength, puts it: 'a lyric is most lyrical when it is most like music and most unlike the best possible paraphrase of itself. Poetry tends to be lyrical when it is furthest from prose, and most inexplicable.' He praises J. M. Synge's poems as 'poetry of the most unquestionable kind, but poetry shrunk almost to its bones'.[9]

Having looked back, the lyric pointed forward. *Fin-de-siècle* stress

on 'The Symbolism of Poetry' lay behind later pro-lyricism, espe-
cially as espoused by the American 'New Critics'. Yet Yeats himself
wrote narrative poems and verse-drama, both of which interacted
with his evolving lyric; and Thomas rejected Arthur Symons's
'revival and extension of [Edgar Allan] Poe's opinion that there could
be no such thing as a long poem'.[10] In effect, the modern period has
witnessed new kinds of dynamic between lyric and longer poems,
between lyric and other 'texts': Thomas's own move from prose
to poetry may be a case in point. And despite – or because of – his
devotion to the Romantic poets (discussed in Chapter 2), Thomas
does not circumscribe the lyric's reach when he speaks of 'core' or
'essence'. The point is that lyric is poetry's *sine qua non*. Thomas
damned a would-be poet by saying that he has 'no lyrical impulse –
if we may use a somewhat indefinite phrase that is nevertheless
suggestive of that essence of poetry for which we have never met
an expression more exact'.[11] His 1901 review qualifies 'The lyric … is
self-expression' with:

> whether by necessity or by mere malice aforethought. Those
> that practise the art include men who have spent a laborious
> life in sounding their own stops, like Shelley or Sidney, and
> also the men (and women) who mistake the lowest form of
> vanity for the highest form of art.

The poets dedicated to 'sounding their own stops' are credited with a
'sense even of common things … so poignant that it must be unique';
while 'art' (as opposed to vanity verse) takes self-expression beyond
the self. To 'sound [one's] stops' is to distance and objectify.

Admittedly, Thomas's creative prose clings to a first-person
perspective in a way that betokens the suppressed lyric poet: witness
Philip Larkin's axiom that 'novels are about other people and poems
are about yourself'.[12] Reviewing John Masefield's novel *The Street of
Today* (1911), Thomas calls it 'a novel by a lyric essayist and therefore
too long by near four hundred pages … He ought … to have chosen

a form in which he could have used the first person singular through-out'. He calls his own *Beautiful Wales* (1905): 'without humanity except what it may owe to a lanky shadow of myself – I stretch over big landscapes just as my shadow does at dawn'. And, regretting that *The South Country* (1909) 'is made up of separable parts', he notes: 'My mind is lyrical or if you like jerky & spasmodic.'[13] Yet who would read lyric poems if they did not resonate with other 'selves' or locate the self in the world? Thomas Pfau, glossing Hegel's *Aesthetics*, describes the lyric as 'drawing out the intersubjective cognitive element that slumbers in the emotive fabric of individual life'.[14] For Mutlu Konuk Blasing, lyric is depersonalised by its complex *linguistic* fabric: lyric 'makes audible a virtual subjectivity in the shape of a given language' by concentrating and maximising that language's possibilities.[15] Perhaps Thomas's problem was not how to get 'myself' out of his writing, but into it. On the threshold of poetry, he wrote an autobiographical 'novel', *The Happy-Go-Lucky Morgans* (1913), and the memoir later published as *The Childhood of Edward Thomas* (see Afterword). Thomas embarked on the latter, he says, signifi-cantly writing about himself in the third person: 'because he thinks he must do something other than reviewing & he can't face the novel concerning people unlike himself which he fancied … he was going to attempt'.[16] For Thomas, autobiography objectified the self. It's a premise of this book that he was among the pioneers who remade the lyric as 'psychodrama' in the light and context of modern psychology. The objectified lyric 'self', not necessarily singular, not really univocal, neither an individual nor a character, representing different facets of 'mind', formally constituted through permuta-tions of word, image, syntax, tone and rhythm, has a wide circumference. To quote Theodor Adorno: 'The force with which the private I is externalised in the work is the I's collective essence.'[17] In Louis MacNeice's long poem *Autumn Journal* (1939), which MacNeice calls 'half-way between the lyric and the didactic poem', the poet's 'various and conflicting/ Selves' are situated in fast-moving history.[18] The same is true of Thomas's poems.

The vocational epiphany of 'An Old Song II' ripples outwards:

> The sun set, the wind fell, the sea
> Was like a mirror shaking:
> The one small wave that clapped the land
> A mile-long snake of foam was making
> Where tide had smoothed and wind had dried
> The vacant sand.
>
> A light divided the swollen clouds
> And lay most perfectly
> Like a straight narrow footbridge bright
> That crossed over the sea to me;
> And no one else in the whole world
> Saw that same sight … (47)

The speaker faces into an arena that awaits his unique imprint, this very poem. 'Most perfectly' chimes with Thomas telling Robert Frost that writing poetry makes him 'conscious of a possible perfection as I never was in prose'.[19] As a pure blank sheet, the 'vacant sand' parallels 'naked frosty blue' in 'The Penny Whistle' (50). But nothing and nobody is ever really vacant. It takes a combination of forces to externalise the 'I'. Sea, mirror and other motifs place Romantic godfathers at Thomas's poetic baptism (see Chapter 2). Meanwhile 'mirror shaking' signals that neither psychodrama, nor the co-option of Nature for that purpose, will be a clear-cut enterprise. Further, besides potentially mirroring the self (as with the sexual arousal implied by 'snake' and 'swollen'), the natural world is also the agent of revelation, awakening first the eye, then the other senses. Like 'The sun used to shine', this poem aligns its own dynamic with 'walking', somehow both an inward and outward action:

> I walked elate, my bridge always
> Just one step from my feet:

A robin sang, a shade in shade:
And all I did was to repeat:
  'I'll go no more a-roving
  With you, fair maid.'

'A robin sang, a shade in shade': this encrypted line is another bridge
between the phenomenal world and the unconscious. It also marks
a transition from eye to ear ('feet' seems metrical as well as kinetic).
Again with Romantic precedent, the speaker now subjects his
subjectivity and ear to the 'collective' of folksong: another 'bridge'.
Thomas sang folk songs. He reviewed collections of them, antholo-
gised them in his *Pocket Book of Poems and Songs for the Open Air*
(1907), and was in touch with the leading collector, Cecil Sharp. He
wondered whether the folk revival might 'give a vigorous impulse
to a new school of poetry', as Sharp hoped it would to an English
school of music.[20] Thomas had already based 'An Old Song I' on 'The
Lincolnshire Poacher'. In both 'songs' we hear the lyrical impulse
being charged by the folk impulse: 'And all I did was to repeat …'.
The 'repeated' word 'shade', like earlier internal tunes (snake/
making, sea/me), prepares for the inference that the poet-initiate is
absorbing folk-structures such as refrain. In the next stanza, bird-
song and folksong intermingle as prompters from outside the self:
'The sailors' song of merry loving/ With dusk and sea-gull's mewing/
Mixed sweet'. The song's chorus is called a 'wild charm'. The
musicians in 'The Penny Whistle' and 'The Gypsy' are similarly
linked with wild Nature (as with poetry's 'crescent' moon) in ways
that respect rather than primitivise their music. All three poems end
with a folksong take-over or make-over. The gypsy's mouth-organ
'people[s] … the hollow wooded land' (59); the penny-whistle player
'Says far more than I am saying' – and the poem ends there. In 'An
Old Song II' the sea-shanty 'Amsterdam' occupies more and more
of each stanza – the last stanza completely. Lyric poem and newborn
lyric poet dissolve back into collective origins.

Thomas's ear will stay tuned to the folk-ghost and to natural sounds as well as to 'talk': inter-aurality rather than inter-textuality. He keeps up a complex dialogue with birdsong (vindicated as analogous to lyric by proof that it shares genetic code with human speech). But wind and water also infiltrate or figure Thomas's poetry in ways that extend the aesthetic dimension of 'Romantic ecology'.[21] 'The Source' is another poem of vocational self-discovery. Here wind and water, underscored by repeated words and sounds, orchestrate the poem's arrival at its own articulation:

> All day the air triumphs with its two voices
> Of wind and rain:
> As loud as if in anger it rejoices,
> Drowning the sound of earth
> That gulps and gulps in choked endeavour vain
> To swallow the rain.
>
> Half the night, too, only the wild air speaks
> With wind and rain,
> Till forth the dumb source of the river breaks
> And drowns the rain and wind,
> Bellows like a giant bathing in mighty mirth
> The triumph of earth. (49)

As the earth-voice 'drowns' air-voices we may hear the release of Thomas's poetic 'impulse' from psychological turmoil and from the 'choked endeavour' of his prose (see p. 233). All 'voices' are again inevitably internal (just as conceptual art can never detach itself from the conceiver). Even so, 'The Source' gives voice to the non-human. Similarly, in the soundscape of 'The Penny Whistle', what the poet is 'saying' emerges from a counterpoint between brooks' 'black hollow voices' and the musician's 'melody'. Thomas mostly confines 'voice' itself to birds and brooks, although wind and water vocalise trees: 'The aspens at the cross-roads talk together' (97). But throughout his poetry words for sound (for lyric) transfer democratically, often disturbingly, between human utterance, bird-noises, weather and water: 'say', 'speak', 'tell', 'talk', 'laugh', 'whistle', 'whisper', 'whimper', 'call', 'cry', 'roar', 'hiss', 'murmur', 'chatter', 'hum', 'sigh', 'moan', 'shout', 'scream', 'shriek'. 'The Hollow Wood' is a strange echo-chamber:

> Out in the sun the goldfinch flits
> Along the thistle-tops, flits and twits
> Above the hollow wood
> Where birds swim like fish –
> Fish that laugh and shriek –
> To and fro, far below
> In the pale hollow wood … (48)

Thomas's 'lyrical impulse' is neither egocentric nor anthropocentric. His early poems establish a lyric ground with porous boundaries.

2. CRITICAL THINKING

That 'An Old Song II' should echo a review written years ago, and apply Thomas's ideas about folksong, suggests how his criticism underpins his poetry. In 1914 his response to Robert Frost's *North of Boston* was as much climax as starting-point. Thomas is barely rated as a 'lyric theorist'. Yet it's a truly exceptional circumstance that, before writing poetry, he wrote so much about it. A prose self-portrait depicts Thomas's teenage discovery of poetry as opening up 'a second world in which he thenceforth moved with a rapture … not often [observed] in the religious'.[22] In giving to criticism what he might otherwise have given to poems, yet thereby laying aesthetic foundations for future poems, Thomas provides a unique lens through which to view poetry in the early twentieth century. His reviews also interpret the contexts in which he did his critical work, as when (in 1908), reviewing a *Book of Living Poets*, he lists the forces ranged against the intelligent reception of 'new poetry':

Reprints of old, well tested, or well guaranteed poetry abound and catch the attention of the most timid and unobservant; and not only poetry, but such prose as satisfies similar needs, as for example *Religio Medici* and *The Opium Eater* … The prose of our own time is also rich in poetic qualities … Foreign literatures and translations add still further defences which new poetry has to scale.

Then the multiplication of authors, and of writers of verse in particular, makes choice very difficult. An imbecile with ten pounds in his pocket can easily add one to the number of the volumes from which the lover of poetry has to choose. Finally, in a centrifugal age, in which principles and aims are numerous, vague, uncertain, confused, and in conflict, the lack of good criticism, or even of moderately good criticism that has any authority, defrauds many noble and beautiful voices of the ears which expect them.[23]

Thomas himself reviewed all of the above, being especially swamped by works destined for the strap-line 'Minor Poetry'. Everyone, it seems, was writing poems: the verse-epidemic after the outbreak of war had a hinterland. Yet Thomas's wide brief led him to historicise and conceptualise poetry in ways that informed his judgment of new work (see Chapter 2). And, despite exhaustion, frustration, 'imbeciles', and serious literati with 'no lyrical impulse', his mysterious investment in poetry never wavered. As for real contenders: Thomas never doubts Yeats's pre-eminence ('above all there is Mr Yeats');[24] he was perhaps the first critic to prefer Hardy's poetry to his novels; and he monitored, even mentored, the development of younger poets in whom he found a spark – principally W. H. Davies and Walter de la Mare. He was a friend of both, but friendship rarely led him to pull his punches. Reviewing *Chambers of Imagery* by his close friend Gordon Bottomley, he said: '[the] verses … are not always wrought up to the condition of poetry, but seem to have been left in a raw state that can appeal to the intelligence only'.[25] The new collections which most excited him were the successive volumes of Charles M. Doughty's *The Dawn in Britain* (see p. 132); Ezra Pound's *Personae* (1909) – here Thomas's 'pure love of praising the new poetry' turned out to be a brief encounter;[26] D. H. Lawrence's *Love Poems and Others* (1913); and, of course, *North of Boston*.

Thomas's poetry criticism prepared for the recognition of Frost that prepared for his recognition of himself. Without compromising or foreclosing his criteria, he navigated a 'centrifugal' poetic period, to which *post hoc* labels like 'Georgian' or 'modernist' are little guide. Swinburne was still publishing (he died in 1909), and the aftermath of the 1890s jostled with the school of Rudyard Kipling. Thomas can be tough on outdated 'aesthetic poetry': he writes of Arthur Symons's *Knave of Hearts* (1913), a selected poems: 'The descriptions of things seen and the personal lyrics are very sensitive reflections of a spirit suffering from the dethronement of aestheticism, and the imperfect acceptance of a successor.'[27] Thomas's book-length critical works, *Maurice Maeterlinck* (1911), *Algernon Charles Swinburne* (1912) and *Walter Pater* (1913), while not conceived as a triadic manifesto, effectively deconstruct the 'aestheticism' that had been a formative influence on his own writing. In their best passages, these studies amount to a theoretical basis for his poems. But if Thomas rejected *fin-de-siècle* remoteness from life, he did not, as we have seen, reject *fin-de-siècle* symbolic intensity. His reviews are tougher on versifiers than on suffering aesthetes. For instance, he hears Kipling (in prose and verse) as 'the ranting and whining of an unpleasantly accented unpleasant voice'; and equally condemns John Davidson's more progressive, neo-Nietzschean rhetoric in works such as *The Triumph of Mammon* (1907): a 'crude and furious pamphlet'.[28] Like Yeats, Thomas is ambivalent (complicated) about poetry's relation to modernity: the force that was making the age 'centrifugal'. While resistant to the exponential growth of London and the massive changes in rural England, he accepts, if with irony, the impossibility of writing 'as if there were no such thing as a Tube, Grape Nuts, love of Nature, a Fabian Society'. In 1902 he said of a consciously modern

Annual of Art and Literature: 'this thing modernity is the strangest medley that was ever put into a cauldron to produce the spirit of an age. Nothing comes amiss to it. All the ends of the world are come upon it; and it is equally at home in Athens, Alexandria, Samoa, and the East-end.'[29] But for Thomas, as for Yeats, it's a matter of poetry needing time to absorb change at a deeper level. Davidson's increasingly 'fatal tendency simply to translate his thoughts and opinions into verse'[30] is at odds with Symbolist principles. Thomas's evangelism on behalf of new poetry was itself visionary. And his longer-term hopes for modern poetry, as for modernity, centred, not on technological or socio-political change but on more inward kinds of progress: '[i]ncreasing complexity of thought and emotion', 'the myriad-minded lyric'.

Thomas was also a critic of criticism. He thought that the emergent literary academy was doing little about 'the lack of good [poetry] criticism', and that the 'scattered pages on poetic diction' in Coleridge's *Biographia Literaria* ('the most profound literary criticism … in English') remained 'all that can at present form the basis of any true criticism of poetry'. Comparing more recent critics with Coleridge, he calls Matthew Arnold 'a journalist'; Pater, 'a dilettante'.[31] But he makes an exception for A. C. Bradley. His review of Bradley's *Poetry for Poetry's Sake* (Bradley's inaugural lecture as Oxford Professor of Poetry) praises Bradley for rescuing 'form' from 'art for art's sake'; for not divorcing it from content; and for defining '*poetic* value' in a way that 'distinguishes between the subject and the substance of a poem'. Bradley's thesis, as summarised by Thomas, would remain a key idea: 'a perfect poem may be written on a sparrow, and a worthless one on the omnipresence of the Deity'. It throws light on Thomas as a critic of criticism that he later says of Bradley's *Oxford Lectures on Poetry*: 'He would make the worst of debaters. He is only troubled about what is true.'[32] The poet-critic Arthur Symons is the only other contemporary critic whom Thomas praises highly. He tells Bottomley that, despite lacking 'originality', Symons 'hardly [has] a superior living as a critic combining instinct

& scholarship'.[33] Thomas finds a narrower stimulus in the work of critics who attempt new approaches to English metre: 'this difficult field, so unhappily alluring to the conservative and the blind'. He commends Mark H. Liddell's *Introduction to the Scientific Study of English Poetry* (1902) because, by highlighting rhythm and stress, it makes the old system of prosody 'ridiculous'. He adds, however, that Liddell 'leaves blank verse, as before, an infinitely varied line usually of ten syllables'.[34]

Thomas was drawn to prosodic theory because he believed that poetry depended on the ear of both poet and reader. 'Lyrical impulse' entails a pulse. To quote his poem 'Old Man', he always seems 'to be listening, lying in wait' for persuasive rhythms. Thus he judges that Davies's poems 'either sing themselves through like an old air or they break up and fall'; and he represents de la Mare's lyricism and his rhythms as virtually the same thing:

> Mr de la Mare's poems are the purest lyrics. Most are very short and rhymed, the majority are no longer than a sonnet, but in a great variety of metres and stanza forms … The movement of his verse is always half-hidden under the thought of which it forms a part. It is at its best in the inward melody, the spiritual or apparently bodiless rhythms, so characteristic of this age, in the work of men like Messrs Bridges, Yeats, and Sturge Moore.[35]

Despite the name-checks here, Thomas never quite endorses the rhythms of either Thomas Sturge Moore or Robert Bridges. Reviewing Moore's *The Gazelles and Other Poems*, he praises Moore for 'still experimenting, still sounding the capacity of language'; but concludes that he fails rhythmically owing to the 'slowness', rather than 'liquidity', of his lines: 'He would seem always to compose word by word, and seldom to be moved to write a whole line at one impulse.' Elsewhere, he calls Moore's rhythms 'heavy-gaited', and identifies a cause, when he says: 'Mr Moore rightly thinks a great deal: perhaps he does not unthink sufficiently.' Thomas finds similar rhythmic faults in Lascelles Abercrombie: 'his ideas rush, but his words never flow. He suggests a man who jumps vertically instead of running ahead.'[36] As for Bridges's elaborate metrical experiments: a 'serious charge' against the Bridges hexameter is 'that it does not admit of the compact, allusive, elliptical and novel quality of style in which poetry differs from prose'.[37] Conversely, the poems that Thomas likes in the *Living Poets* anthology 'sound notes which were never heard before'.[38] So does his own 'Unknown Bird' in a poem of aural vocational revelation: 'No one saw him: I alone could hear him/ Though many listened' (55). Echoing his de la Mare review, Thomas calls the bird's notes 'bodiless sweet'.

Well before Frost came on the scene, Thomas saw poetic rhythm as constituted by permutations of speech and metre; blank verse as 'an infinitely varied line'. Writing *Walter Pater* strangely focused his ideas about speech, rhythm and poetry. The 'exquisite unnaturalness' of Pater's style, its stifling of pulse and impulse, prompted the crucial insight that literature must 'do all that a speaker can do by innumerable gestures and their innumerable shades, by tone and pitch of voice, by speed, by pauses, by all that he is and all that he will become'. (This sounds like 'the myriad-minded lyric' again.) If Pater's prose has the vices of 'heavy-gaited' poetry, Swinburne's often-manic rhythms bypass speech by running to the opposite extreme: 'in *Atalanta in Calydon* rhythm [is] paramount, in rule sole and undivided'; 'Swinburne [tends] towards a musical jargon that includes human snatches, but is not and never could be speech'.[39] Yeats, however, gets the balance right. Thomas wrote in 1904: '"Speech delighted with its own music" is the best definition of Mr Yeats's verse' (the quotation is from Yeats's play 'The King's Threshold'). He calls Yeats's blank verse an 'infinitely varied measure' in which 'No two lines are alike.'[40] Later, praising the 'extraordinarily original close-packed poems' in Lawrence's *Love Poems and Others*, he singles out those where 'the metre changes three or four times':

[I]t is obvious at once that the poems would be impossible in
'In Memoriam' stanzas, for example. Their metrical changes,
like their broken or hesitating rhythms, are part of a personal-
ity that will sink nothing of itself in what is common. They
have the effect which Whitman only got now and then after a
thousand efforts of rhymeless lawlessness.[41]

Thomas's initial attraction to Pound was also based on the shock
of new rhythms: on Pound's '[c]arelessness of sweet sound and of
all the old tricks'. While his three reviews of *Personae* (1909) note
'prickliness', 'faults' and 'eccentricities', Thomas yet says: 'It is the old
miracle that cannot be defined, nothing more than a subtle entangle-
ment of words, so that they rise out of their graves and sing.' He
commends Pound for getting beyond 'the superficial good qualities
of modern versifiers ... the smooth regularity of the Tennysonian
tradition [and] the wavering, uncertain languor of the new [the
Celtic Twilight]'. Thomas's *volte face* over Pound, 'having allowed the
turbulent opacity of his peculiarities to sink down', again hinges on
rhythm. His review of *Exultations* (also 1909) cites 'stiff rhythms and
no rhythms at all' as the ultimate symptom of Pound's artistic inco-
herence: of his being too 'pestered with possible ways of saying a
thing'. (Another symptom is the poly-lingual diction which 'dapples'
the poems.)[42] Five years later, applauding Frost's 'sentence-sounds',
Thomas took a smack at Poundian as well as Tennysonian rhythms:
'The metre avoids not only the old-fashioned pomp and sweetness,
but the later fashion also of discord and fuss.'[43] Frost and Thomas
agreed that the eye-based or eye-biased Imagist aesthetic, then being
promoted by Pound, denied poetry's roots in speech. To quote Frost:
'The ear is the only true writer and the only true reader.'[44] It's relevant
to contemporary anti-lyricism, which takes some cues from Pound
that, having initially hailed Pound's 'revolt' against 'all but meaning-
less suavity and skill', Thomas ended by finding it empty: 'we believe
that we see very nearly nothing at all'. As for Pound's criticism:
Thomas praises *The Spirit of Romance* (1910) for its originality and

translations, but finds it 'restlessly opinionated … His personality is negative, and rises to the appearance of being positive only by contradiction.'[45] Both as lyric theorist and lyric practitioner, Thomas was well aware of contrary aesthetic positions: 'discord and fuss'. He might be termed 'an anti-anti-lyricist' *avant la lettre.*

Thomas's most sustained poetic credo predates both his poems and his meeting with Frost. It occurs in *Maurice Maeterlinck,* and was provoked by Maeterlinck's poem 'Serres Chaudes': an atomised 'catalogue of symbols'. Here Thomas speaks for a more holistic brand of symbolism, to which rhythm is integral, and for 'intensity'. He again exposes the subject-matter fallacy (sparrow/ Deity); and insists, as in his critique of Pater, that single words are inert until animated by their relation to one other:

> [N]o word, outside works of information, has any value beyond its surface value except what it receives from its neighbours and its position among them. Each man makes his own language in the main unconsciously and inexplicably, unless he is still at an age when he is an admiring but purely aesthetic collector of words … and there are a hundred peculiarities in his rhythms and groupings to be discovered. In the mainly instinctive use of his language the words will all support one another, and, if the writing is good, the result of this support is that each word is living its intensest life … Any writer whose words have this power may make a poem of anything – a story, a dream, a thought, a picture, an ejaculation, a conversation. Whatever be the subject, the poem must not depend for its main effect upon anything outside itself except the humanity of the reader. It may please for the moment by the aid of some irrelevant and transitory interest – political interest, for example; but, sooner or later, it will be left naked and solitary, and will so be judged, and if it does not create about itself a world of its own it is condemned to endure the death which is its element. These worlds of living

poems may be of many different kinds. As a rule they are regions of the earth now for the first time separated from the rest and made independent; they may be lit by the sun of every one, or by another, or by the moon, or by a green lantern: whatever they are, they are stronger than this world, and their light more steadfast than sun or moon ... Anything, however small, may make a poem; nothing, however great, is certain to. Concentration, intensity of mood, is the one necessary condition in the poet and in the poem.[46]

These principles, which pre-empt the anti-lyricism that leans towards disjunctive syntax, or even disjoins words themselves, have a reflexive presence in Thomas's complementary poems 'Words' and 'The Word'.

'Words' acts out the proposition that poetry is where mutual 'support' between words reaches its apotheosis; where each word 'lives its intensest life'. The opening lines, a vocational invocation, convey a sense of the poem itself being written, of 'English words' being shaped into an English lyric:

Out of us all
That make rhymes,
Will you choose
Sometimes –
As the winds use
A crack in a wall
Or a drain,
Their joy or their pain
To whistle through –
Choose me,
You English words? ... (91)

Although the short line might seem to highlight single words, the elongated form equally highlights their interdependence, both as links in a syntactical chain and as steps in a rhythmic dance: in the last stanza the poet-speaker says: 'Let me sometimes dance/ With you'. Rhyme-words dance across stanzas: two are twenty-four lines apart. In the first stanza, the syntactical placing of the one-word line 'Sometimes' and its rhyme with 'rhymes' provide a rhetorical/ metrical stress, which, by reinforcing the plea, may mark its fulfilment. 'Words' calls words 'Worn new/ Again and again'. This is so, in both history and poetry, because they constantly refresh their association with 'things' as well as with one another: 'Young as our streams/ After rain'. Here again, the form, the short line, adds emphasis: while 'things' can only be vicariously present as 'words', the poem's dynamic intertwines them, as does metaphor: 'Tough as oak,/ Precious as gold,/ As poppies and corn,/ Or an old cloak'. The speaker goes on to plead:

Make me content
With some sweetness
From Wales
Whose nightingales
Have no wings, –
From Wiltshire and Kent
And Herefordshire,
And the villages there, –
From the names, and the things
No less.

Yet, since 'names' and 'things' are non-identical, since they belong to different orders, they may also become dissociated: form liaisons that time makes unintelligible. Thomas's poem 'Women he liked' concerns a farmer who loves trees and plants them along a lane which they later engulf: 'the name alone survives, Bob's Lane' (127).

At the beginning of 'The Word' hardly anything survives: 'There are so many things I have forgot' (93). The speaker has disconcertingly forgotten a huge jumble of things and names (including 'names

of the mighty men/ That fought and lost or won in the old wars'),
all swallowed by an 'Abyss of what can never be again'. Yet, as
with 'Bob's Lane', forgetting proves to be a way of remembering –
or proves poetry as a way of remembering. 'The Word' acts out
Thomas's proposition in *Maurice Maeterlinck* that: 'Anything, however
small, may make a poem; nothing, however great, is certain to.' The
poem continues:

> One name that I have not –
> Though 'tis an empty thingless name – forgot
> Never can die because Spring after Spring
> Some thrushes learn to say it as they sing.
> There is always one at midday saying it clear
> And tart – the name, only the name, I hear.
> While perhaps I am thinking of the elder scent
> That is like food, or while I am content
> With the wild rose scent that is like memory,
> This name suddenly is cried out to me
> From somewhere in the bushes by a bird
> Over and over again, a pure thrush word.

As in 'Words', we sense a poem being composed. But this implied
poem ('an empty thingless name') reverses the presumed norm
whereby things acquire names. It takes its origin from something
other than subjection to language as a historical web of associations.
The poem is reflexively figured by birdsong ('pure' sound) and deep
memory. Peter McDonald observes that the 'energies of repetition'
within the verse structure 'become themselves almost the poem's
subject'.[47] '[S]uddenly … cried out' enacts the surprise of the sounds
that arrive from the abyss, the mystery of what 'may make a poem' –
not necessarily 'things'. This again is 'lyric': in his review of Schelling's
English Lyric Thomas thinks lyric 'most lyrical when it brings before
us what we knew nothing of until then, dispensing with great
things and famous names'.[48] Lyric's alternative naming will survive

('Never can die') its unpredictable or indefinable ('perhaps') occa-
sions; although, as we see, it may carry their traces. But even if no
poem can be entirely 'thingless' or 'bodiless', here poetry becomes
'The Word' rather than 'Words'. In *Maurice Maeterlinck* Thomas
says that words in a 'work of art' may be 'words only, or images, or
spirits'.[49] The spiritual, quasi-biblical title of 'The Word' defines
poetry as vision rather than as language, or defines it as the language
of vision: 'a pure thrush word'. At once 'said' and 'sung', a 'thrush
word' emerges from the '[c]oncentration, intensity of mood' that
creates the 'worlds of living poems': 'what we knew nothing of until
then'. To compare 'the wild rose scent' with 'memory' (not *vice versa*)
is to put the metaphysical before the physical: to question poems
that depend on short-term memory or 'transient interests' like
'mighty men' at war. By the same token (not only here) Thomas's
critical thinking has been absorbed into poetic structure.

3. QUINTESSENTIAL LINES

Thomas also considers a lyric 'most lyrical' when 'furthest from
prose', 'most unlike the best … paraphrase of itself'. If so, the moment
when he found his own '[c]oncentration, intensity of mood' should
tell us something about what 'makes a poem' – what makes it
different from prose. In a sense, this moment (a moment his poetry
revisits) reprised the lyric's genesis, its formation out of chaos, its big
bang. Thomas becoming a poet is more than a personal case-history
with an ambiguously happy ending. What happened in December
1914 was extraordinary on several fronts: a modal change from lyric
theory to practice; an interior change from psychological illness
to psychodrama (see Chapter 5); a contextual change from peace
to war; the all-encompassing change from prose to poetry. None
of these changes (except possibly war) came about overnight. And –
to return to 'the same moon' – they all shape 'The sun used to
shine' as a poem about poetic origins. This poem began as notebook
jottings in August 1914, and took its first shape as the essay 'This

England', published in the *Nation* (7 November 1914). A staging-post on Thomas's road from prose to poetry and war, the essay ends with a quasi-manifesto:

> Then one evening the new moon made a difference ... At one stroke, I thought, like many other people, what things that same new moon sees eastward about the Meuse in France ... I was deluged, in a second stroke, by another thought, or something that overpowered thought. All I can tell is, it seemed to me that either I had never loved England, or I had loved it foolishly, aesthetically, like a slave, not having realised that it was not mine unless I was willing and prepared to die rather than leave it as Belgian women and old men and children had left their country. Something I had omitted. Something, I felt, had to be done before I could look again composedly at English landscape, at the elms and poplars about the houses, at the purple-headed wood-betony with two pairs of dark leaves on a stiff stem, who stood sentinel among the grasses or bracken by hedge-side or wood's-edge. What he stood sentinel for I did not know, any more than what I had got to do.[50]

The something 'to be done' would include rewriting 'This England' as 'The sun used to shine'. What changed? Thomas is always curiously interested in prose-writers who turn to poetry, but remarks: 'As a rule, this verse is neither so pleasing nor so interesting as a verse-writer's prose.'[51] There are poets who start with prose drafts (Yeats); poets who write fiction and poetry concurrently (Hardy, Lawrence). Thomas is a rare instance of a poet who recasts materials from an extensive body of prose written over years. Keith Douglas insists that in poetry 'every word must work for its keep'. Obviously words work hard in prose too, but to different ends; or, differently, to an end. Thomas says that writing poetry is 'like doing the best parts of my prose in verse... & leaving out the connecting futile parts'.[52] All that the speaker of 'The Word' 'forgets' may belong to prose. Being required to make up (and more) for that loss, words in poetry 'live their intensest life' by multi-tasking. It follows that Thomas's poems do more than précis his prose. As 'Words' and 'The Word' affirm, language ceases to be any kind of vehicle. For example, 'wood-betony' has a different career in 'The sun used to shine':

… We turned from men or poetry

To rumours of the war remote
Only till both stood disinclined
For aught but the yellow flavorous coat
Of an apple wasps had undermined;

Or a sentry of dark betonies,
The stateliest of small flowers on earth,
At the forest verge; or crocuses
Pale purple as if they had their birth

In sunless Hades fields. The war
Came back to mind with the moonrise
Which soldiers in the east afar
Beheld then … (122)

It's as if a lens, fit for its initial purpose, has found sharper focus: the need for this to happen being integral to the prose. Betonies become 'dark' in a double sense, while 'purple' qualifies 'crocuses' (absent from the prose) and prepares for Hades. 'Pale', 'dark' and 'remote' belong to different objects in the prose, to topographical features unmentioned and unnecessary in the poem: 'the island hills of North Monmouthshire, dark and massive, the remote Black Mountains pale and cloud-like'. Colour-adjectives now map the direction·in which the poem is moving. Similarly, Thomas replaces his uncertain 'sentinel' with a more war-like 'sentry', more closely attached to 'betonies': 'a sentry of dark betonies'. The blend of singular and plural nouns enhances the metaphorical oddity of a phrase that condenses a shift to 'war pastoral', Thomas's shift to soldier-poet. Then 'wood's-edge' becomes 'forest verge', not simply a location, while 'on earth' marks a landscape that has become microcosmic, the landscape of poetry: Eden (the apple), sun, moon, Hades.

Above all, 'wood-betony' has become entangled in line, stanza and rhythm. To quote Frost: a poet 'must learn to get cadences by skilfully breaking the sounds of sense with all their irregularity of accent across the regular beat of the metre'.[53] In 'The sun used to shine' sentence-sounds are broken across a mainly four-stress line and eight quatrains, rhymed ABAB. In the first three quatrains (see p. 13), 'slow' expansive rhythms ally 'walking and talking' with an Edenic suspension of time: 'We never disagreed/ Which gate to rest on'. The tone of the remembering voice simultaneously relishes August 1914 up to the slight chill when memory surfaces within memory: 'The war/ Came back to mind'. The lines about the betonies occur as the mid-point of sense-impressions that dwell on (and in) the life that war threatens. But the rhythm, co-extensively with the image, is already starting to change: a change accentuated by alliterative/assonantal stresses that derive from 'sentry'. The tempo is briefly slowed again by the parenthetic line/phrase, 'The stateliest of small flowers on earth': a poised pentameter that encodes the poets contemplating the flower. 'At the forest verge', which revives the sounds of 'sentry', starts the next line with a forward impetus, although the caesura aptly gives us pause after 'verge'. Then the half-rhyming of 'crocuses' with 'betonies' reinforces the link between these symbolic flora. The quatrain's other rhyme-words, 'earth'/'birth', might seem more positively linked, but the syntax-break at the stanza-break contributes to an unsettling oxymoron which prepares for 'The war'. Line and stanza, the rhythm created by breaking 'sounds of sense' across metre, are crucial to the calculus whereby the poem says 'something' more, or more things at once, than the prose.

Thomas's involvement with prose was critical as well creative.

In 1900, having started to publish country books, meditative essays and rather wan fictional sketches, he was already, as Jean Moorcroft Wilson observes, calling himself a 'prose-poet'.[54] That is, he was skirting 'The Frontiers of English Prose': title of an article he published in 1899, aged twenty-one. The article flags up what Thomas sees as a relatively new literary phenomenon: 'the apparent destruction of the boundaries between poetry and prose, if not between verse and prose'. Thomas especially credits poets (Wordsworth, Coleridge, Shelley) with extending prose's remit, but ends by declaring: 'The field has been won; prose shares it with verse, having in her grasp the lyre of life and claiming to touch every string by right …'.[55] How do we interpret this? Having tried verse, Thomas has seemingly opted for prose. In saying that prose 'shares the lyre', is he making the best of a bad job while suffering from undiagnosed 'poet's block' (see p. 252)? Or does he have a real sense that boundaries are being pushed, that his own prose can help to push them? Indeed, Thomas often represents contemporary prose, 'rich in poetic qualities', as a serious rival to poetry (see p. 25). His attraction to Hardy and Lawrence, writers with whom he might be grouped on the 'frontier', seems relevant. Yet generic confusion co-exists with his hopes for fusion: 'There is no form that suits me, & I doubt if I can make a new form.'[56]

Between 1899 and 1914 Thomas's testing of the frontier evolved. At the outset, he had a 'millennial' vision for prose as well as poetry. In another review of Liddell's book on prosody, he complains that it 'fails to reveal a quality in verse which has not been, or in future may not be, achieved in prose':

Perfect prose has always a music of ideas, and its stresses are, or should be, as subtle and constant as in verse. The millennial prose may unfold a rhythm, and possibly even a rhyme, of grander music than Dante's or Homer's, availing itself, nevertheless, of all their mighty inventions.[57]

Thomas becomes critically excited whenever he finds prose and poetry advancing in tandem. Hence, in part, his high regard for the Irish Literary Revival, particularly for Yeats and Synge. He says of *The Playboy of the Western World*: 'By nature or by art, we must achieve a speech something like this which corresponds with the thought almost onomata-poetically, or fail.'[58] Here Thomas favours dramatic prose that approaches the condition of poetry, rather than prose that has developed equivalent qualities. The year before (1906), he had urged writers to capitalise on the achievement of Baudelaire's prose-poems: 'We believe that a prose form as honest, as consistent, as impressionistic as Whistler's painting must arise ... Borrow really wrote about six prose-poems; yet he now wearies us with six bad books.'[59] Five years later, Thomas turned this perception back towards poetry, when he wrote of Lawrence's poems: 'More than half are the quintessences of novels. Not mere novels in little, not mere sketches or embryos of novels; but, as it were, the tiny but solid beings of which novels are the shadows artificially made gigantic.'[60] This, interestingly, returns full circle to 1901: to a review in which Thomas sets poetry's 'brevity' and 'elliptical intensity' above prose ('There is something slinking about prose'), and cites another frontiersman, George Meredith: 'Some of us may think ... that in "Modern Love" Mr Meredith has proved that a psychological motive may be completed as well in three or four thousand words as in a hundred times as many.'[61] Once again, there are two possibilities: either Thomas repeatedly mistook his métier; or his situation between prose and poetry was a destructive/constructive element in which it was somehow necessary to immerse – critically too. His critique of Pater's prose (also self-criticism) translated into immediate sympathy with Frost's theory and practice. He told Frost: 'my "Pater" would show you I had got onto the scent already'.[62] Thomas also condemns other prose-writers' styles as out of touch with speech and life: Robert Louis Stevenson's words 'are perilously near the ghostliness of mere words'.[63]

Thomas repeats 'quintessence' when he compares his first poems

to 'quintessences of the best parts of my prose books'.[64] The word
has a history in (or as) *fin-de-siècle* aesthetics – which again shows
that Thomas has not entirely left them behind. For Arthur Symons,
the 'ideal of Decadence', epitomised by Paul Verlaine's poetry, is 'To
fix the last fine shade, the quintessence of things'. And Pater cele-
brates 'The School of Giorgione' for painting 'ideal instants', which
'are like some consummate extract or quintessence of life'.[65] 'Ideal
instants' is a reminder that that Thomas's epiphanies, like those of
other early twentieth-century writers (Joyce, Woolf), owe something
to Pater's formulation of the 'moment' as well as to Wordsworth's.
'Quintessence' belongs with 'concentration' and 'intensity': a quality
that Thomas attributes to *North of Boston*. Even Frost's eclogues he
calls 'drama with a lyric intensity which borders on magic'. In fact,
his reviews of *North of Boston* mark a conceptual shift. Rather than
(as in 1899) anticipating a new prose 'music' or (as in 1906) extolling
the prose poem, Thomas is now advocating poetry that takes
supposedly prosaic qualities and raises them to a higher pitch:

> He will be accused of keeping monotonously at a low level,
> because his characters are quiet people, and he has chosen
> the unresisting medium of blank verse. I will only remark
> that he would lose far less than most modern writers by being
> printed as prose. If his work were so printed, it would have
> little in common with the kind of prose that runs to blank
> verse: in fact, it would turn out to be closer knit and more
> intimate than the finest prose is except in its finest passages.
> It is poetry because it is better than prose.

Thomas also says that Frost has 'gone back, as Whitman and as
Wordsworth went back, through the paraphernalia of poetry into
poetry again' (as Thomas himself may have gone through the
paraphernalia of prose).[66] In effect, Frost's 'sentence-sound' builds
a bridge from prose to poetry. It's no paradox that Thomas's prose
became more prosaic as well as more autobiographical in 1913–14.

When writing *The Childhood of Edward Thomas*, he said: 'It's very lean but I feel the shape of the sentences & alter continually with some unseen end in view.'[67] Meanwhile, besides providing a template for sentence-shaped poems, Frost was divining the poet in Thomas, and urging him to rewrite, as poetry, passages in his prose-work *In Pursuit of Spring* (1914). By early 1914, several conditions for frontier-crossing were in place.

There is no single or simple pattern whereby Thomas extracts 'quintessences' from a vast prose backlist, which includes critical writings, notebook-entries and letters. What crosses over may be a word, a phrase, an image, a scene, an incident, a character, a perception, an idea: 'Anything, however small …'. For instance, two early poems, 'March' and 'The Other', draw differently on *In Pursuit of Spring*. 'March', to which sense-impressions are primary, condenses Thomas's prose-record of successive spring days into one evening 'hour'; much birdsong into a thrush-chorus. The symbolism latent in the book's concept is realised as a contest between weather and 'song' – also another act in the psychodrama of Thomas becoming a poet:

> … What did the thrushes know? Rain, snow, sleet, hail,
> Had kept them quiet as the primroses.
> They had but an hour to sing. On boughs they sang,
> On gates, on ground; they sang while they changed perches
> And while they fought, if they remembered to fight:
> So earnest were they to pack into that hour
> Their unwilling hoard of song before the moon
> Grew brighter than the clouds … (35)

'The Other' brings psychodrama and symbol centre-stage. A quasi-fictional thread in *In Pursuit of Spring*, the narrator's encounters with an alter ego dubbed 'the Other Man', becomes an allegory of the divided self. Landscapes from the book are not converted into sensory texture, but stylised to figure interior states: 'Here was both

road and inn, the sum/ Of what's not forest' (40). But even notes,
a single paragraph, a brief essay, can fertilise more than one poem
or kind of poem. 'This England' also foreshadows 'This is no case
of petty right or wrong', Thomas's most explicitly patriotic poem
(see p. 137). Of course, we usually cannot know whether Thomas has
deliberately revisited or consciously recalled a specific passage, or
whether it has floated up from the unconscious mind. A notebook-
entry for 24 June 1914 undoubtedly helped him to 'remember
Adlestrop'. But the poem also takes details from other stops on
the way, and has links with a prose sketch in which a train pauses
while a thrush is 'singing, calling out very loud, clear things in his
language over and over again' (this thrush gets into 'The Word' too).[68]
'Man and Dog', a poem mainly documented from recent notes, and
contextualised by the war, also harks back to earlier portraits of itin-
erant labourers in Thomas's prose – it is, indeed, their quintessence
(see p. 223). Again, prose and poem may have common pre-verbal
sources, and none of this means that Thomas's poetry is not wholly
alive to and in the present: 'Today I think/ Only with scents …' (79).

  Distilling the past is an activity of present 'thinking'. This very
poem, 'Digging', echoes autumnal scenarios in Thomas's prose; and
some poems are palimpsest upon palimpsest: compacted layers of
experience and representation. Certainly, no poem is the poem that
Thomas might have written a decade earlier. The acute historical
sense, which extends to every area of his poetry, seems indexed to its
multi-layered sources as well as to the war. Perhaps Thomas's delayed
poetic birth, the history it carries, the history it faces into, led him
to intensify and articulate the basis of (lyric) poetry in memory: 'In
my memory/ Again and again I see it' (89). The word itself recurs,
as do variants like 'recall', 'call back', 'came back'. Memory is a
cognitive form that both forms, and is re-formed by, a poem. In 1903,
reviewing an unsatisfactory book about the Lake District, Thomas
had referred to 'the maturing in the vat of memory which makes
a difference as great as that between a photograph and a Titian'.[69]
His poetry, so long matured, is thus partly occupied with its own

mystery: with the transactions between conscious and unconscious memory that result in 'a pure thrush word' being suddenly cried out. Jean Moorcroft Wilson shows that Thomas's poem 'Beauty' is primarily based on a notebook entry from 1910 (see p. 256).[70] But what sent Thomas back to that notebook? What simultaneously brought to mind an image he had once quoted from a letter of Shelley's? What made 'Beauty' itself a poem about going back beyond loss to somewhere unspecified, perhaps to the locus of poetry? 'Not like a pewit that returns to wail/ For something it has lost, but like a dove/ That slants unswerving to its home and love …' (58).

Memory shuttles between the structural background and foreground of Thomas's poetry – as it does in 'Old Man'. This celebrated poem, which has many sources in Thomas's prose, may have begun as a palimpsest but ends as an *ars poetica*. 'Old Man' suggests not only how memory inhabits the conundrum of 'name' and 'thing' (including 'no-thing'), but also how it engages with that conundrum to create a poem:

Old Man or Lad's-love, – in the name there's nothing
To one that knows not Lad's-love, or Old Man,
The hoar-green feathery herb, almost a tree,
Growing with rosemary and lavender.
Even to one that knows it well, the names
Half decorate, half perplex, the thing it is:
At least, what that is clings not to the names
In spite of time. And yet I like the names.

The herb itself I like not, but for certain
I love it, as some day the child will love it
Who plucks a feather from the door-side bush
Whenever she goes in or out of the house.
Often she waits there, snipping the tips and shrivelling
The shreds at last on to the path, perhaps
Thinking, perhaps of nothing, till she sniffs

Her fingers and runs off. The bush is still
But half as tall as she, though it is as old;
So well she clips it … (36)

The oddly named plant opens up cognitive 'paths' to conscious and unconscious loci. Those paths are constituted by different rhythms, and may imply different kinds of poem. The first path, the path of metaphysical 'perplexity', is associated with a meditative tone and a syntax that circles around recurrent terms. As the speaker argues with himself, the stresses fall on such recurrence: name(s)/ nothing/ one/ knows; the chiasmus between the start of the first line and end of the second. In the lines where the speaker observes the child, repetition, stress and assonance work with present participles to emphasise habit rather than dialectics. The path 'in or out of the house' forms the basis for an epiphanic poem within the poem. Then, speculation about what the child 'will remember' (and the role of words therein) renders the epiphany kinetic, and projects it into the future: 'a bent path to a door'. The poem becomes a stream of consciousness, both speaker's and child's:

> Not a word she says;
> And I can only wonder how much hereafter
> She will remember, with that bitter scent,
> Of garden rows, and ancient damson-trees
> Topping a hedge, a bent path to a door,
> A low thick bush beside the door, and me
> Forbidding her to pick.

Here syntax (a single sentence) combines with blank verse to represent the making of memory (poetry) as a fluid accumulation, at once sensory and psychological. Yet there is tension between the cohesive rhythm and the possibility that the elements it carries may not ultimately cohere or endure. They may vanish down the poem's final cognitive path:

As for myself,
Where first I met the bitter scent is lost.
I, too, often shrivel the grey shreds,
Sniff them and think and sniff again and try
Once more to think what it is I am remembering,
Always in vain. I cannot like the scent,
Yet I would rather give up others more sweet,
With no meaning, than this bitter one.

I have mislaid the key. I sniff the spray
And think of nothing; I see and I hear nothing;
Yet seem, too, to be listening, lying in wait
For what I should, yet never can, remember:
No garden appears, no path, no hoar-green bush
Of Lad's-love, or Old Man, no child beside,
Neither father nor mother, nor any playmate;
Only an avenue, dark, nameless, without end.

'Old Man' ends as a shadow-path into a meaningless void, where the self-as-memory disintegrates. Yet anti-epiphany is one of the places where poetry goes. And this path, even if it figures darkness beyond human reach, is given presence by the verse-movement. The repeated 'no', the strongly stressed adjectival triple shot (one, two and three syllables), and the resonant ending on 'end' render the 'avenue' eerily tangible: a naming of the nameless, the climax of a memorable poem. At its very root, Thomas's poetry 'perplexes' the relation between memory and language, and suggests the complex epistemological paths that run between memory and lyric. In this he is a modern relativist. Yet, by not wholly detaching words from things, he also gives poetry a special status as memory, and memory a special status as poetry: 'the things are forgotten, and it is an aspect of them, a recreation of them, a finer development of them, which endures in the written words'.[71]

'Old Man' may sit close to poetic mysteries, because it is one of two poems, which, in November 1914, Thomas first wrote as prose-sketches. The other is 'Up in the Wind': his poem that most resembles a Frost eclogue. Yet these poems and their prototypes owe something to stylistic effects in Thomas's earlier prose. The orchestration of the paths in 'Old Man' recalls passages where Thomas goes deeply into, and hence elaborately constructs, a specific image. A paragraph in *The South Country* begins: 'I like trees for the cool evening voices of their many leaves, for their cloudy forms linked to earth by stately stems – for the pale lifting of the sycamore leaves in breezes and also their drooping, hushed and massed repose, for the myriad division of the light ash leaves – for their straight pillars and for the twisted branch work …' This single-sentence paragraph culminates in: 'the sycamores, which are the chief tree of Cornwall, as the beeches and yews are of the Downs, the oaks of the Weald, the elms of the Wiltshire vales'. A similar crescendo can occur where Thomas pursues an idea that later melts into his poetry's aesthetics/metaphysics; as when he ponders poetic 'worlds' or wishes: 'If only those poems which are place-names could be translated at last … What a flavour there is about the Bassetts, the Boughtons, the Worthys, the Tarrants, Winterbournes, Deverills, Manningfords, the Suttons …'.[72] Perhaps in such 'prose-music' Thomas achieves some unique 'rhythms and groupings' (see p. 31), some elements of a future poetic syntax – if not yet a relation between syntax and line. As 'Old Man' shows, it's not true that he eliminated all the rhetorical tropes of his prose style.

Compared with 'Old Man', the prose-sketch 'Old Man's Beard' suggests a plane taxi-ing rather than taking off. This is the first half:

Just as she is turning in to the house or leaving it, the baby plucks a feather of old man's beard. The bush grows just across the path from the door. Sometimes she stands by it squeezing off tip after tip from the branches and shrivelling them between her fingers on to the path in grey-green shreds. So the bush is still only half as tall as she is, though it is the same age. She never talks of it, but I wonder how much of the garden she will remember, the hedge with the old damson trees topping it, the vegetable rows, the path bending round the house corner, the old man's beard opposite the door, and me sometimes forbidding her to touch it, if she lives to my years. (149)

'Old Man' compresses phrases and clauses from 'Old Man's Beard': 'the same age'/'as old' ('old' echoes 'Old Man'); 'Just as she is turning into the house or leaving it'/'Whenever she goes in or out of the house'; 'touch it'/'pick'. Yet expansion can concentrate too: 'Old Man's Beard', in which the question of 'names' does not arise, ends merely: 'a dark avenue without an end'. Assonance is one trigger or agent of poetic concentration: mutually attracting words ('shrivel-ling'/'shreds'), drawing in new words: 'snipping' for 'tips'. But what powers all verbal changes is the new rhythmic spark between syntax and verse. While aspects of the poem's syntax are latent in 'Old Man's Beard', Thomas now exploits poetry's greater freedom as regards word order, its ability to bring English closer to an inflected language. We can already see that inversions of clause or phrase will be neither archaism nor occasional device but a mode of struc-tural concentration, integral to Thomas's unique way of breaking sentences across lines. Thus 'if she lives to my years', at the end of a prose sentence, becomes 'hereafter' near the start, and precedes rather than follows 'she will remember'. Then 'with that bitter scent' is tucked in between 'remember' and 'Of'. Compressed syntax effects a subtler interweaving of past and present, and tightens the liaison between 'scent' and memory. By beginning the next line with 'Of garden rows', Thomas also adds propulsion to the catalogue this phrase initiates. Later, 'As for myself I cannot remember when I first smelt that green bitterness' becomes: 'As for myself,/ Where first I met the bitter scent is lost'. Meeting now precedes loss, and asso-nance as well as stress connects/opposes 'first' and 'lost'. 'Hereafter' and 'lost' (more semantically suggestive than 'cannot remember') are also placed at line-endings. The line, engendered by the spark between syntax and verse, is where Thomas crosses the frontier. 'Free verse' does not necessarily bestow prose freedoms or 'open' endings. Any line in any poem must work as a line: a distinctive unit of poetic meaning within an overall movement. An effective line makes us fractionally pause it to grasp its role in that movement. All line-endings 'end' something; 'run-on' lines do not really run on (which is why most actors voice poems inaccurately). Rather, the pause focuses attention on what a specific syntactical continuity might mean. Hence the reflexive run-ons in 'The sun used to shine': 'paused and started/ Again', 'parted// Each night'. In 'Old Man' 'shrivelling' as end-word highlights the assonance with 'shreds'; while 'perhaps/ Thinking', which loads stress onto 'think-ing', differs in rhythm as well as nuance from 'perhaps of nothing' within the line. By making words work harder, Thomas's poems liberate possibilities locked up in his prose: 'Fixed and free/ In a rhyme' ('Words').

Thomas's blank verse, like that of Yeats and Frost, is an 'infinitely varied measure': free blank verse. His blank-verse poems range in length from 'Up in the Wind' (115 lines) to 'The Combe' (twelve lines), but all share a shadowy form of rhyming: assonance and repeated words, not always at line-endings, knit the verse. It's possible that Thomas's reading of Lawrence, as well as Frost, rubbed off. In 'Up in the Wind', two speakers tell the story of the isolated White Horse inn: a Thomas-like visitor and a 'wild girl' who works there. This poem's 'line' (nine to twelve syllables with a high quota of mono-syllabic words) is more conversationally pitched, less rhetorically intense, than that of 'Old Man'. It corresponds more exactly to what Thomas says about the blank verse of *North of Boston*:

> At first sight, some will pronounce simply that anyone can write this kind of blank verse, with all its tame common words, straightforward constructions, and innumerable perfectly normal lines … [Yet] the effect of each poem is one

and indivisible. You can hardly pick out a single line more than a single word. There are no show words or lines. The concentration has been upon the whole, not the parts. Decoration has been forgotten …[73]

Witness such lines in 'Up in the Wind' as:

> On all sides then, as now, paths ran to the inn;
> And now a farm-track takes you from a gate.
> Two roads cross, and not a house in sight
> Except 'The White Horse' in this clump of beeches.
> It hides from either road, a field's breadth back;
> And it's the trees you see, and not the house,
> Both near and far, when the clump's the highest thing
> And homely, too, upon a far horizon
> To one that knows there is an inn within. (31)

The setting of 'Up in the Wind' is the Froxfield plateau above Steep. The poem complements 'Old Man' by exploring historical rather than personal memory, and in not being 'pure lyric'. Reviewing *North of Boston*, Thomas concedes that the inspiration behind Frost's eclogues 'might, under other circumstances, have made pure lyric on the one hand or drama on the other'.[74] 'Up in the Wind', although modelled on the Frost eclogue (see p. 203), remains true to 'lyrical impulse' since it is 'one and indivisible' (every line works for its keep), and again presents cognitive mysteries: the inn 'hides from either road'. Another poem of paths, 'Up in the Wind' approaches 'the thing it is' via historicised, but not documentary, topography. The repeated nouns in the lines quoted above, the back-tracking clauses of the third sentence, involve the reader in slightly puzzling co-ordinates ('see', 'knows'), which pivot on relations between house and trees. The alliteration of 'highest', 'homely' and 'horizon' brings those relations to a climax, as do the assonantal line-endings: 'thing', 'horizon', the enfolded 'inn within'.

'The White Horse', prose origin of 'Up in the Wind', assembles environmental, social and familial history: interwoven, rather than juxtaposed, in the poem. This sketch (five times longer than 'Old Man's Beard') is significantly self-conscious about its genre:

> … Once, I think, the roads crossed in the midst of a tract of common which perhaps ended where now the inn is. But as things are it might well seem to have been hidden there out of someone's perversity. 'I should like to wring the old girl's neck for coming away here.' So said the woman who fetched my beer when I found myself at the inn first. She was a daughter of the house, fresh from a long absence in service in London, a bright wildish slattern with a cockney accent and her hair half down. She spoke angrily. If she did not get away before long, she said, she would go mad with the loneliness. She looked out sharply: all she could see was the beeches and the tiny pond beneath them and the calves standing in it drinking, alternately grazing the water here and there and thinking, and at last going out and standing still on the bank thinking … Every year I used to go there once or twice, never so often as to overcome the original feeling it had given me. I was always on the verge of turning that feeling or having it turned by a natural process, into a story. Whoever the characters would have been I do not think they would have included either the 'old girl' or the landlord's indignant cockney daughter … (144)

In fact, both women survive into the poem; which begins by making a blank-verse line out of the latter's anger with the former for turning a one-time smithy into the inn:

> 'I could wring the old thing's neck that put it here!
> A public-house! It may be public for birds,
> Squirrels and such-like, ghosts of charcoal-burners

And highwaymen.' The wild girl laughed. 'But I
Hate it since I came back from Kennington.
I gave up a good place.' Her Cockney accent
Made her and the house seem wilder by calling up –
Only to be subdued at once by wildness –
The idea of London, there in that forest parlour,
Low and small among the towering beeches
And the one bulging butt that's like a font … (31)

The switch from 'old girl' to 'old thing' ('thing' had been Thomas's first thought or transcription in the prose) gives the first line an internal rhyme that strengthens the 'wild' girl's attitude. The verse blends stress, tone and register to create a speaking presence. When the girl speaks again, the line-break highlights a second strong verb ('I/ Hate it'). Her vocabulary unites vigorous colloquialism ('old thing', 'such-like', 'a good place') with thematic signals for the poem as a whole ('ghosts'). 'A good place' has further meaning, given that the other narrator's comment attaches 'accent' to location, and merges inner and outer 'wildness'. Both kinds of wildness prevail over a city voice, and the paradoxical 'forest parlour' implies less stable living-conditions than 'Kennington'. The girl also sets the scene by linking natural and human history. Whereas 'Old Man' begins with the riddle of 'name' and 'thing', 'Up in the Wind' begins with socio-linguistics: with language environmentally located. Speech, the 'font' of Thomas's and Frost's poetry, establishes the poem's overall 'voice' as a counterpoint of voices. Yet 'common words' and 'straightforward constructions' may also involve riddles.

As the girl tells her story, inn, landscape and weather become increasingly interior:

'… Here I was born,
And I've a notion on these windy nights
Here I shall die. Perhaps I want to die here.

I reckon I shall stay. But I do wish
The road was nearer and the wind farther off …'

The simple utterance has a dark underlay. The girl subsequently deflects her problems, or gives them a new focus, by saying: 'Look at those calves'. Repeated at the end of the poem, this becomes refrain, just as her speech at the start is heightened by rhyme. Thomas has clearly looked at the calves in his prose, and recognised their symbolic and conclusive potential. A cumulative movement in prose-syntax again proves to have been revving up for poetry:

'… Look at those calves.'

> Between the open door
> And the trees two calves were wading in the pond,
> Grazing the water here and there and thinking,
> Sipping and thinking, both happily, neither long.
> The water wrinkled, but they sipped and thought,
> As careless of the wind as it of us.
> 'Look at those calves. Hark at the trees again.'

This climax, slower-paced than that of 'Old Man', more ruminative and oblique, is nonetheless rhetorically calculated. It starts with a run of present participles, and repeats 'trees', 'calves', 'water', 'Sipping and thinking'. Assonance binds 'thinking' to 'wrinkled', and reinforces the syntactical poise of the penultimate line. The girl's two-sentence line ends the poem as gnomically as she began it. Her apparently casual instruction to look and listen, along with the 'thinking' calves (compare the 'perhaps/ Thinking' child in 'Old Man'), leaves voices, perspectives and images in a still-mysterious tension established by means unavailable to prose. 'Hark at the trees again' includes 'Hark at the poem again.'

Thomas's prose had 'paraphrased' his future poems. Accordingly, his poems suggest what makes poetry 'most unlike' prose, even if the frontier remains fruitfully unstable. In 1908 he differentiated poetry from prose by aligning prose with 'explanation': 'Poetry shows results rather than processes, never explains; and, instead of explaining, compels.'[75]

4. INTRICATE FORMS

Blank verse was central to Thomas's transition from prose. Yet so was 'song': in 'An Old Song II' song becomes stanza and *vice versa*. Song underlies the lyric's 'intricacies of form'. Ten of the fifteen poems that Thomas wrote in December 1914 are rhymed; six, stanzaic. He told Frost on 15 December: 'I have been shy of blank verse tho (or because) I like it best. But the rhymes have dictated themselves decidedly'.[76] Indeed, it seems a matter of formal cross-overs rather than strict boundaries. A blank-verse poem may have a hidden stanzaic backbone, as well as shadowy or occasional rhyme; a rhymed poem may parallel the dynamics of a blank-verse paragraph. Some structures (such as the counterpoint between line and syntax) cross between different forms.

The four blank-verse sections of 'Old Man' have links with the eight-line stanza. The first and last sections consist of eight lines; the second section, of fifteen-and-a-half. Thomas splits the last line here between 'Forbidding her to pick' and 'As for myself', which begins a new seven-and-a-half line section. This irregularity at the heart of the poem prepares for what 'is lost'. Three other early blank-verse poems have structural parallels with 'Old Man' in that they involve epiphanic scenes and carry traces of stanza-form: 'March', 'The Manor Farm' and 'The Combe'. The three verse-paragraphs of 'March' expand in tandem with Spring's progress, starting from a three-line synopsis that covers both poem and Spring:

> Now I know that Spring will come again,
> Perhaps tomorrow: however late I've patience
> After this night following on such a day. (35)

The poem's second section (twelve lines) fills out 'such a day'. The final section (seventeen lines) centres on 'this night'. The question 'What did the thrushes know?' starts a build-up to a conclusion which, borrowing refrain from song, circles back to the first line: 'a silence/ Saying that Spring returns, perhaps tomorrow' (see p. 42). Here Thomas's blank-verse line is doing something different again. The reflexive thrush-soundscape is aptly 'packed' with sensory resonance, based on repetitions of Spring, sing/sang/song, silence: 'So they could keep off silence/ And night, they cared not what they sang or screamed'. 'The Manor Farm', too, places sensory effects in the foreground, but slower rhythms and more harmonious assonance herald a less provisional epiphany:

> The rock-like mud unfroze a little and rills
> Ran and sparkled down each side of the road
> Under the catkins wagging in the hedge.
> But earth would have her sleep out, spite of the sun;
> Nor did I value that thin gilding beam
> More than a pretty February thing
> Till I came down to the old Manor Farm,
> And church and yew-tree opposite, in age
> Its equals and in size … (45)

These lines, which move towards the poem's symbolic locus, are the first of two eight-and-a-half line units that make up its first section. Its briefer second section turns the scene into a sunlit vision, stretching back to when 'This England, Old already, was called Merry'. This section relates to the first as sestet to octet. Although wary of the sonnet's constraints, Thomas often uses sonnet-form, like stanza-form, as a hidden grid (see p. 103). 'The Combe' more tightly parallels the sonnet's 'turn'. A truncated 'sestet', beginning mid-line with 'But', completes a 'dark' involuted epiphany, which (formally too) counters that of 'The Manor Farm':

The Combe was ever dark, ancient and dark.
Its mouth is stopped with bramble, thorn, and briar;
And no one scrambles over the sliding chalk
By beech and yew and perishing juniper
Down the half precipices of its sides, with roots
And rabbit holes for steps. The sun of Winter,
The moon of Summer, and all the singing birds
Except the missel-thrush that loves juniper,
Are quite shut out. But far more ancient and dark
 The Combe looks since they killed the badger there,
Dug him out and gave him to the hounds,
That most ancient Briton of English beasts. (48)

Perhaps the poem's four sentences also compose a mutated stanza-structure within blank verse; itself densely textured by repeated words and sounds, sometimes at line-endings: 'briar', 'juniper', Winter', 'there'.

Quatrain and couplet, future staples of Thomas's formal repertoire, are there from the start, along with their roots in folk-expression. 'An Old Song I' takes off from the quatrains of 'The Lincolnshire Poacher', and echoes of proverbial rhyme lend ballast to the irregular couplets (and inner voices) of 'The Signpost':

I read the sign. Which way shall I go?
A voice says: You would not have doubted so
At twenty. Another voice gentle with scorn
Says: At twenty you wished you had never been born ... (37)

The couplets of 'November' can also be syllabically uneven: 'Twig, leaf, flint, thorn,/ Straw, feather, all that men scorn'. For 'After Rain' Thomas invents a halting couplet, which befits a lull in weather and feeling:

The rain of a night and a day and a night
Stops at the light
Of this pale choked day. The peering sun
Sees what has been done … (38)

Like his couplets, Thomas's quatrains and quatrain-poems do not
repeat their cadences. The first lines of 'Interval' and 'Birds' Nests'
lay down contrasting movements: 'Gone the wild day'; 'The summer
nests uncovered by autumn wind' (39, 43). More extended stanzas
are also tailor-made. The seven-liner of 'The Hollow Wood' (see
p. 24), symmetrical in neither rhyme-scheme nor line-length, takes
its cue from the goldfinch's 'flitting' and 'twitting'. The stanza of 'The
Other' is designed to blend narrative with reflection. The first six
lines are rhymed ABABAB (perhaps a nod to the ballad-quatrain);
the last four, CBCC (perhaps a nod to the sonnet). The closing
couplet, which may be narrative or reflective or both, punctuates the
stages of an inner journey that ends: 'He goes: I follow: no release/
Until he ceases. Then I also shall cease.' (42). Thomas is already
shaping the couplet into as flexible an instrument as blank verse.
Like the blank-verse poems discussed above, 'The Signpost' and
'November' consist of uneven sections that approximate to stanzas.
Conversely, 'After Rain' and 'The Mountain Chapel' combine rhyme
with a single fluid movement of long and short lines. 'The Mountain
Chapel' is based on three-line units: two four-beat lines followed
by a two-beat line, rhymed ABA, CDC etc. Its 42 lines, impelled by
sentences that often begin mid-line, also owe something to sonnet-
form and submerged stanza-form:

Chapel and gravestones, old and few,
Are shrouded by a mountain fold
From sound and view
Of life. The loss of the brook's voice
Falls like a shadow. All they hear is
The eternal noise

Of wind whistling in grass more shrill
Than aught as human as a sword,
And saying still:
'Tis but a moment since man's birth
And in another moment more
Man lies in earth …' (43)

Formal variables, including the unrhymed lines, seem intrinsic to the poem's shifting angles on 'sound and view/ Of life'.

Thomas, then, did not cling to blank verse (supposedly 'prosaic') before venturing into rhyme and stanza. He began as formally various as he would go on. He also began by introducing both symmetry and irregularity across every element of form, in both its narrower and larger sense. Each poem has a distinctive shape to which each line makes a distinctive contribution. That applies to poems in blank verse, couplets and quatrains, as well as to one-off verse-forms like those of 'The Hollow Wood', 'The Other', 'After Rain' and 'The Mountain Chapel' – although Thomas's fertile creation of new poem-shapes suggests that he is making deep formal discoveries. Those discoveries may owe something, though not everything, to poetic sibling-differentiation. Thomas's aesthetic relations with Frost will be discussed in Chapter 4. But it's relevant to his emergent lyric that he distinguished his practice from Frost's by adducing brevity and 'avoidance' of blank verse: 'I have tried as often as possible to avoid the facilities offered by blank verse and I try not to be long – I even have an ambition to keep under 12 lines (but rarely succeed)'.[77]

Perhaps to purge oneself of prose is to release an 'impulse' which, in being wholly poetic, might be called 'lyrical'. 'Concentration, intensity of mood' binds every aspect of a poem to such an impulse, and thus creates symbol. For Thomas, his various prose-modes had never fitted everything in. Ironically, the 'separable parts' of The South Country would cohere as lyric 'spasms'. This is an epistemological sense in which his extraction of poetry from prose defines lyric. A 'form that suits me' signifies a means of joining up, and mutually complicating, everything that engages Thomas's sensibility: the natural world, metaphysics, rural culture, literary culture, history, war, himself. Not that every poem brings those elements into play in the same proportion or from the same angle. In 1901 Thomas had indexed 'intricacies of form' to intricacies of genre: 'the myriad-minded lyric'. Perhaps owing to the meaningless portmanteau-category 'Nature poet', to the seeming homogeneity of his poetic cosmos, Thomas's generic range has been as under-estimated as his formal range. His first poems span lyric sub-genres that activate different dispositions of 'mind': 'think' and 'know' are recurrent verbs.

For instance, some poems are what MacNeice calls 'varieties of parable'.[78] They broach metaphysical and/or psychological questions by means of Everyman personae, emblematic imagery and a microcosmic setting. 'The Other' is Thomas's most elaborate parable-poem, but 'The Signpost' and 'November' also present existential conundrums. 'The Signpost' is as emblematic as its title: the speaker/seeker stands in a spooky wintry landscape ('The dim sea glints chill. The white sun is shy'), asking: 'Which way shall I go?' The two 'voices' frame different answers, the most persuasive voice advocating 'earth' and life. 'November' contrasts 'One', to whom November skies represent a 'heavenly' 'refuge', with 'Another' who 'loves even the mud whose dyes/ Renounce all brightness to the skies' (34). Thomas would go on writing 'To be or not to be' poems, but more obliquely. 'After Rain' and 'Interval' inaugurate perhaps the key aspect of his lyric mind: where statement recedes, where image works with form to lay foundations for symbol. Yet, generically, as formally, there are no hard-and-fast boundaries. Thus epiphany, close to Thomas's lyric core, is a pervasive structure. 'The Mountain Chapel' blends parable (the focus on 'man') with epiphany (mountain scene) en route to its bleak conclusion: 'When gods were young/ This wind was old.'

As Thomas's early poems move between genres, the 'I' speaker plays various parts from the merest perceptual prop to psychological lead. Lyric drama stirs facets of ourselves as observer, thinker, lover, artist, mortal being. In ' Up in the Wind' 'I' occupies the cusp between narrative and lyric; in 'The Signpost' he is extraverted into signs and voices. The 'I' of 'The Other' is Rimbaud's 'un autre'. In both 'old songs' 'I' speaks for (evolving) tradition as much as for any self. 'I' comes late in 'Interval' to confirm that the oxymoronic 'roaring peace' of a windy scene has been internalised. But 'I' is absent from, or understood in, 'November', 'After Rain', 'The Mountain Chapel', 'The Hollow Wood' and 'The Combe'. In effect, a named 'I' is not the only actor on Thomas's (mostly lyric) stage. The speech-act matters more than 'who speaks'. One might expect the poems discussed above as 'epiphanies' to pivot on 'I'. Yet only 'Old Man', partly about epiphany or its absence, places 'I' at the psychodramatic centre. Who 'looks' into 'The Combe' is not identified; 'March' displaces the arrival of Spring onto what 'the thrushes know'. The epiphanies of 'The Manor Farm' and 'The Combe' are primarily cultural, although (like all these early poems) they advance Thomas's revelation to himself as poet.

In making a split 'I' its theme, 'The Other' signals the dispersal of Thomas's poetic self into everything that a poem's 'intricacies of form' encompass:

> … I learnt his road and, ere they were
> Sure I was I, left the dark wood
> Behind, kestrel and woodpecker,
> The inn in the sun, the happy mood
> When first I tasted sunlight there.
> I travelled fast, in hopes I should
> Outrun that other. What to do
> When caught, I planned not. I pursued
> To prove the likeness, and, if true,
> To watch until myself I knew … (40)

Rhymed contraries, 'dark wood'/ 'happy mood', stake out the fork-ing road. The second half of the stanza crams in three sentences that particularly confuse Self and Other, as when ambiguous syntac-tical units begin and end lines: 'When caught', 'until myself I knew'. The porous boundaries (visionary, formal, generic) of Thomas's lyric ground originate in such antinomies. In December 1914 it was already clear that dialectics/ drama would shape relations between, as within, his poems. His late start and pressing horizon may have concentrated his poetry as a whole into a lyric sequence or sequence of interlacing sequences. Poems are set at multiple angles to one another: the nearest contemporary equivalent was Yeats's practice. It's proof of urgency ('I travelled fast') that poems such as 'The Other' and 'Old Man' encode, as well as initiate, this larger intricate geometry. Like 'An Old Song II', 'After Rain' harks back to Thomas writing about lyric form in 1901: 'Increasing complexity of thought and emotion will find no such outlet as the myriad-minded lyric, with its intricacies of form as numerous and as exquisite as those of a birch-tree in the wind.' The poem ends:

> The leaflets out of the ash-tree shed
> Are thinly spread
> In the road, like little black fish, inlaid,
> As if they played.
> What hangs from the myriad branches down there
> So hard and bare
> Is twelve yellow apples lovely to see
> On one crab-tree,
> And on each twig of every tree in the dell
> Uncountable
> Crystals both dark and bright of the rain
> That begins again. (38)

In that liquidly musical finale 'myriad branches' and 'Uncountable' echo Thomas's critical credo, but it is primarily felt or heard as form. At the climax, where rain and rhythm are paused, the word/ line 'Uncountable' bears a self-relishing stress between 'dell' and 'Crystals'. And 'rain', which begins by symbolising a force that has 'choked' expression, ends as art: 'leaflets' might be poems. 'Crystals both dark and bright of the rain' suggests 'complexity of thought and emotion' becoming intricate form. And this process will 'begin again'.

CHAPTER 2

Remixing the Romantics

'We cannot dissociate ourselves from Keats and his contemporaries. We are bone of their bone and flesh of their flesh.'[1] So wrote Edward Thomas in 1910. In 1901, when boosting the emergent modern lyric, he had also invoked Romantic origins:

> Early last century it was boldly prophesied that dramatic poetry would supersede all other branches of the art. Lyric and epic were classed as outworn, barbarous forms, incapable of expounding the complexity of modern life … At that very time the lyric was asserting a supremacy which it has never lost. The very dramas of the day were often lyrical, and had only lyrical good qualities. 'Prometheus Unbound' is actually called by Shelley 'a lyrical drama'. The noblest literary achievements were in the lyric. So puissant was it that its caress entrapped philosophy. Coleridge, Wordsworth, Shelley and their great contemporaries revealed its adaptability to every mode of thought and emotion.[2]

To prove the lyric's post-Romantic sway, Thomas cites 'Swinburne and Meredith, of a passing age', and comes up to date with: 'above all there is Mr Yeats'. Since his values as a critic, if not yet as a poet, were so rooted in the Romantics, Thomas understood how Yeats was extending their achievement: 'He seems to have got beyond our critical interest in old things, folk-lore, spiritualism, etc., as much as Wordsworth got beyond Percy['s *Reliques*] … his glorious work …

plays and must play a great part in the movement of this age towards a finer and deeper spirit'.[3]

Today we are more sceptical about 'finer and deeper spirits'. When Thomas read the Romantic poets, 'Romantic ideology' had yet to be deconstructed – not that he is always 'brain of their brain'. Jerome J. McGann, in his influential study *The Romantic Ideology* (1983), argues that most Romantic works 'displace' the socio-political context of 'the actual human issues with which the poetry is concerned'; that they transfer those issues to 'idealised localities'; and that 'an uncritical absorption in Romanticism's own self-representations' has made critics complicit in this manoeuvre. McGann's book challenged an approach to Romantic poetry, which had allegedly repressed historical context by fixating on subjectivity, transcendence and, indeed, poetry.[4] Nicholas Roe sums up (with irony) the resultant shift in academic perspectives: 'Wordsworth, for example, writes in "Tintern Abbey" of "something far more deeply interfused" as a way of not writing about the failure of the French Revolution or poverty in the Wye valley.'[5] As the Romantic poets are linked with lyric, so Anti-Romanticism merges into Anti-Lyricism (both belong to the same quarrel between two schools of criticism). Thus Gene W. Ruoff, in a post-McGann book on the 'major lyrics' of Wordsworth and Coleridge, is reluctant to call a poem a 'poem'. Ruoff has no 'belief that either the use or end of language within poetic discourse is radically different'.[6] Yet, for all the (often salutary) academic attention to other 'texts' in the Romantic period, the 'major lyrics' have not gone away. And various critics have portrayed those lyrics as less in contextual denial than McGann contends. For instance, Michael Löwy and Robert Sayre argue that 'analyses inspired by McGann … often miss the crucial point, namely, the power of the Romantic anti-bourgeois critique and its liberating aspirations'. And, in *Lyric and Labour in the Romantic Tradition*, Anne Janowitz stresses the 'communitarian' as well as 'individualist' element in the Romantic matrix. She shows that 'lyrical ballad' need not be an oxymoron.[7] Yeats, Thomas and other modern poets have remade the lyrical ballad: perhaps a mark of its vitality. Poems have something to tell academic criticism about their precursors. When McGann maximises the 'differentials' between Romantic consciousness and 'our' more 'advanced' culture, he discounts what poetry can do with differentials.[8]

This chapter will suggest that Thomas (like Yeats and Wallace Stevens) marks the spot where, in English-language poetry, Romantic aesthetics undergo a modern metamorphosis. Beneath the academy's radar, Romantic structures may still be part of poetry's bone and flesh. It's not just a matter of individual poets taking the odd cue from Wordsworth or Keats, but of epochal tides: 'something far more deeply interfused'. Perhaps only poems, including Romantic poems, truly test 'Romantic ideology' – if in a different (deeper) sense than McGann's. Indeed, whenever scholars in the field modify the historicist approach, which binds readers as well as poems to a particular context, they seem to rediscover something distinctive about what poetry does. For instance, Richard Eldridge argues that the 'specifically situated protagonist' of Romantic poems uniquely 'embodies' the quest to elicit 'value [from] scrutiny of our human possibilities'. Eldridge illustrates his point by exploring Wordsworth's 'dialectical movement of thought', which can 'transfigure and deepen our sense of the possibilities and practice of both philosophy and poetry'.[9] As this chapter will show, Romantic 'possibilities' have a key role in the metaphysics of Thomas's poetry. Yet Thomas is as sensitive to the difference between poetry and the philosophy it 'caresses' as to that between poetry and prose. He writes of a collection by John Davidson: 'We ought to guess the philosophy from the poetry no more than we guess the athlete's meals from the length of his leap.'[10] This resembles Coleridge complaining that 'metaphysical trains of Thought … when I wished to write a poem, beat up Game of far other kind – instead of a Covey of poetic Partridges with whirring wings of music, or wild Ducks *shaping* their rapid flight in forms always regular (a still better image of Verse) up came a metaphysical Bustard, urging its slow, heavy, laborious, earth-skimming Flight, over dreary & level Wastes.'[11] The deconstruction of 'Romantic ideology' may be 'a metaphysical Bustard' which seeks to strip poetry of its truth-claims.

1. 'SACRED BOOKS'

For Edward Thomas as for Yeats and Stevens, Romantic poetry was not remote literary history. In Britain and Ireland the 'Symbolist movement' of the later nineteenth century had a neo-Romantic dynamic, which fuelled, and was fuelled by, critical and scholarly developments. Editions, biographies and studies of the poets poured forth. Thomas often reviewed this spate of publications, to which poets contributed. For instance, Swinburne, Yeats, Arthur Symons (author of *The Symbolist Movement in Literature*) and Laurence Binyon promoted what Seamus Perry calls 'the rise and rise of Blake'.[12] Although Thomas complained that reprints in general were swamping new poetry (see p. 25), the necessity to rethink the Romantic poets, while being exposed to work which variously derived from them, lengthened his critical perspectives and braced his critical standards. In autumn 1906 we find him reviewing an edition of Blake's poems, and, soon after, Symons's collection *The Fool of the World* (1906). Perhaps Blake's 'beautiful poetry and powerful ideas', as well as the poets named, are fresh in Thomas's mind when he qualifies his praise of Symons by saying that his poems 'have not the intellectual abandonment of Wordsworth's, nor the sensuous abandonment of Keats's', and 'lack that divine impulse which makes poetry something entirely different from prose'. He writes in similar terms of a neo-Romantic collection by AE (George Russell), actually called *The Divine Vision*: 'The poet has intellect, he has emotion, observation, imagination, but they seldom lose their identities and become art.'[13] Thomas touches Romantic base from another angle when he compares the utter typicality of William Watson's *New Poems* with eighteenth-century poetry's appeal to 'ordinary men'. Thomas claims that 'Pope might have talked the "Essay on Man" before writing it'; whereas 'no ordinary man could fancy himself writing the "Ode to the West Wind", or "Kubla Khan"'. That nothing by Watson 'causes the least surprise when understood' aligns the Romantic poets (and Thomas) with continuing Symbolist revolt against 'exteriority' and 'rhetoric'.[14]

In the early 1900s 'Romantic ideology' undoubtedly spawned much lazy criticism and derivative poetry: 'gifted people who do nothing but continue or weaken in verse the attitude of Shelley … or of Keats, sometimes with the addition of a vaguer mournfulness and a less intelligible choice of words'.[15] But poems cannot be held responsible for the uses to which they are put. Being so alive to the Romantic poets as source and touchstone for contemporary poetry, Thomas kept an eye on their reception. He never forgave Matthew Arnold for calling Shelley a 'beautiful and ineffectual angel' (a 'splenetic adventure in depreciation').[16] And it was W. J. Courthope, Oxford Professor of Poetry in the 1890s, who provoked the affirmation 'bone of their bone and flesh of their flesh'. Reviewing Courthope's *History of English Poetry*, Thomas dismisses his argument, driven by neo-Augustanism and anti-Jacobinism, that 'Wordsworth and Keats [are] astray from the development of English poetry through Chaucer, Shakespeare, Milton, Dryden, Pope, Gray, and Johnson'; and that 'the last century's progress in poetry has been upon mistaken lines'. He says of Courthope's 'reactionary revolt': 'Too much Pope has spoiled him for poetry – Pope and his theory that poet and poetry must be obviously connected with social life'.[17] The Romantics still attracted moral as well as political suspicion. Thomas writes in his brief study *Keats* (1916):

[W]e have been deceived into suspecting evil of ['Ode to a Nightingale'] because it is beautiful and attributes divinity to what we think a weakness. None today would complain if the thought had remained in this lyrical form:

Welcome joy, and welcome sorrow,
　Lethe's weed and Hermes' feather;
Come today, and come tomorrow,
　I do love you both together!

we should begin to talk earnestly of the gospel of pain.[18]

Some younger critics, partly in reaction against *fin-de-siècle*
'decadence', put a new spin on Victorian moral disapproval. One
such was Irving Babbitt: the anti-Romantic American critic who
influenced the 'classicism' professed by T. S. Eliot, and whose polemic
The New Laokoon (1910) anticipated aspects of *The Romantic Ideology*.
As Thomas notes in his review of *The New Laokoon*, Babbitt questions
the value set on 'spontaneity' and 'expressiveness'; attacks 'indeter-
minate enthusiasms' and 'vapid emotionalism'; and complains that
'literature has lost "virility and seriousness" in losing "standards and
discipline"'. Thomas comments: 'he has plenty of acid for attack;
only we doubt whether he would look so well had he less hostile
criticism to do, and we should be afraid of the creative activity of
one who believes it to be the work of the imagination "to throw as it
were a veil of divine illusion over some essential truth"'. He wonders
whether the book is 'anything more than an uncommonly ingenious
and laboured expression of the academic objection to life'.[19] Resistant
to critics who categorise, Thomas rarely employs even the adjective
'Romantic', let alone 'Romanticism'. Rather, he discusses individual
poets and poems, specific links and differences. When reviewing
Symons's critical survey *The Romantic Movement in English Poetry*
(1909) he accepts the titular term, but says approvingly: 'The
movement is not treated as a movement at all. Each writer is taken
separately, and for the most part Mr Symons leaves it to his readers
to flounder in generalisations if they will, for he gives them few.'[20]
Yet Thomas 'generalises' in the sense that he is chiefly interested
in nineteenth-century poetry that has split from the aesthetic
premises of an era when only Crabbe's works gave much evidence

of 'tangible and recognisable human life'. He never doubts that a necessary revolution occurred: 'How glorious it must have been … to have welcomed, with mind just fresh from eighteenth-century miscellanies, the *Lyrical Ballads!*'[21] It's significant for Thomas's aesthetics (and shows his indifference to over-arching 'Romanticism') that he detaches Byron from such glories: 'his was a crude eighteenth century stomach with a genuine craving for nineteenth century food'. He accuses Byron of 'binding the lovely verse, not as Keats, with flowers and such painless bonds, but with chains that cut'.[22] While Thomas sees most eighteenth-century poets as shrinking poetry's vision and constricting its forms, he writes of Blake (thirty years Byron's senior): 'An intelligent man who has once read a large part of Blake with patience can never again settle down with just the same dusty creases in his mind as before. He drenches the mind with eternity.'[23] But it's Shelley who was Thomas's first love, and who exemplifies his neo-Romantic affiliations with Yeats. Yeats himself would eventually recognise that Shelley 'and not Blake, whom I had studied more and with more approval, had shaped my life'; and recall that 'unlike Blake, isolated by an arbitrary symbolism, [Shelley had] seemed to sum up all that was metaphysical in English poetry'. In fact, Yeats's massive debt to Shelley had been obvious since his 1900 essay 'The Philosophy of Shelley's Poetry' (praised by Thomas), where philosophy and poetry are coterminous: 'whatever of philosophy has been made poetry is alone permanent'. Here, having re-read *Prometheus Unbound*, Yeats assigns it 'an even more certain place than I had thought, among the sacred books of the world'.[24] Shelley's shaping effect on Thomas is suggested by this eulogy (1905):

> Keats may be a greater poet. Wordsworth and Byron may be more effectual. Matthew Arnold has said as much, and there are many who believe in the efficacy of repeating it, although it is not clear whether the critic condemned Shelley for any better reason than that he did not wear side-whiskers …
>
> Shelley is an immortal sentiment. Men may forget to

repeat his verses; they can never be as if Shelley had never been. He is present wherever youth and love and rapture are. He is a part of all high-spirited and pure audacity of the intellect and imagination, of all clean-handed rebellion, of all infinite endeavour and hope. The remembered splendour of his face is more to us than the Houses of Parliament …

[I]t comes as the final defeat, when Shelley is left dusty on the shelf; and the defection of a poet from the tribe of Shelley is the great apostasy of the nineteenth century.[25]

Thomas's copy of *The Lyric Poems of Shelley* was not 'left dusty'. It survives, to quote Guy Cuthbertson, 'with flowers and leaves between the pages, and fly-leaves entirely covered by copies in his hand-writing of the best-loved poems and passages'. In *The Happy-Go-Lucky Morgans* (1913) Thomas's *alter ego* Philip Morgan spends the last Spring before he dies ('a poet's Spring') quoting Shelley: the 'sad bliss' and 'wild wisdom' of 'the greatest lyrics that ever were'. Perhaps Philip's Shelleyan death underlies Thomas's poetic birth.[26]

Thomas read the Romantic poets so closely that his reviews of an edited *Collected Poems* are liable to dwell on variants and changes. When he notices Keats's 'developing tact and self-criticism … during composition', is he unconsciously interested in composing poems?[27] More broadly, here again Thomas's critical emphases prefigure his creative practice and assume new configurations within it. Byron and Blake are the Romantic poets furthest from his core aesthetic values: Byron, owing to his Augustan affinities, because his spectacular life exceeds his 'careless' art, and because he 'preferred writing about himself to self-expression';[28] Blake, because he is *sui generis*:

[H]e stands and works alone. He is out of the stream of English literature. His one true predecessor, Thomas Traherne, he never knew.

His most characteristic work seems to owe nothing to anyone else, but to spring straight from the brain of Blake or from the universe which he contemplated, or from an electric union of the two.

Blake, like Byron, is an imperfect artist: 'Although he could always catch the heavenly harmony of thoughts, he could seldom mount them on a fitting chariot of rhythm and rhyme.'[29] Thomas sees Wordsworth, in his best poems, as both artist and visionary, yet does not write extensively about him. Perhaps too much had already been said; perhaps others reviewed the new editions; perhaps comparative silence marks deep influence. Thomas's debt to Wordsworth is shown by the degree to which he both reconceives Wordsworth's 'Romantic ecology' and reworks Wordsworthian tropes (see below); also by his certainty that *Lyrical Ballads* changed the game. He takes as given the conceptual shift whereby Wordsworth 'made of nature a neighbour commonwealth to our own'; the structural shift whereby Wordsworth 'writes a poem in the hope of making it give the same impression as a certain hawthorn-tree gives to him'; and the demotic-folk shift which reintroduced speech to poetry, ballad to lyric. His highest praise of W. H. Davies is to say that it can be 'natural to him to write, much as Wordsworth wrote, with the clearness, compactness, and felicity which make a man think with shame how unworthily … he manages his native tongue'.[30] Thomas identifies most closely with Wordsworth in his reviews of *North of Boston*: that is, he virtually hails Frost's poetry (and proleptically his own and Frost's together) as *Lyrical Ballads* Mark 2: 'Mr Frost has, in fact, gone back, as Whitman and as Wordsworth went back, through the paraphernalia of poetry into poetry again'; 'speech … possessing a kind of healthy, natural delicacy like Wordsworth's'.

Yet Thomas also thinks that Frost, in his new 'experiment like Wordsworth's', 'sympathises where Wordsworth contemplates'.[31] Thomas's symbolist leanings make him resistant to Wordsworthian 'contemplation', as to Arnold's view that Wordsworth and Byron are more 'effectual' than Shelley. His own writings on Shelley, Keats and Coleridge take a more inward turn than his writings on Wordsworth.

He engages more minutely with the intrinsically 'poetic' qualities of their work. Thus in one review Thomas argues against the belief that Shelley's poems wholly lack the sensory power of Keats's. As unwilling to make false divisions as false connections, he juxtaposes quotations designed to show what these poets have in common 'as prisms to the sunlight, lyres to the winds, still and living mirrors to catch and transform the pageantry of earth and heaven' (compare 'mirror shaking' in Thomas's 'An Old Song II'). But Thomas is equally acute about the distinctive role of 'sensuous things' in each poet's work, given Shelley's 'innate tendency ... to transmute visible things into spirits and abstractions', whereas Keats 'saw things themselves and not their spirits'.[32] Thomas also distinguishes between Coleridge's practice and Keats's 'sensuous eye': 'It is characteristic of Coleridge ... not to produce elaborate pictures, but rather to set the mind alight by a few strokes.' All these comments suggest the sensory palette that had impressed Thomas before he wrote his own poems, including the further dimension of 'sensuous things' in Romantic poetry. He writes of Coleridge's poetic make-up:

> Coleridge loved mildness and wildness equally. Mildness, meekness, gentleness, softness, made sensuous and spiritual appeals to his chaste and voluptuous affections and to something homely in him, while his spirituality, responding to wildness, branched out into metaphysics and into natural magic.[33]

Thomas's poem 'The Chalk-Pit' contains a self-portrait in which he figures as 'Mild and yet wild too'. Like other poems by Thomas, it also involves 'some ghost': 'ghostliness' being an aspect of Coleridgean wildness. Ultimately, with regard to all the Romantic poets, Thomas is interested in the (sometimes ghostly) chemistry between man and work, and in how a poem's structures effect, or do not effect, transformation into a poetic 'self'. His summation of Keats's odes is a key passage: 'in the odes the poet made for himself a form in which the essence of all his thought, feeling, and observation, could be stored without overflowing or disorder; of its sources in his daily life there was no more shown than made his poems quick instead of dead'.[34]

Yet it's about poetry's apotheosis too: about what Yeats calls 'sacred books'. Romantic aesthetics invest, or seek to invest, poetry with powers transferred from God to the poet's mind. For Thomas, Shelley personifies such powers. And he says of Coleridge's 'combination' of 'richness and delicacy, of sweetness and freshness, of sensuousness and wildness, of spirit and sense' that these qualities can be 'raised again and again to a peculiar harmony from the innermost parts of our poetry's holy of holies'. But perhaps Keats, for whom the poetry of the past had such 'intense reality', represents something that Thomas replicates in his whole attraction to the Romantic poets and to their own remixings: Keats 'lived more passionately in the company of the dead than any other man ever did … in [his poems] we see the poets all as one company'.[35]

2. 'THE DESIRE OF THE EYE'

Romantic poets aspire to 'vision'. It's as visionaries that Thomas celebrates Shelley and Blake. He writes of Blake: 'The microscope is a toy compared with his vision. He made human the stars and the seasons, and he made starry the flower and the grass.'[36] Although 'vision' encompasses the other senses that mediate between mind and universe, M. H. Abrams notices 'the extraordinary emphasis throughout this era on the eye and the object and the relation between them'.[37] Thomas's poetry understands and manifests what 'The Lofty Sky' calls 'The desire of the eye' (53). He also sets high standards for 'seeing'. 'And now I see as I look' is the climactic line of 'First known when lost' (61). With reference to Blake, Thomas defines imagination as 'the clear seeing of things in the brain, whether those things exist (and have been seen) in nature, or … only in the brain'. He says in his biography of Richard Jefferies: 'The clearness of the physical is allied to the penetration of the spiritual vision'; and stresses that 'the habit of concentration' is essential to both. Jefferies, whom Thomas compares with Blake, Shelley and Wordsworth, was a further channel through which he absorbed the Romantics' 'intense communion ... with the earth, the sun and sky'.[38] Yet, as in 'Ode to a Nightingale', Romantic poems do not take vision for granted: 'Was it a vision, or a waking dream?' Shelley ends 'Mont Blanc' with a more complex question: 'And what wert thou, and earth, and stars, and sea,/ If to the human mind's imaginings/ Silence and solitude were vacancy?' (In *The Happy-Go-Lucky Morgans*, this is mooted as an epitaph for David Morgan: another 'poetical' Morgan brother who dies.)[39] Even McGann concedes that 'Romantic poetry incorporates Romantic ideology as a drama of the contradictions which are inherent to that ideology', although he regards this drama as largely outwith the poetry's consciousness or control.[40] Thomas's poetry revisits the dialectics that complicate Romantic vision (Blake's 'contraries'), Romantic aspiration to vision (Wordsworth's flickering 'intimations') and Romantic apotheosising of poetic vision: Shelley torn between reason and 'imaginings'. For Thomas, all these dialectics have been further complicated by modernity.

Thomas's poems sometimes approach Blake's visionary immediacy. 'The Dark Forest' springs 'from the universe': 'Dark is the forest and deep, and overhead/ Hang stars like seeds of light ...' (130). 'Cock-Crow', written just after Thomas enlisted, while not unambiguous about the war, transmits a 'Jerusalem'-like intensity:

> Out of the wood of thoughts that grows by night
> To be cut down by the sharp axe of light, –
> Out of the night, two cocks together crow,
> Cleaving the darkness with a silver blow:
> And bright before my eyes twin trumpeters stand,
> Heralds of splendour, one at either hand,
> Each facing each as in a coat of arms:
> The milkers lace their boots up at the farms. (101)

Thomas attributes to Blake 'a settled mystic patriotism, which wars could not disturb',[41] and the deepest England sounded in his own poems may have Blakean vibrations. 'Good-night', which endows the London streets of Thomas's youth with a timeless music, echoes Blake's 'The Echoing Green': 'the call of children in the unfamiliar streets/ That echo with a familiar twilight echoing' (67). Contrariwise, 'February Afternoon' (as contrasted with 'Cock-Crow' too) parallels the negative face of Blake's millenarianism. Here a war-mongering Moloch-like God looms over English landscape: 'And God still sits aloft in the array/ That we have wrought him, stone-deaf and stone-blind' (109).

In three poems with abstract titles – 'Ambition', 'Health' and 'The Glory' – Thomas explicitly broaches the question of vision, perhaps of 'Romantic ideology'. These poems revisit the 'situated' Romantic protagonist who projects a varying mix of metaphysical, psychological and aesthetic needs onto the phenomenal world. Like the protagonist in Coleridge's 'Dejection: An Ode', Thomas's troubled 'I' faces the difficulty of internalising 'outward forms' as spiritual or poetic vision. There's also a sense that the difficulty, like entropy, increases. 'Ambition' begins by doubting its very subject:

Unless it was that day I never knew
Ambition. After a night of frost, before
The March sun brightened and the South-west blew,
Jackdaws began to shout and float and soar
Already, and one was racing straight and high
Alone, shouting like a black warrior
Challenges and menaces to the wide sky ... (59)

The birds in flight and song reprise the inspirational energy of Shelley's 'Skylark'. This kinetic effect, driven by monosyllabic verbs and run-on lines, gives way to slower rhythms associated with (mainly visual) imagery of stasis: 'plumes of pearly smoke', 'a motionless white bower/ Of purest cloud, from end to end close-knit', a train's roar 'touched … with silence'. Here, moving from inspiration to practice, Thomas again implicitly writes a poem within a poem: 'ambition' is realised as a 'close-knit' artwork. Yet, like the previous sound and movement, which verges on violence ('warrior', 'menaces'), this smoke-and-mirrors effect seems to over-reach itself. Its stillness is destabilised by inflated metaphor and by the speaker's self-ironical confession of creative hubris:

> Time
> Was powerless while that lasted. I could sit
> And think I had made the loveliness of prime,
> Breathed its life into it and were its lord,
> And no mind lived save this 'twixt clouds and rime.
> Omnipotent I was, nor even deplored
> That I did nothing. But the end fell like a bell:
> The bower was scattered; far off the train roared.
> But if this was ambition I cannot tell.
> What 'twas ambition for I know not well.

'Ambition' confronts a gap between Romantic aspiration/ inspiration and its fulfilment. The poem reflexively 'ends' by puncturing the vision it has engendered. Mind and universe manage only an illusory liaison, not Wordsworth's ideal marriage. Michael Kirkham argues: 'This is, surely, a Lucifer's dream of usurpation, the pride that comes before the fall, *the* Fall. This Lucifer, besides, is a Romantic poet, blurring distinctions between perception and conception, imagining that his work reproduces the act of Creation.' For Kirkham, the pun on 'rime' is 'Thomas's critique of his *'romantic self'*.[42] Yet Thomas's larger 'Romantic self' includes such critique. Indeed, an earlier form of it can be found in Shelley's concern with 'the perennial divorce of inspiration and composition', to quote Angela Leighton. This divorce Leighton sees as impelling an 'aesthetic of the sublime', which (as at the end of 'Mont Blanc') is more ambivalent than Wordsworth's: '[Shelley] still looks on the landscapes of infinity, but … expresses the possibility, in his poems, that they do not "look at us in return"'.[43] In 'Ambition', 'Omnipotent I was' may echo Keats attacking 'the wordsworthian or egotistical sublime'.[44] The poem certainly alludes to Keats, when bringing the God-like speaker down to earth with a heavier bump than 'Forlorn! The very word is like a bell/ To toll me back from thee to my sole self' in 'Ode to a Nightingale'. 'Ambition' is one of the 'Phantoms' that Keats repudiates in 'Ode on Indolence'.

In 'The Glory' Thomas will return to the gap between clouds and rhyme, and mention the 'sublime'. But his intermediate poem 'Health' proposes a more positive, because less ambitious, version of vision. This is also the poem where he comes nearest to free verse, perhaps because its speculative cast requires a looser medium:

Four miles at a leap, over the dark hollow land,
To the frosted steep of the down and its junipers black,
Travels my eye with equal ease and delight:
And scarce could my body leap four yards.

This is the best and the worst of it –
Never to know,
Yet to imagine gloriously, pure health.

Today, had I suddenly health,
I could not satisfy the desire of my heart
Unless health abated it … (82)

At the outset, 'Health' registers, but accepts, a gap. The speaker begins by separating vision – the poet's leaping 'eye', its capacity for glorious imagining – from other physical and metaphysical faculties. This exerts some control over aspiration: now in its more visceral Romantic mode as 'desire'. The desires specified are for 'beauty' (art), 'peace' (psychic equilibrium), ultimately for 'power':

Yet I am not satisfied
Even with knowing I never could be satisfied.
With health and all the power that lies
In maiden beauty, poet and warrior,
In Caesar, Shakespeare, Alcibiades,
Mazeppa, Leonardo, Michelangelo […]
I could not be as the wagtail running up and down
The warm tiles of the roof slope, twittering
Happily and sweetly as if the sun itself
Extracted the song …

'Ambition' contains the words 'powerless' and 'omnipotence'. In 'Health', 'power' has Byronic and Nietzschean rather than (or as well as) Faustian contexts. Discussing Byron's poem 'Mazeppa', Thomas says: 'There are finer poems … but [the poet] is the equal of that wild lover [and] of the great king who slept while the tale was told'. Nietzsche's exemplars for his Ubermensch include Caesar and Michelangelo. Comparing Jefferies to Nietzsche, Thomas remarks that Jefferies 'would not have made the mistake of so admiring the unfettered great man's prowess as not to see the beauty of the conquered and all the other forms of life which the powerful would destroy if they might'.[45] 'Health' effectively reins in Romantic ambition by resisting the idea of the poet as superhero or 'warrior': another word repeated from 'Ambition'. Thomas will soon be a soldier-poet, but no D'Annunzio. The speaker rejects solipsistic hubris and focuses on focus: on the capacity of the poet's eye to assimilate, rather than beget, its objects:

I could not be as the sun.
Nor should I be content to be
As little as the bird or as mighty as the sun.
For the bird knows not of the sun,
And the sun regards not the bird.

But I am almost proud to love both bird and sun,
Though scarce this Spring could my body leap four yards.

Thomas plays with proportion as in 'The Word' (see p. 34), and Keats may again supply an aesthetic counterweight to Romantic over-reaching. The sun 'extracting' the song redefines power as 'Negative Capability', while 'bird and sun' together recall Keats's: 'I scarce remember counting upon any Happiness – I look not for it if it be not in the present hour … The setting sun will always set me to rights – or if a Sparrow come before my Window I take part in its existence and pick about the Gravel.'[46] In 'lov[ing] both bird and sun', which cannot 'know' each other, Thomas's speaker positions himself where vision can indeed bridge gaps: where a poem might be written (or is being written). This present-tense poem ends with a more achieved 'poem within a poem' than that of 'Ambition'.

Aspirational words common to 'Health' and 'The Glory' are gloriously/glory, beauty, content, lovelier/lovely. Common to 'The Glory' and 'Ambition' are happy/happiness, pure[est], lovely/loveliness. The quasi-religious 'glory', perhaps the most aspirational word of all, pervades Wordsworth's 'Intimations' ode: 'The glory and the freshness of a dream', 'The sunshine is a glorious birth', 'trailing clouds of glory do we come', 'Whither is fled the visionary gleam?/ Where is it gone, the glory and the dream?' 'The Glory' is another early-morning poem with birds. But these birds set the stage for a more exploratory approach to the gap between poet-speaker and 'outward forms', and to the metaphysical, psychological and aesthetic terms that interpenetrate in all three poems:

The glory of the beauty of the morning, –
The cuckoo crying over the untouched dew;
The blackbird that has found it, and the dove
That tempts me on to something sweeter than love;
White clouds ranged even and fair as new-mown hay;
The heat, the stir, the sublime vacancy

Of sky and meadow and forest and my own heart: –
The glory invites me, yet it leaves me scorning
All I can ever do, all I can be,
Beside the lovely of motion, shape, and hue,
The happiness I fancy fit to dwell
In beauty's presence … (87)

'Sublime vacancy' may be partly an oxymoron or irony: it's certainly much closer to Shelley's 'vacancy' at the end of 'Mont Blanc' than to Wordsworth's 'sense sublime' in 'Tintern Abbey'. The less sublime 'vacant sand' in Thomas's 'An Old Song II' is more productive (see p. 21). Reviewing an anthology of mountain-poems, Thomas had criticised the aesthetics of the Sublime: 'The mind of the poet and his reader annihilates the mountains'.[47] In his own poem 'The Mountain Chapel' a mountain virtually annihilates humanity: 'When gods were young/ This wind was old' (44). For Angela Leighton, Shelley's 'Mont Blanc' and 'Hymn to Intellectual Beauty' are 'testing inquiries into the workings of the imagination as it confronts a landscape that is desolating in its emptiness'.[48] The landscape of 'The Glory', unlike that of 'The Mountain Chapel', is hardly 'desolating'. Yet it presents a 'vacancy' that seemingly cannot be filled by the subjectivity of a protagonist who desires his art and life to match 'the lovely of motion, shape, and hue'; but for whom glory/sublimity sets an impossible standard. In fact, 'beauty' (repeated four times) seems to matter more than the Sublime: to be the keyword here as 'power' in 'Health'. Doing (making poems) and being are indivisible in what follows:

Shall I now this day
Begin to seek as far as heaven, as hell,
Wisdom or strength to match this beauty, start
And tread the pale dust pitted with small dark drops,
In hope to find whatever it is I seek,
Hearkening to short-lived happy-seeming things

80

That we know naught of, in the hazel copse?
Or must I be content with discontent
As larks and swallows are perhaps with wings?
And shall I ask at the day's end once more
What beauty is, and what I can have meant
By happiness? And shall I let all go,
Glad, weary, or both? Or shall I perhaps know
That I was happy oft and oft before,
Awhile forgetting how I am fast pent,
How dreary-swift, with naught to travel to,
Is Time? I cannot bite the day to the core.

'The Glory' is a double sonnet which takes rhymes as they come. The first sonnet 'turns' in the eighth line, but the overall turn violates sonnet-form by asymmetrically starting halfway through the twelfth line with 'Shall', and by posing a series of questions, in irregular sentence-units, rather than finding resolution. 'I cannot bite the day to the core' is an admission of Romantic failure. 'Health' ends with an implied shift from inspiration to composition. 'The Glory', another present-tense, work-in-progress poem, takes matters further. The questions that leave it open-ended propose a range of scenarios for both poems and life: a dedicated quest 'to find whatever it is I seek'; inhabiting an oxymoronic status quo ('content with discontent'); epistemological enquiry into the terms of Romantic aspiration ('What beauty is'); ceasing to 'seek' or 'ask'; tapping into the (here merely palliative) resources of memory. Thomas has poems that correspond to all five scenarios.[49] But perhaps, taken together as *ars poetica*, these unanswered questions, with their syntactical twists, approximate to the scenario proposed by the first question. That is, they represent Thomas's poetry as a relativistic journey in an uncertain direction: 'to find whatever it is I seek'. To put it another way: the Romantic protagonist has morphed into a modern protagonist.

Yet, in the same instant, Thomas proves the adaptability of Romantic structures to new contexts. That includes structures of thought as they affect poetic genre and form. Indeed, the journey or quest is itself a key Romantic trope, although Thomas's forking paths discard the immanent teleology which Romantic journeys take from the Christian narrative. Again (as in these three poems), Wordsworth's illuminating 'moment' becomes a more precarious staging-post. A Thomas epiphany may be negative or 'nothing'. In effect, the fallout of Romantic 'vision' contributes to Thomas's relativistic dialectics about perception, and to the shifting perspectives within and between his poems. Some poems bring those dialectics and shifts to the surface. Like 'Ambition', 'The Path' ends with a conscious ending that seems a Romantic dead-end.

> ... the eye
> Has but the road, the wood that overhangs
> And underyawns it, and the path that looks
> As if it led on to some legendary
> Or fancied place where men have wished to go
> And stay; till, sudden, it ends where the wood ends. (72)

Yet this is also Romantic critique. 'Fancied', like 'I fancy' in 'The Glory', encodes Coleridge's view of 'Fancy' as inferior to imagination. The delusive 'legendary/ Or fancied place' simplifies the perceptual twists of a journey that begins:

> Running along a bank, a parapet
> That saves from the precipitous wood below
> The level road, there is a path. It serves
> Children for looking down the long smooth steep,
> Between the legs of beech and yew, to where
> A fallen tree checks the sight ...

From 'Running', which takes time to locate its noun, the run of syntax and rhythm constitutes the 'path' as that of cognitive and poetic complexity. This path also skirts the unconscious zone, which

Thomas so often symbolises by wood or forest: 'precipitous' and 'underyawns' are unsettling. A Romantic 'eye' has opened up the path, and travels some way along it, as in the phrase 'winding like silver'. Yet moss fails 'to cover roots and crumbling chalk/ With gold, olive, and emerald', and the possibility of vision is variously 'checked': perhaps a reality-check; perhaps a sign that 'vision' is moving into new psychological territory (see Chapter 5).

Conversely, positive epiphany can arrive unexpectedly, as in two poems with contrary starting-points: 'Home', which begins 'Often I had gone this way before', and 'I never saw that land before'. These 'Prelude' poems, epiphanies of poetry itself, locate Thomas's vocational self-discovery in circumstances remote from the sublime:

> Often I had gone this way before:
> But now it seemed I never could be
> And never had been anywhere else;
> 'Twas home; one nationality
> We had, I and the birds that sang,
> One memory.
>
> They welcomed me. I had come back
> That eve somehow from somewhere far:
> The April mist, the chill, the calm,
> Meant the same thing familiar
> And pleasant to us, and strange too,
> Yet with no bar … (81)

Here a known landscape, one of Thomas's vocal landscapes, stages an achieved interchange between mind and world. Perhaps this interchange works because it has an environmental basis. The visionary 'oneness' between poet and birds is ratified, the orchestration of the little cosmos completed, by a 'labourer' also arriving home: 'from his shed,/ The sound of sawing rounded all/ That silence said'. 'Home', with its democratic inter-species relations, figures what might be termed Thomas's 'lyric ecology'. So does 'I never saw that land before' where a hitherto unknown landscape, again with labourer and birdsong, ultimately discloses an unspecified 'goal' which resembles 'home':

> … The blackthorns down along the brook
> With wounds yellow as crocuses
> Where yesterday the labourer's hook
> Had sliced them cleanly; and the breeze
> That hinted all and nothing spoke.
>
> I neither expected anything
> Nor yet remembered: but some goal
> I touched then; and if I could sing
> What would not even whisper my soul
> As I went on my journeying,
>
> I should use, as the trees and birds did,
> A language not to be betrayed;
> And what was hid should still be hid
> Excepting from those like me made
> Who answer when such whispers bid. (120)

Perhaps these poems dispose of aspiration along with teleology by implying that poetry itself is vision enough; by challenging us to decode their wholly poetic substance ('silence', 'hid'). The poet-speaker is again defined by Keatsian receptivity rather than by soaring ambition. Thomas strengthens the aesthetic point by implicitly recasting a key objective of *Lyrical Ballads*: to remove 'the film of familiarity' from 'things of every day' ('Anything, however small …').[50] His poetic epistemology primarily moves between the antinomies 'strange' and 'familiar', known and unknown, rather than heights and depths. As Thomas gets closer to the war and the Front, darker epiphanies or other poetic formats tend to prevail. Yet he wrote 'I never saw that land before' in May 1916, just before 'The sun used to shine'. The memory that crystallises as the poem may look back over the whole – unexpected – landscape of his poetry so far: 'and if I could sing …'. Like 'The sun used to shine', this poem anticipates death ('I never saw that land before,/And now can never see it again'), and ends with oblique legacy. The speaker's Keats-like demeanour is not the only Romantic contribution to that legacy. The Romantic substratum of all Thomas's 'journeying' is marked by the initial (initiatory) stress on 'seeing'; by 'soul'; and by 'hints' of Wordsworth's 'corresponding mild creative breeze' from *The Prelude* and Coleridge's 'intellectual breeze' from 'The Eolian Harp' in 'the breeze/ That hinted all and nothing spoke'.

3. EARTH AND SKY

Wind symbolises inspiration in several of Thomas's poems. Its most Shelleyan appearance is in 'The Wind's Song', which ends: 'My heart that had been still as the dead tree/ Awakened by the West wind was made free' (118). Perhaps this also invokes Shelley himself as 'awakener'. Elsewhere, Thomas generally brings inspirational wind down to earth and to practice. 'Words' rewrites 'Make me thy lyre, even as the forest is' in the simile: 'As the winds use/ A crack in a wall/ Or a drain,/ Their joy or their pain/ To whistle through' (91). 'Aspens', Thomas's most complex reworking of Coleridge's harp and Shelley's lyre, revisits his tree-image for lyric 'intricacies' (see p. 106):

> All day and night, save winter, every weather,
> Above the inn, the smithy, and the shop,
> The aspens at the cross-roads talk together
> Of rain, until their last leaves fall from the top … (97)

In 'Aspens' the Romantic windharp figures the modern lyric by fusing inspiration with form. Wind not only animates the trees/ poem but – in the same breath – imparts distinctive sounds, speech, and symbolism. This *ars poetica* also attaches poetry to earthly affairs: 'the inn, the smithy, and the shop'.

Inspirational 'wind' is a rough guide to how Thomas re-sets the co-ordinates of 'sky' and 'earth' in Romantic cosmography. They are dialectically contrasted in his early parable-poems, 'November' and 'The Signpost', but with an ultimate bias towards the condition of being, as a 'voice' in 'The Signpost' proposes: 'No matter what the weather, on earth,/ At any age between death and birth' (37). Thomas liked to quote Wordsworth's insistence, in his poem on the French Revolution, that 'this very world' (Thomas substitutes 'earth') is where 'We find our happiness, or not at all'. 'The Source' ends with 'The triumph of earth' over 'wild air'. The disturbed protagonist of 'Wind and Mist' says: 'I did not know it was the earth I loved/ Until I tried to live there in the clouds' (74). Evidently 'earth' is not just one thing in Thomas's poetry. Its meanings are psychological and metaphysical as well as physical or ecological, as are the meanings of 'sky'. In 'The Source' 'earth' seems tantamount to poetry itself. Sky, important to the aspirational panoramas of 'Ambition', 'Health' and 'The Glory', is more Shelley's sphere than Wordsworth's: the sphere of whirling cosmic energies. At one level, 'The Lofty Sky' may be a comment on Thomas's lofty and less lofty Romantic influences – and on their interdependence. The poem has links with a prose passage about reading Keats, whom Thomas elsewhere calls 'though a lover of the moon, a most sublunary poet, earthly, substantial, and precise'.[51] Loftiness wins out in the poem, yet seems an occasional if ineradicable need; while 'the wealden clay' represents a more habitual aesthetic element:

> Today I want the sky,
> The tops of the high hills,
> Above the last man's house,
> His hedges, and his cows,
> Where, if I will, I look
> Down even on sheep and rook,

And of all things that move
See buzzards only above: –
Past all trees, past furze
And thorn, where naught deters
The desire of the eye
For sky, nothing but sky.
I sicken of the woods
And all the multitudes
Of hedge-trees. They are no more
Than weeds upon this floor
Of the river of air
Leagues deep, leagues wide, where
I am like a fish that lives
In weeds and mud and gives
What's above him no thought.
I might be a tench for aught
That I can do today
Down on the wealden clay … (53)

The tension between 'river of air' and 'weeds and mud' parallels the 'aery surge' of Shelley's West Wind ruffling 'sea-blooms' and 'oozy woods' below. 'Two Pewits', in which these birds 'Plunging earthward, tossing high' symbolise Thomas's creative orbit, contains the phrase 'dark surge' (70). In 'The Lofty Sky', the 'desire of the eye' pulls more strongly against gravity: the rhythm makes transcendence a dynamic rather than a leap of faith. In contrast to the perception-distorting clouds of 'Wind and Mist', the psychological aspect of this skyward movement suggests the superego extricating itself from the id. Syntax works with the short line and repeated words to create a crescendo that recalls Thomas's regard for 'a complex sentence in which the stops are as valuable as the division of a stanza of verse into lines, or as the hedges and littered crags and out-cropping rock by which the eye travels up a mountain to the clouds'.[52] 'The Lofty Sky' ends by echoing another poem that updates Romantic desire,

Yeats's 'Lake Isle of Innisfree': 'I/ Would arise and go far/ To where the lilies are'. But this most Shelleyan of Thomas's poems has already gone far.

In Thomas's poetry 'sky' becomes a less frequent word, and less important conceptual complex, than 'earth'. In 'Aspens' 'Empty as sky' is an image for ghostly vacancy. Darwin, agnosticism and relativism have de-sacralised Thomas's Romantic bearings, usually ruling out transcendental 'visionary gleams'. The 'bodiless sweet' song of his 'Unknown Bird' echoes the 'unbodied joy' of Shelley's lark. But later, in 'After you speak', it's as 'a black star' and 'mote/ Of singing dust' that the lark now 'embodies' poetry (124). This poet-lark seems truer to Wordsworth's 'kindred points of Heaven and Home' than to Shelley. Even so, Thomas's post-Darwinian 'earth', as outer and inner 'home', differs from Wordsworth's: primarily, in being more historical. That affects what his poetry takes from Wordsworth as regards the nexus between memory – in all its aspects – and poem. Chapter 1 argued that Thomas's late birth as a poet has left structural marks, whereby his poems both mobilise memory and underscore the lyric's origins in memory (and forgetting). But an underlying dialogue with Wordsworth is part of this too. In 'I never saw that land before', 'I neither expected anything/ Nor yet remembered' may dispose of Wordsworthian memory along with Shelleyan aspiration.

'Over the Hills' and 'The Ash Grove' involve a more direct dialogue: specifically, with the epiphanic 'spots of time' central to Wordsworth's aesthetic. Each poem is overtly constructed as an act of remembering and a reflection on that act. In 'Over the Hills', the speaker seems to make the correct Wordsworthian moves. Besides remembering a particular 'spot of time', he remembers turning it into an epiphany:

> Often and often it came back again
> To mind, the day I passed the horizon ridge
> To a new country, the path I had to find

By half-gaps that were stiles once in the hedge,
The pack of scarlet clouds running across
The harvest evening that seemed endless then
And after, and the inn where all were kind,
All were strangers. I did not know my loss
Till one day twelve months later suddenly
I leaned upon my spade and saw it all,
Though far beyond the sky-line. It became
Almost a habit through the year for me
To lean and see it and think to do the same
Again for two days and a night ... (52)

Critics dispute the extent to which Wordsworth, in 'Tintern Abbey' and elsewhere, conceives 'recollection' as compensating for 'loss'.[53] But 'Over the Hills' wholly denies recompense: to 'see it all' is simultaneously to 'know ... loss'. The poem ends:

Recall
Was vain: no more could the restless brook
Ever turn back and climb the waterfall
To the lake that rests and stirs not in its nook,
As in the hollow of the collar-bone
Under the mountain's head of rush and stone.

In effect, the epiphany has failed to do its job. If the initial 'path-finding' has been oddly difficult, the impossible final path bars any return to any source. At the same time, as with the shadow-path at the end of 'Old Man', rhythm makes absence tangible. It seals the poem itself as the only trace of something irrecoverable. In contrast, 'The Ash Grove' recalls (and calls itself) a 'moment', an 'interval', which still informs the speaker's life: 'Scarce a hundred paces under the trees was the interval'. This is an epiphany that goes on giving:

… And now an ash grove far from those hills can bring
The same tranquillity in which I wander a ghost
With a ghostly gladness, as if I heard a girl sing

The song of the Ash Grove soft as love uncrossed,
And then in a crowd or in distance it were lost,
But the moment unveiled something unwilling to die
And I had what most I desired, without search or desert or cost.
(108)

Yet, although memory-based 'feelings' of 'tranquil restoration' seem to be avowed here, as in 'Tintern Abbey', 'The Ash Grove' also reverses Wordsworth's 'emotion recollected in tranquillity'. To enter another grove is to remember (a rare) 'tranquillity'; while the grove was/is a locus in space and time that paradoxically holds memory at bay: 'Not even the spirits of memory and fear with restless wing,/ Could climb down in to molest me over the wall// That I passed through at either end without noticing'. Memory is clearly not an unqualified good. And this recurrence, like the original grove, seems enormously fragile. It renders the speaker a 'ghost, while the song-simile alludes to something 'lost' as soon as found. The epiphany is further qualified by the oblique terms in which it affirms life or satisfies 'desire'. Yet perhaps the moment's residual quality proves its enduring power. The 'interval' is ultimately the poem/song itself, which has 'passed through' some inner barrier to transform its material origins. 'The Ash Grove' dramatises what 'Over the Hills' implies, and 'something unwilling to die' again marks the unexpected 'unveiling' of poetry: 'the things are forgotten, and it is an aspect of them, a recreation of them, a finer development of them, which endures in the written words'.[54] These two poems do not renounce the Wordsworthian 'moment'. But they deconstruct and reconstruct it by making it more contingent, fragile and fallible; and by distinguishing between experience ('things'), memory, and poetry: the surviving trace of both ('written words'). In effect, what refuses to die is poetry. 'The Bridge', in which the speaker again inhabits a virtual nano-second of 'rest' between memory and expectation, presents itself as 'this moment brief between/ Two lives'. Here 'The dark-lit stream has drowned the Future and the Past' (66). *Inter alia* 'dark-lit stream' figures the duality and fluidity of epiphanies as points on Thomas's poetic journey.

As with personal memory, so with socio-cultural memory and longer-term human memory – neither divorced from personal memory: all part of the 'dark-lit stream'. Mindful of history and pre-history, Thomas's 'Digging' deepens, in two senses, these lines about flowers from Wordsworth's Prologue to *Peter Bell*: 'The common growth of mother-earth/ Suffices me – her tears, her mirth':

What matter makes my spade for tears or mirth,
Letting down two clay pipes into the earth?
The one I smoked, the other a soldier
Of Blenheim, Ramillies, and Malplaquet
Perhaps. The dead man's immortality
Lies represented lightly with my own,
A yard or two nearer the living air
Than bones of ancients who, amazed to see
Almighty God erect the mastodon,
Once laughed, or wept, in this same light of day. (99)

'Digging' takes a post-Darwinian as well as wartime dig at 'God', but without postulating a wholly beneficent 'mother-earth'. 'Living air' is transferred from 'Tintern Abbey' ('the round ocean and the living air') to mean something more like the earthly biosphere. A passage in *The South Country*, a passage where prose-rhythms intensify towards poetry, theorises Thomas's eco-historical approach to landscape:

[I]f we but knew or cared, every swelling of the grass, every wavering line of hedge or path or road were an inscription, brief as an epitaph, in many languages and characters … The eye that sees the things of today, and the ear that hears, the mind that contemplates or dreams, is itself an instrument of an antiquity equal to whatever it is called upon to apprehend. We are not merely twentieth-century Londoners or Kentish men or Welshmen … of these many folds in our nature the face of the earth reminds us, and perhaps, even where there are no more marks visible upon the land than there were in Eden, we are aware of the passing of time in ways too difficult and strange for the explanation of historian and zoologist and philosopher. It is this manifold nature that responds with such indescribable depth and variety to the appeals of many landscapes.[55]

'Up in the Wind' begins Thomas's poetry by reading 'inscriptions' that centre on the 'forest parlour' of The White Horse pub. In probing the historical interaction between a place and its inhabitants, in defining history *as* such interaction, the poem reworks the Wordsworthian 'encounter-poem' as well as the Frost eclogue. Thomas's poetic encounters with rural people are not confined to eclogue, but occur in a range of generic contexts. And the people encountered are not only solitary 'wandering men' (as in 'It was upon') or lonely women, like the 'wild girl' in 'Up in the Wind'. His poetry's social make-up includes farm-labourers, ploughmen, woodmen, shepherds, gipsies, inn-keepers, charcoal-burners, a happy 'huxter' and his wife. Yet Thomas seems especially liable to remodel Wordsworth's solitary old men: perhaps owing to their potential as history-bearers on his historicised earth. In 'Lob', it's an old Wiltshireman who triggers a mythic personification of English history from 'barrows' to Shakespeare to No Man's Land. The 'old man bent' in 'The New Year' is less mythic, as the poem's temporal title might suggest, but still emblematic:

He was the one man I met up in the woods
That stormy New Year's morning; and at first sight,
Fifty yards off, I could not tell how much

Of the strange tripod was a man. His body,
Bowed horizontal, was supported equally
By legs at one end, by a rake at the other:
Thus he rested, far less like a man than
His wheel-barrow in profile was like a pig … (49)

The 'stormy' New Year is 1915, and 'the strange tripod', which reminds the speaker of boy's games (like leap-frog) and animals (pig, tortoise) is an enigma that may befit the historical moment. The poem ends:

His head rolled under his cape like a tortoise's;
He took an unlit pipe out of his mouth
Politely ere I wished him 'A Happy New Year',
And with his head cast upward sideways muttered –
So far as I could hear through the trees' roar –
'Happy New Year, and may it come fastish, too,'
While I strode by and he turned to raking leaves.

Ominous signs include the 'roar', which muffles or prevents the dialogue that usually occupies such encounters; the younger man 'striding by' as if to war; the absence of any concluding comment. 'The New Year' alludes to Wordsworth's 'Resolution and Independence': its 'roaring in the wind all night', the poet-speaker's conversation with the stooped leech-gatherer.[56] But that 'roar' has become something else in another time, and Thomas's poem lacks the 'contemplative' comfort, the clinching moral, the stable future, represented by Wordsworth's ending: a vow to 'think of the Leech-gatherer on the lonely moor'. Similarly, in Thomas's 'Man and Dog' the old itinerant labourer, who carries personal and socio-political history from a difficult past into a future destabilised by war, tells his story with a stoicism that leaves us to draw our own conclusions (see p. 223). There is a parallel with Wordsworth's 'A Discharged Soldier', but Wordsworth emphasises the pathos of this 'ghostly figure' rather than his historical relation to earth and war.

On its road to war, Thomas's poetry often 'remembers the future' via the past. The archaeology of 'Digging' links the soldier-poet with Marlborough's soldiers and 'bones of ancients'. In 'The Green Roads', another 'path' poem – the path of eco-historical consciousness – the deep past, with its 'lost' memories, doubles as an omen:

> The green roads that end in the forest
> Are strewn with white goose feathers this June,
>
> Like marks left behind by someone gone to the forest
> To show his track. But he has never come back.
>
> Down each green road a cottage looks at the forest.
> Round one the nettle towers; two are bathed in flowers.
>
> An old man along the green road to the forest
> Strays from one, from another a child alone […]
>
> That oak saw the ages pass in the forest:
> They were a host, but their memories are lost,
>
> For the tree is dead: all things forget the forest
> Excepting perhaps me, when now I see
>
> The old man, the child, the goose feathers at the edge of the forest,
> And hear all day long the thrush repeat his song. (128-9)

Thomas is no prophet-poet like Wordsworth. Nor does he 'warn' like Wilfred Owen. But the speaker of 'The Green Roads' is a poet who cannot 'forget the forest' and our human situation on its 'edge'. Here the symbolic spectrum of 'forest' in Thomas's poetry tilts more towards oblivion than towards the unconscious self, although the latter dimension is present too. This emblematic poem, with its old man and child, its dualistic dwellings, its unremitting refrain-word, its hints of extinction, suggests the 'many folds in our nature' shaped by earthly life. Some rural people in Thomas's poetry seem at home on the earth, whatever its hardships. The man in 'Man and Dog' likes 'anything to do with trees', despite having been lamed by falling from a poplar. 'A Private' begins: 'This ploughman dead in battle slept out of doors/ Many a frosty night' (50). But the man in 'House and Man' is unsettled, not just metaphorically, by trees, by forest, by living in a house 'Which the trees looked upon from every side' (60). His seeming paranoia does not diminish a sense of earth's inhospitality or indifference to human dwelling and consciousness. The man (mankind) dissolves in the speaker's (dissolving) memory too: 'as dim he and his house now look/ As a reflection in a rippling brook'. Thomas's poems can be ambivalent about humanity's 'inscriptions' on landscape. He had written in 1908: 'Man seems to me a very little part of Nature and the part I enjoy least.'[57] His poems veer between applauding, and being disturbed by, Nature reclaiming ground from human constructions. The cottages in 'The Green Roads' are set at a questioning angle to 'forest'.

Agnosticism and Darwinism, even an acceptance of humanity's redundancy, do not eradicate 'mystery'. 'The Chalk-Pit' ends: '"… imperfect friends, we men/ And trees since time began; and nevertheless/ Between us still we breed a mystery"' (89). Thomas's 'green roads' are mysterious too. As a post-Christian metaphysic, this contrasts with Yeats's recourse to an alternative systematic *Vision*. Thomas replaces the sacral element in Romantic visions with an ecological sense of earth-history and earth-mystery. We may witness this happening in three climactic stanzas of 'The Other', where Salisbury Plain supplies the locale, although transcendence ('sky', 'everlasting') has not entirely left the stage:

I sought then in solitude.
The wind had fallen with the night; as still
The roads lay as the ploughland rude,
Dark and naked, on the hill.

Had there been ever any feud
'Twixt earth and sky, a mighty will
Closed it: the crocketed dark trees,
A dark house, dark impossible
Cloud-towers, one star, one lamp, one peace
Held on an everlasting lease:

And all was earth's, or all was sky's;
No difference endured between
The two. A dog barked on a hidden rise;
A marshbird whistled high unseen;
The latest waking blackbird's cries
Perished upon the silence keen.
The last light filled a narrow firth
Among the clouds. I stood serene,
And with a solemn quiet mirth,
An old inhabitant of earth.

Once the name I gave to hours
Like this was melancholy, when
It was not happiness and powers
Coming like exiles home again,
And weaknesses quitting their bowers,
Smiled and enjoyed, far off from men,
Moments of everlastingness.
And fortunate my search was then
While what I sought, nevertheless,
That I was seeking, I did not guess. (41-2)

In 'The Other', pursuit of 'the unseen moving goal' seems impelled
by psychological rather than metaphysical 'desire'. Yet Thomas's
paths are never rigidly segregated. Tracks can switch or join. In
the stanzas quoted above, the split protagonist is integrated by the
conceptual as well as emotional meaning of his self-realisation as

'An old inhabitant of earth'. This is also a historical realisation: 'We are not merely twentieth-century Londoners …'. A 'moment' of all-inclusive vision, which again implies the unexpected advent of poetry, reconciles and interconnects Self and Other, subject and object, past and present, earth and sky. The invisible birds and dog also contribute to a mysterious harmony, a lyric ecology.

Literary reconciliations may be taking place too. This climactic epiphany, founded on 'naked' exposure to crepuscular sights and sounds, has links with Keats's 'earthliness' as well as Wordsworth's. The speaker internalises the earth as 'home' by means of sensory immersion and existential intensity ('happiness'/ 'melancholy'). The 'unseen' bird, like an earlier allusion to 'never-foamless shores', recalls the 'Darkling' scenario of 'Ode to a Nightingale'. Again, 'Moments of everlastingness' suggests a full-blown Wordsworthian epiphany, but 'everlasting' also has a more directly religious context in Henry Vaughan's 'The Retreat' ('And felt through all this fleshly dress/ Bright shoots of everlastingness') and in Thomas Traherne. Thomas liked to quote from Traherne's *Centuries of Meditation*: 'The corn was orient and immortal wheat … I thought it had stood from everlasting to everlasting'. In one aspect, these stanzas condense a metaphysical trajectory from Christian mysticism to Romantic Nature to Gaia. They also echo an early eighteenth-century poem: 'A Nocturnal Reverie' by Anne Finch, Countess of Winchilsea. This poem Thomas (like Wordsworth) considered proto-Romantic, and born of struggle 'against the artificiality of the age':

> … the free Soul to a compos'dness charm'd,
> Finding the Elements of Rage disarm'd,
> O'er all below a solemn quiet grown,
> Joys in th' inferior World, and thinks it like her own.[58]

'The Other' has broader parallels with Shelley's 'Hymn to Intellectual Beauty', where 'The awful shadow of some unseen Power' precipitates a dedicated quest, through 'life's unquiet dream', for another kind of otherness. 'Solemn' and 'serene' appear in Shelley's reconcil-iatory final stanza:

> The day becomes more solemn and serene
>   When noon is past – there is a harmony
>   In autumn and a lustre in its sky
>   Which through the summer is not heard or seen,
>   As if it could not be, as if it had not been! …

Facets of Thomas's 'Romantic self' thus come together at a pivotal point in a poem which inaugurates and epitomises the inner journey of his modern self. The epiphany summed up as 'one star, one lamp, one peace' (metaphysics, aesthetics, psychology), perhaps a Romantic meta-epiphany, remains on the horizon, marking a source as well as a goal. But no earthly 'lease' or 'moment' can really be 'everlasting': both phrases are oxymoronic. The next stanza begins: 'That time was brief …'.

4. KEATS AND LYRIC FORM

The aesthetic self-commentary of Thomas's poetry brings him closer to Keats than to other Romantic poets. His criticism always stresses Keats's art. Attacking poets and prose-writers who advocate 'Nature' too evangelically, he says: 'Keats, almost alone, entirely lacks inartistic intention.'[59] To quote again his summation of Keats's odes: 'in the odes the poet made for himself a form in which the essence of all his thought, feeling, and observation, could be stored without overflowing or disorder; of its sources in his daily life there was no more shown than made his poems quick instead of dead'.[60] Here the odes provide a template for lyric intensity, lyric psychodrama; while the bond between 'form' and 'essence' renders Keats a proto-Symbolist. John Burrow may press too far his argument, in 'Keats and Edward Thomas': that the 'particular strength' of Thomas's poems 'testifies as much to an intelligent reading of Keats as to the acknowledged friendship and advice of Robert Frost'.[61] Yet in 1913–14 Thomas was indeed thinking and writing about Keats; Keats exemplifies (perhaps distils) a literary hinterland where he usually goes it alone without Frost; and Thomas's special feeling for the odes is aesthetically significant: he makes no comparable comment on the forms of Wordsworth, Coleridge or Shelley. The odes maximise two aspects of Keats's aesthetic to which Thomas seems especially indebted: the sensory intensity that Keats brings to the physics and metaphysics of earthly habitation; Keats's deep engagement with traditional verse-forms: specifically, with sonnet and couplet.

In poetry, all sense-impressions depend on a single sense. The ear regains power from the eye since 'vision' has to be heard and not seen. Thomas's poems have their own distinctive ways of constituting 'prisms to the sunlight, lyres to the winds, and living mirrors', and his evocation of 'sensuous things' ranges from Coleridgean 'strokes' to 'elaborate pictures'. This can happen in a single poem, as when the lightly stroked 'hoar-green feathery herb, almost a tree' in 'Old Man' gives way to a fuller mapping of the garden. Yet we may detect Keats's imprint when density of sound and rhythm thickens; when synaesthesia is at work; when poems become conscious of their own sensory qualities or origins. In 'The Word', the 'pure thrush word' arrives when the poet-speaker might be 'thinking' of 'scents'. 'Digging' implies a similar genesis:

Today I think
Only with scents, – scents dead leaves yield,
And bracken, and wild carrot's seed,
And the square mustard field;

Odours that rise
When the spade wounds the root of tree,
Rose, currant, raspberry, or goutweed,
Rhubarb or celery … (79)

It's not a matter of loading every rift with sensuousness, but of the whole poetic fabric. For Thomas, 'Ode to a Nightingale' and 'Ode on a Grecian Urn' 'are of a texture so consummate and consistent that the simple line, "The grass, the thicket, and the fruit-tree wild," in one of them, and an equally simple line in the other, "With forest branches, and the trodden weed," both gain from their environment an astonishing beauty, profound and touching.' Consummate verbal texture subliminally activates all our senses (perhaps the hallmark-test of poetry), but Thomas's ear is also attuned to how Keats uses stress and assonance to orchestrate rhythm for particular sensory purposes. In the last line of 'To Autumn' he hears 'something light, thin, cold, and vanishing, especially by comparison with the mellowness and slowness of the other verses, with all their long "oo" and "ou" and "aw" and "z" sounds'.[62]

Thomas's rhythms have their own special effects. In 'But these things also', consonantal frictions and echoes blend the visual and the tactile into the auditory: 'The shell of a little snail bleached/ In the grass; chip of flint, and mite/ Of chalk' (67). Smell and its sibling, taste, are the hardest senses to convey by aural means. Despite 'soft incense' in 'Ode to a Nightingale', Thomas may be the poet who has done most for smell, as (often at the same time) for memory. 'Digging' makes smell vivid by attaching it to the robustly assonant plant-names ('Rose, currant, raspberry, or goutweed') and kineti-cally active spade. Kinesis is of the rhythmic essence: 'The movement of [Cobbett's] prose is a bodily thing. His sentences do not precisely suggest the swing of an arm or a leg, but they have something in common with it.'[63] Hence the pulse of 'walking' and 'talking' in 'The sun used to shine'. A different walker, with a different rhythmic foot-print, is the labourer in 'Home': 'A labourer went along, his tread/ Slow, half with weariness, half with ease' (82). The placing of 'Slow' before the half-symmetrical, half-unsymmetrical phrases, the asso-nance of 'Slow' with 'weariness' and 'ease', underline the weight of the labourer's homecoming 'tread' along with the relief of his arrival. When Thomas's poetry dwells on a particular sense, or 'thinks …

with scents' or with any other sense ('scents' may cover 'sense'), this mode of reflexivity implies that poetry not only brings 'the whole soul of man into activity'[64] but brings the body too. 'The Other' begins with an impression that the speaker has just been born or reborn into a physical world, or is surfacing from an unconscious state. The assonantal language seems a component, as well as transmitter, of sensory existence: 'Glad I was/ To feel the light, and hear the hum/ Of bees, and smell the drying grass' (40). '[T]asted sunlight' (a tasting of these words in mouth and ear, too) occurs later. It's hard to judge the ratio of Thomas's Romantic remixings. But, in his most positive epiphanies, the speaker tends to have a Keatsian bodily presence, to seem at home in his own skin – as do labourer and poet-speaker in 'Home'. Body and mind, the mind in itself, are undivided. A poem's sounds and rhythm become integral to inhabiting the earth. In 'Digging': 'It is enough/ To smell, to crumble the dark earth'. 'Smell' melts into touch by way of the word's echo in 'crumble'. 'Sowing' is another synaesthetic quatrain-poem that takes its rhythmic cue from earth's literal feel and smell: 'just/ As sweet and dry was the ground/ As tobacco-dust'. In the next two stanzas, the prolonged adjectives before 'cry', the alternating line-lengths and tucked-in participial phrases, help to suggest a body (and hence mind) 'stretching' after toil. *Vice versa* the effect reprises the bodily origin of poetic rhythm:

I tasted deep the hour
Between the far
Owl's chuckling first soft cry
And the first star.

A long stretched hour it was;
Nothing undone
Remained; the early seeds
All safely sown ... (69)

Thomas's poem 'The Brook' is conscious of its own construction in a way that also seems conscious of Keats's art. At one level, the 'beguiled' speaker is writing a poem, seeking the epiphanic 'word' for a mysterious experience. Sensory immersion doubles as the creation of a synaesthetic scene:

> Seated once by a brook, watching a child
> Chiefly that paddled, I was thus beguiled.
> Mellow the blackbird sang and sharp the thrush
> Not far off in the oak and hazel brush,
> Unseen. There was a scent like honeycomb
> From mugwort dull. And down upon the dome
> Of the stone the cart-horse kicks against so oft
> A butterfly alighted. From aloft
> He took the heat of the sun, and from below.
> On the hot stone he perched contented so,
> As if never a cart would pass again
> That way; as if I were the last of men
> And he the first of insects to have earth
> And sun together and to know their worth … (96)

As so often, birds set the tone: here a tonal range ('mellow' recalls Thomas on 'To Autumn') which prefigures a blend of at-homeness and unease in the poem's imagery. The assonance paddled/beguiled/mellow/blackbird is interrupted by the 'sharper', monosyllabic 'sharp the thrush'. There is a related mimetic contrast between the cart-horse's kinetic 'kicks', and 'A butterfly alighted', although it's the butterfly that introduces the sense of touch: 'From aloft/ He took the heat of the sun, and from below'. The balanced phrases contribute to (bio-) rhythms which underline the point that we are co-inhabitants of the earth: that, through our senses, we share 'earth/ And sun' with other species. Then the timeless holistic balance symbolised by the butterfly, the eschatological hint in 'first' and 'last', give way to flux:

I was divided between him and the gleam,
The motion, and the voices, of the stream,
The waters running frizzled over gravel,
That never vanish and for ever travel.
A grey flycatcher silent on a fence
And I sat as if we had been there since
The horseman and the horse lying beneath
The fir-tree-covered barrow on the heath,
The horseman and the horse with silver shoes,
Galloped the downs last. All that I could lose
I lost. And then the child's voice raised the dead.
'No one's been here before' was what she said
And what I felt, yet never should have found
A word for, while I gathered sight and sound.

The 'stream' is a historical, Heraclitean (and again synaesthetic) image for life and poetry: including the poem in progress as 'motion' and 'voices'. It connects with other such streams in Thomas's poetry: the 'dark-lit' stream of 'The Bridge', the 'strange stream' of 'A Dream' (see p. 219). Immersion in space gives way to immersion in time. After the intense onomatopoeia of 'frizzled', the senses recede into the background of an eco-historical reverie that reaches back past the 'barrow' to the primal earth ('No one's been here before') and possibly again forward to 'the last of men'. Yet this reverie depends on the sensory basis initially established for the interconnectedness of earth's inhabitants through different time-zones and culture-zones: cart-horse and 'horse with silver shoes'. In the last three lines, contrary to what is said, 'gather[ing] sight and sound' has created the poem that this phrase completes. Here poetry's 'word' is neither historical nor symbolic but existentially exact.

'The Brook' is a double sonnet in couplets. That might seem doubly odd, given Thomas's dislike of the eighteenth-century heroic couplet and his critical onslaughts on sonnet-form: 'a man must be a tremendous poet or a cold mathematician if he can accommodate his thoughts to such a condition'.[65] But perhaps Keats is the mediator here. Peter McDonald writes of Keats and the sonnet (and the couplet):

> [I]n his poetry [Keats] investigates and deepens the form's meaning and capacities in a profound way. Inevitably, a large part of this achievement relies upon the encounter with rhyme which the sonnet, for Keats, made so pressingly the business of composition. As much as the closed couplet, sonnet forms expose rhyme by foregrounding its demands as a challenge to the construction of a contained statement. Keats's re-figuring of that containment … is towards a poem in which everything seems to share the same space and time, in which the past and the future collapse into the sheer activity of the present: and that present is one in which rhymes are the tests and tokens of a voice's improvisatory living in the moment.[66]

As we have seen, sonnet-form quickly became a hidden keystone of Thomas's structures. It can stiffen both his blank verse and his rhymed poems in paragraph-blocks. When sonnet and couplet come together, as in 'The Brook', the ways in which verse-form or rhyme or syntax might 'contain' a poem's substance are multiplied, as are the possibilities of mutual subversion. On the one hand, each sonnet follows its own structural path. On the other, the couplets take on their own momentum. The rhymed-couplet sonnet is itself a distinctive variant: its dynamic less involuted, more geared to 'The motion, and the voices, of the stream'. In 'The Brook', the line beginning 'I was divided' marks a conscious 'turn' between the two sonnets, between thematic phases. Within each sonnet, the turn occurs irregularly (see below). The 'mathematics' of sonnet and couplet are further complicated by the cross-currents between sentence and metre. Frost had then written few couplet-poems that Thomas could have used as a model, although 'The Brook' may recall Frost's 'The Tuft of Flowers' ('The butterfly and I had lit upon,/ Nevertheless, a message from the dawn …').[67] Hence, perhaps, Thomas's recourse to the Romantic couplet: the 'open' couplet, fluently rhymed, which Keats developed in reaction against its 'closed' eighteenth-century predecessor. Although Thomas's couplet-poems sometimes remember Chaucer (as 'Lob' does), they are all true to his distinction between Byron 'binding the lovely verse … with chains that cut', and Keats binding it 'with flowers and such painless bonds'. Even where the couplet might appear 'closed', as in 'Early one morning', the rhythm is fully 'open' to its particular occasion: 'A gate banged in a fence and banged in my head./ "A fine morning, sir," a shepherd said' (126). The repeated 'banged' stirs the rhythm in a way that accentuates the poem's road to war. Thomas adapts the open couplet to different occasions and genres, with different rhythmic consequences, as in 'Man and Dog' and 'Beauty': written on successive days. 'Man and Dog' establishes an easy-going couplet in which narrative takes its cue from conversational speech, and the rhymes slip past: '"'twill take some getting." "Sir, I think 'Twill so."/ The old man stared up at the mistletoe/ That hung too high in the poplar's crest for plunder …' (56). 'Beauty', a psycho-dramatic soliloquy (see p. 256), begins by pushing hard against the couplet, and by making rhyme a stepping-stone of rhetorical momentum: 'What does it mean? Tired, angry, and ill at ease,/ No man, woman, or child alive could please/ Me now …' (58).

Endymion (1818) launched Keats's open couplet. Honeycombs and butterflies appear in a passage from Endymion, which Thomas quotes in Keats, and glosses as 'knitting … choice things' into 'a country basket'. The passage begins: 'O thou to whom/ Broad-leaved fig-trees even now foredoom/ Their ripen'd fruitage; yellow girted bees/ Their golden honeycombs …' Thomas quotes these lines to support his view that Keats's couplets can be too 'open'. Noting 'a lack of continuity in construction, no doubt fostered by [Keats's] habit of dealing with separate beauties instead of organic ideas', he adds: 'a trick of style, which puts a full stop anywhere but at the end of a line, only exaggerates this discontinuity'. Yet he says later: 'Where … beauty has sway the verse disencumbers itself, running fresh as well as full, either massive or light and clear, with pauses of natural fitness whether at the end of a line or not'.[68] That might be a blueprint for how 'The Brook' moves. The poem begins with an enclosed couplet, but the next few sentences run across couplets, with 'Unseen' conspicuously full-stopped. After using this 'trick of style' to knit the scene, Thomas 'turns' his first sonnet mid-couplet in the tenth line. He initiates a one-sentence 'sestet', propelled into a metaphysical zone by the repeated 'as if'. Keats's trick reappears at the turn of the second sonnet, where the riddling 'All that I could lose/ I lost', climax of the whole poem, places a full stop inside two lines from different couplets. The assonance 'lose'/'lost' (picking up 'last') is enhanced by the words' position in the line. Although the senses are not directly involved here, the poem's consummate 'texture' reaches its apotheosis.

Not all Thomas's couplet-poems have a hotline to Keats. But perhaps Keats alerted him to the form's potential variety. It's interesting that three consecutive poems linked with his enlistment – 'Haymaking', 'A Dream' and 'The Brook' – respond to the 'stream' of history by variously combining sonnet-form and couplet, irregularity and containment. Immediately after 'The Brook', Thomas wrote the quatrain-poem 'Aspens'. This darker *ars poetica* again implicates Keats (along with Shelley). The receptive aspens suggest Negative Capability at work, but more negatively than in 'The Brook':

> … The whisper of the aspens is not drowned,
> And over lightless pane and footless road,
> Empty as sky, with every other sound
> Not ceasing, calls their ghosts from their abode,
>
> A silent smithy, a silent inn, nor fails
> In the bare moonlight or the thick-furred gloom,

In tempest or the night of nightingales,
To turn the cross-roads to a ghostly room.

And it would be the same were no house near.
Over all sorts of weather, men, and times,
Aspens must shake their leaves and men may hear
But need not listen, more than to my rhymes.

Whatever wind blows, while they and I have leaves
We cannot other than an aspen be
That ceaselessly, unreasonably grieves,
Or so men think who like a different tree, (97)

Whereas 'gathering sight and sound' involves an element of choice, here the tree/poet seems programmed to 'grieve'. Aspens '*must* shake their leaves'. Poetry must receive and transmit ominous signals as sights and sounds press in upon its receptors. 'Thick-furred gloom' is a bleaker take, as the poem is generally, on how the senses function amid the 'verdurous glooms' of 'Ode to a Nightingale'. Thomas's nightingales appear to make night no less 'ghostly'. Frost (another Keats fan) had some influence on Thomas's sensory effects. The aspen-whisper, which pervades this poem, may pick up 'My long scythe whispered' in Frost's 'Mowing'.[69] Yet perhaps Keats awoke Thomas's ear to 'the sound of sense' in a different sense from Frost.

5. 'THE NAME OF MELANCHOLY'

'For these' is a prospectus for the ideal earthly home:

An acre of land between the shore and the hills,
Upon a ledge that shows my kingdoms three,
The lovely visible earth and sky and sea,
Where what the curlew needs not, the farmer tills … (99)

Spanning local 'acre' and global 'kingdoms', Thomas's microcosm might be the ground of 'visionary gleams' or lyric ecology. The next two quatrains zoom in on a house and garden, which again exemplify an ideally balanced existence: 'A house that shall love me as I love it', 'A garden I need never go beyond'. Yet the last quatrain finds something missing: something that this Eden (and Romantic ideology) may symbolise but fails to deliver:

> For these I ask not, but, neither too late
> Nor yet too early, for what men call content,
> And also that something may be sent
> To be contented with, I ask of fate.

Thomas's psychodrama, with its rarely attained goals of 'content', 'happiness' and 'gladness', corresponds in outline to Abrams's account of the 'circuitous' or 'spiral' Romantic quest, which begins with self-division and hopefully ends with (re-)integration: 'one star, one lamp, one peace'.[70] There are particular links with Coleridge's self-division in 'Dejection: An Ode':

> And still I gaze – and with how blank an eye! […]
> I see them all so excellently fair,
> I see, not feel, how beautiful they are!

In his essay 'Ecstasy', Thomas identifies with 'Dejection',[71] and his own 'Beauty' presents depressive symptoms similar to Coleridge's 'dull pain' and 'grief without a pang'. Coleridge's fear that he will lose his 'shaping spirit of Imagination', even while able to shape a poem about this fear, parallels Thomas's condition before he found poetry. 'Beauty' ends with poetry seemingly coming to the rescue of the speaker who compares himself to 'a river/ At fall of evening while it seems that never/ Has the sun lighted it or warmed it' (58).

'Melancholy' is the most prominent Romantic term for a depressed state. 'The Other', more circuitous than spiral, dramatises self-division in ways that connect with emergent psychoanalysis (see Chapter 5). Yet the poem refers to 'melancholy', and the word recurs in Thomas's self-diagnosis. For all its accumulated associations, 'melancholy' has a plasticity, which suits his wariness of psychological labels. In 'The Other' it changes places with 'happiness', and 'October' ends:

> … and now I might
> As happy be as earth is beautiful,
> Were I some other or with earth could turn
> In alternation of violet and rose,
> Harebell and snowdrop, at their season due,
> And gorse that has no time not to be gay.
> But if this be not happiness, – who knows?
> Some day I shall think this a happy day,
> And this mood by the name of melancholy
> Shall no more blackened and obscured be. (101)

The last two lines recast Thomas's remark that 'melancholy (in spite of the ode) is too disparaging a name' for the 'mood' of 'Ode to a Nightingale'. Yet he describes that mood as founded on 'pain, desire, and impatience [for death]'.[72] Thomas is well aware of the historical baggage carried by 'Melancholia' (root: black bile). Burton's encyclopaedic *Anatomy of Melancholy* (1621), which he celebrates as arousing 'the joy of reading, beyond all other books', may have influenced the plasticity of 'melancholy' in his poetry: 'No book so much as his gives us a sense of the immensity of the past, of the infinite numbers of the dead, the littleness of the living generation, the brevity of now.' Thomas quotes Burton's remark: 'I writ of melancholy, by being busy to avoid melancholy.'[73]

Historically, 'melancholy' has shifted in meaning between psychological illness and literary sensibility, and those two aspects can move together or apart. The jury is still out as to whether we should identify 'centuries-old descriptions of melancholy and melancholia' with the disorder 'later … known as clinical depression'.[74] 'Romantic melancholy' is the apotheosis of melancholy as literary sensibility, because Romantic subjectivity takes self-consciousness to the limit. And here literary melancholy more clearly becomes not one thing, but a complex or spectrum. Emily Brady and Arto Haapalo call it 'an aesthetic emotion', with both 'negative and positive aspects', to which 'the pleasure of [solitary] reflection and contemplation' is integral.[75] Not always pleasure: in Romantic works melancholic self-contemplation can induce an 'exaggerated emphasis … on feelings of solitude, darkness, grief, suffering, despair, longing, and elegiac sadness'.[76] Such feelings may derive from, or be projected onto, the objective world. For Thomas Pfau, 'melancholy' is one of Romanticism's three, historically situated governing moods (the others being trauma and paranoia). And for Löwy and Sayre:

> Romanticism [is] illuminated by the dual light of the star of revolt and what Gérard de Nerval called the 'black sun of melancholy' … The Romantic critique is bound up with an experience of loss. The Romantic vision is characterised by the painful and melancholic conviction that in modern reality something precious has been lost, at the level of both individuals and humanity at large; certain essential human values have been alienated. This alienation … is often experienced as exile ….[77]

'Loss' is one of Thomas's recurrent words, and 'exile' appears as 'powers/ Coming like exiles home again' in 'The Other'. In some prose writings he updates melancholy alienation by adopting, and applying to himself, Ivan Turgenev's concept of 'the superfluous man'.[78] For Thomas, 'The superfluous are those who cannot find society with which they are in some sort of harmony.' Discussing (and praising) Ernest Dowson, he says: 'Deep within the dark background of [his poems] is the comic, terrible cry of the superfluous man.' He ends by calling Dowson 'an unbodied melancholy'.[79] Melancholy is the flipside of Romantic ideology as well as of Enlightenment optimism: 'Ay, in the very temple of Delight/ Veil'd Melancholy has her sovran shrine'. Writing on Keats's melancholy, Pfau refers to 'a new and shocking consciousness of the human as denatured, stripped of genuine spiritual agency and self-determination'.[80]

One way in which Thomas modernises 'melancholy' is by configuring its complexity as literary sensibility with its application to psychological disorder – to his own mental problems: 'I writ of melancholy, by being busy to avoid melancholy.' The melancholy of 'October' is both 'aesthetic' – a framing perspective – and a real condition in search of a name. 'Mood' can be another aesthetic term. The Symbolist 1890s had given 'mood', often linked with lyric, fresh literary currency. Yeats's brief essay 'The Moods' (1895) begins: 'Literature differs from explanatory and scientific writing in being wrought about a mood, or a community of moods, as the body is wrought about an invisible soul'.[81] When Thomas names a poem 'October', names 'melancholy' and names it as a 'mood', he all-but names Keats: the poet who did most to make 'the melancholy fit' a primary mood and 'aesthetic emotion' of Romanticism. Wordsworth's phrase 'earth's diurnal course', from 'A slumber did my spirit seal', may lurk in 'with earth could turn'. But a Keats-defined 'melancholy' matches the speaker's state better than a Wordsworth-defined 'Nature'. 'October' revisits the aspirations of 'The Glory' in condensed form: 'and now I might/ As happy be as earth is beautiful'. But its principal focus is self-estrangement bound up with an autumnal sense of mortality.

Earlier, Thomas had written a poem actually called 'Melancholy', another intersection between his criticism and his poetry:

The 'Ode on Melancholy' is one of the central poems of this period, admitting, as it does so fully, and celebrating, the relationship between melancholy and certain still pleasures. Nowhere is the connoisseurship of the quiet, withdrawn spectator so extremely and remorselessly put … Richer juice could not be extracted from poison-flowers.[82]

Thomas's poem, like his prose, represents melancholy as an emotion 'so extremely' aesthetic that it abandons its larger literary claims to be a complex mood conditioned by 'modern reality':

> The rain and wind, the rain and wind, raved endlessly.
> On me the Summer storm, and fever, and melancholy
> Wrought magic, so that if I feared the solitude
> Far more I feared all company: too sharp, too rude,
> Had been the wisest or the dearest human voice.
> What I desired I knew not, but whate'er my choice
> Vain it must be, I knew. Yet naught did my despair
> But sweeten the strange sweetness, while through the wild air
> All day long I heard a distant cuckoo calling
> And, soft as dulcimers, sounds of near water falling,
> And, softer, and remote as if in history,
> Rumours of what had touched my friends, my foes, or me. (85)

Thomas translates his critique of Keats's 'Ode' into poetry by creating a melancholic persona who, with subtextual self-criticism, indulges dangerous feelings: dangerous because 'aesthetic' in the narrowest sense, because they aestheticise Nature along with the Self. Brady and Harpaalo note that melancholy can include 'self-indulgent, almost narcissistic pleasure'.[83] Thomas exaggerates Keats's already exaggerated recipe for how to behave 'when the melancholy fit shall fall'. The poem's Keatsian echoes include its being a near-sonnet in (hexameter) couplets, and being devoted to sensory immersion. But this speaker who luxuriates in natural sounds, this poem that luxuriates in its own sounds, take immersion too far: they banish 'voice': usually crucial to Thomas's poetry. Meanwhile Romantic 'desire' reaches peak-vagueness and peak-frustration, and the polarity 'sweetness'/'despair' pushes 'happiness'/

'melancholy' to an unhealthy limit. The masochistic melancholy on display (as display) derives from Keats by way of 1890s Aestheticism (Dowson), as perhaps does Thomas's reading of the 'Ode'. The speaker's supine surrender to 'magic' may encode Thomas using opium as a young man. His demeanour certainly exemplifies the *fin-de-siècle* 'connoisseurship' and 'spectatorship', which Thomas's criticism always condemns. Thus he says of Keats's 'Isabella': 'The inactive pity, the unreluctant and even complacent melancholy, that see in the increasing sorrow of their heroine or victim a richer zest, were new then to poetry, though the nineteenth century staled them.'[84] Solipsistic and irresponsible, relishing 'despair', this kind of melancholy puts 'history' and real feeling on hold. And it's with conscious 'staleness' that 'Melancholy' remixes words from 'Ode on Melancholy', 'Ode to a Nightingale' and 'La Belle Dame sans Merci': 'soft', 'rave', 'fever', 'despair', 'wild', 'strange'. For good measure, Thomas stirs into his toxic Romantic cocktail a Wordsworthian cuckoo and Coleridgean dulcimer.

'October' is one of three poems, written in Autumn 1915, which reconnect melancholy and Keats with history. The other two are 'There's nothing like the sun' and 'Liberty'. All the poems come within the orbit of Thomas's comment on Keats's odes and 'The Eve of St Agnes': 'Love for vanished, inaccessible, inhuman things, almost for death itself – regret – and the consolations offered by the intensity which makes pleasure and pain so much alike – are the principal moods of these poems.'[85] Besides applying concepts from *Keats*, Thomas's poems allude to the odes. They do so formally as well as thematically, even though no poem is stanzaic, and line-length does not vary much. 'October' consists of uneven blocks (nine and twelve lines); 'There's nothing like the sun' is a twenty-line block; 'Liberty', a twenty-seven line block. Yet those statistics hover in the sonnet's vicinity, and every block is intricately rhymed. As Chapter 1 noted, Thomas often binds blank verse with assonance or repeated words. Similarly, in his non-stanzaic rhymed poems, the rhyme keeps departing from any scheme it seems to establish

('Ambition' and 'The Glory' are examples). The unpredictable rhymes of 'October', 'There's nothing like the sun' and 'Liberty' especially fit McDonald's model of Keats's odes as a formal dynamic 'in which rhymes are the tests and tokens of a voice's improvisatory living in the moment'. It's as if Thomas takes back the elaborately rhymed ode-stanza into the freer modes of paragraphing and syntax enabled by blank verse. All three poems are in the first person and the present tense. While not 'odes', they implicitly address a month, the sun, the moon.

'October' begins:

> The green elm with the one great bough of gold
> Lets leaves into the grass slip, one by one, –
> The short hill grass, the mushrooms small milk-white,
> Harebell and scabious and tormentil,
> That blackberry and gorse, in dew and sun,
> Bow down to; and the wind travels too light
> To shake the fallen birch leaves from the fern;
> The gossamers wander at their own will.
> At heavier steps than birds' the squirrels scold.
>
> The rich scene has grown fresh again and new
> As Spring … (101)

The rhyme-scheme of the first nine lines is ABCDBCEDA. It's at a certain distance that 'gold' and 'scold' frame the 'rich scene'. The one-sentence line clinches the scene, but also seems a semi-detached preparation for what follows. Again, 'fern' hangs without a rhyme until it finds both an end-rhyme and internal rhyme seven lines later: 'Were I some other or with earth could turn/ In alternation of violet and rose …'. A reflexive pun is involved here too, since 'alternation' follows a sonnet-like 'turn'. This rhyme's unexpected course takes the poem into new structural and existential possibilities. It belongs to a rhythm which, contrary to what is said, draws speaker and poem towards the earth's movement. Like a Shakespearian sonnet, 'October' ends with a couplet: 'And this mood by the name of melancholy/ Shall no more blackened and obscured be'. The alliterative stress on 'mood' and 'melancholy', the rhyme of four-syllable word and monosyllable, create a bio-rhythmic bounce which helps a possibly happier future to shadow seasonal 'alternation': rhyme as 'improvisatory living' (McDonald), perhaps. Certainly, this changes the mood-music of 'Melancholy'.

For Coleridge, 'whirring wings of music' distinguish poetry from philosophy. Thomas contrasts the simplistic verse-movement of Keats's 'Welcome joy, and welcome sorrow' with that of 'Ode to a Nightingale'. The varying 'mood' of his own autumnal poems connects with 'outward forms' through distinctive rhythms: rhythms that are partly thematic since each poem seeks to correlate human and natural cycles:

> There's nothing like the sun as the year dies,
> Kind as it can be, this world being made so,
> To stones and men and beasts and birds and flies,
> To all things that it touches except snow,
> Whether on mountain side or street of town.
> The south wall warms me: November has begun,
> Yet never shone the sun as fair as now
> While the sweet last-left damsons from the bough
> With spangles of the morning's storm drop down
> Because the starling shakes it, whistling what
> Once swallows sang … (102)

> The last light has gone out of the world, except
> This moonlight lying on the grass like frost
> Beyond the brink of the tall elm's shadow.
> It is as if everything else had slept
> Many an age, unforgotten and lost
> The men that were, the things done, long ago,

All I have thought; and but the moon and I
Live yet and here stand idle over the grave
Where all is buried. Both have liberty
To dream what we could do if we were free
To do some thing we had desired long,
The moon and I. There's none less free than who
Does nothing and has nothing else to do,
Being free only for what is not to his mind,
And nothing is to his mind ... ('Liberty', 103)

As 'There's nothing like the sun' itemises earthly life, iambic mono-syllables flatten the rhythm. This helps to make humanity part of the natural world, although denied any higher status than 'stones' or 'flies'. The emphatic ABAB rhymes of the first four lines add to the finality of this proposition, but rhythm and rhyme-scheme change as the speaker 'warms' to the sun. Subsequently, the rhythm is complicated by a catalogue of the months which relishes their names along with their differences: 'But I have not forgot/ That there is nothing, too, like March's sun,/ Like April's, or July's, or June's, or May's'. Perhaps this self-echoing series ('August, September, October, and December') is the poem 'listening to itself', as McDonald says Keats's odes do.[86] But the last four lines, with their return to strong rhymes, hear something different. The refrain changes course; rhythm flattens out again; and the last two lines distinguish between what the speaker says and what the poem says:

No day of any month but I have said –
Or, if I could live long enough, should say –
'There's nothing like the sun that shines today.'
There's nothing like the sun till we are dead.

The ode- or sonnet-like rhyming at the beginning of 'Liberty' (ABCABC) contributes to a slower, elegiac build-up of two sentences that move from darkness to burial. 'Liberty' includes intricate rhyme, unrhymed lines, couplets. For the speculation about freedom at the centre of the poem, the open couplet is used to disruptive effect: 'There's none less free than who …'. 'Liberty' ends with a reversion to intricacy (discussed below). Perhaps what Thomas does is 'free rhyme'.

Several things might have 'grown fresh again and new' in these three poems, but Thomas's literary relation to Keats is certainly one of them. Direct allusion flags this up. In 'October', for instance, 'the wind travels too light' echoes 'sinking as the light wind lives or dies' in 'To Autumn'. Allusion marks the conscious 'belatedness' that Guy Cuthbertson attributes to 'There's nothing like the sun'. For Cuthbertson, this November poem knows that it comes late in the season and in literary history: Thomas's 'sweet last-left damsons' show him 'taking some of the fruit from Keats's fruit-filled autumn scene'. It's relevant that the (imitative) starling should be 'whistling what/ Once swallows sang'.[87] Yet 'late' or 'last-left' need not mean 'too late'. It can mean 'what yet lives' – as do other Romantic poets in Thomas's Keatsian orbit. 'October' complicates the rhythm of Wordsworth's 'The river glideth at his own sweet will' as well as of 'earth's diurnal course'. 'Liberty' is (perhaps ironically) pan-Romantic in its very title; and its first line, nocturnal setting and melancholic solitude recall Coleridge's 'Frost at Midnight', where the speaker is 'left … to that solitude, which suits/ Abstruser musings', while 'all the numberless goings-on of life' become 'Inaudible as dreams'. 'Liberty' goes further: burying the past in one of Thomas's amnesiac vortices. 'Frost at Midnight' invokes a flame rather than the moon as implied auditor, but ends with icicles 'Quietly shining to the quiet Moon'. 'Liberty' ends with 'this moon that leaves me dark within the door'. The poets meet 'under the same moon'.

These poems also remix elements from poems by Thomas that have already remixed the Romantics: poems that involve desire, beauty, loss, otherness, seasons, sun and moon. He had written many prose sketches of autumn too. Why, now, such exceptionally layered palimpsests, such quintessence of quintessence? Perhaps these poems indeed mark a further distillation. Perhaps they renew or re-inscribe motifs, structures and influences from the matrix which has made Thomas a poet – and a 'war poet'. Keats has already obliquely (formally) entered his poems of July 1915. 'October', written in mid-October, is the first poem that Thomas wrote in army camp. Everyday commitment to the war may have heightened his sense of Keats along with his sense of mortality: 'the brevity of now'. He may have come to identify with Keats's own urgent horizon: 'There's nothing like the sun till we are dead'. Certainly Thomas's 'Autumn' is a season when 'leaves … slip', 'the year dies', 'last-left damsons … drop down' and ultimately: 'The last light has gone out of the world'.

The second half of 'Liberty' is where Thomas especially rewrites Keats's melancholic love 'almost for death itself – regret – and the consolations offered by the intensity which makes pleasure and pain so much alike' (see p. 113). The poem's knottiness stems from its status as a reflection on freedom by a poet who has made a choice that both liberates and circumscribes him:

If every hour

Like this one passing that I have spent among
The wiser others when I have forgot
To wonder whether I was free or not,
Were piled before me, and not lost behind,
And I could take and carry them away
I should be rich; or if I had the power
To wipe out every one and not again
Regret, I should be rich to be so poor.
And yet I still am half in love with pain,
With what is imperfect, with both tears and mirth,
With things that have an end, with life and earth,
And this moon that leaves me dark within the door. (104)

'And yet': the syntactical/ rhythmic release of the last sentence implies that contraries are being as reconciled as is mortally possible. In thus glossing and positively redirecting Keats's 'half in love with easeful Death', perhaps Thomas answers the complaint of 'For these'. Subtly nuanced and cadenced anapaestic phrases ('what is imperfect', 'things that have an end') are buttressed by couplet-rhymed iambic stresses: 'tears and mirth', 'life and earth'. In the final line, stress again falls on key monosyllables ('moon', 'dark', 'door'), but anapaests predominate, and the line half-rhymes with a slightly remote word. The poem's rhythm is left in some darkness too.

Thomas's autumnal anatomy of melancholy culminates in 'Liberty': perhaps partly a manifesto. Melancholy, if not quite his 'sovran shrine', seems a capacious enough spectrum to cover much of his sensibility. The rhetorical questions in 'The Glory' have a melancholic starting-point; and terms that recur in accounts of melancholy, including Thomas's own accounts, fit his poetry: solitude, darkness, sadness, loss, despair, longing, pleasure and pain, absence of 'spiritual agency' (see p. 111). He identifies with the tree that 'ceaselessly, unreasonably grieves'. His 'Melancholy' poem is self-parody as well as critique. The word does not occur again, perhaps because its meanings have been absorbed. But melancholy continues to be implicitly redefined, and some poems at the blackest end of its spectrum lie ahead. 'Rain', set in a 'bleak' army 'hut', tugs against any element of 'Welcome joy, and welcome sorrow' in 'Liberty':

> Rain, midnight rain, nothing but the wild rain
> On this bleak hut, and solitude, and me
> Remembering again that I shall die
> And neither hear the rain nor give it thanks
> For washing me cleaner than I have been
> Since I was born into this solitude … (105)

This melancholic return to solitary nocturnal reflection merges inner dissolution with a vista of the war-dead: 'Myriads of broken reeds all still and stiff' (Burton's *Anatomy* evokes 'the infinite numbers of the dead'). There is ultimately

> ... no love which this wild rain
> Has not dissolved except the love of death,
> If love it be towards what is perfect and
> Cannot, the tempest tells me, disappoint.

Here and elsewhere, Thomas redefines Romantic melancholy with reference to the Great War. 'Dissolve' is a quasi-suicidal verb in 'Ode to a Nightingale' too, and 'Rain' ends by darkening both Keats's 'half in love with easeful Death' and Thomas's 'half in love with pain,/ With what is imperfect'. The irony of 'perfect' revisits melancholy as an 'aesthetic emotion' in a context where it is clearly so much more.

CHAPTER 3

'The compact essential real truth': Thomas and Great War Poetry

Besides discussing Thomas as a 'war poet', this chapter will look at other Great War poets, and at concepts of Great War poetry, from the perspective of his poems and criticism. What difference does it make if Thomas (rather than, say, Wilfred Owen or Isaac Rosenberg) is our primary lens? Did the fact that he became a poet in December 1914 lay down a marker for what followed? Thomas's involvement with war poetry implicitly began under the moon of August 1914. It explicitly began when he wrote a review-article, 'War Poetry', which appeared in the December 1914 issue of Harold Monro's journal *Poetry and Drama*. His notes for the article include the following:

> The war national but as yet dark and chaotic in brain – e.g. no good poems early in Napoleonic wars. Some writers can't go on with old work but no reason why they should at once be able to admit war into subject matter. Poetry excepting cheapest kind shows this dark chaotic character.
>
> People expressing all sorts of <u>views</u> and trumping up old canting catchwords, but not yet the compact essential real truth to this occasion alone.[1]

This suggests that poetry has a unique job to do, and that war does not change (even if it conditions) the nature of that job. In the article itself Thomas says: 'by becoming ripe for poetry the poet's thoughts may recede far from their original resemblance to all the world's, and may seem to have little to do with daily events. They may retain hardly any colour from 1798 or 1914.'[2] When Thomas conceived the article, he was neither poet nor soldier. Perhaps his double metamorphosis owes something to his starting to think critically about 'war poetry' with the war 'as yet dark and chaotic in brain'.

Wilfred Owen, too, sees what he has learned to call 'war poetry' as having a special relation or obligation to 'truth': 'the true Poets must be truthful'. Writing to his sister, Owen says of Siegfried Sassoon's 'trench life sketches': 'except in one or two of my letters … you will find nothing so perfectly truthfully descriptive of war. Cinemas, cartoons, photographs, tales, plays – Na-poo. Now you see why I have always extolled Poetry'.[3] If trench-French backs up Owen's claims, so does his status as 'truth-teller', and the attacks on that status, in the continuing struggle for control of Great War representation. Like Thomas, Owen sets poetry's 'truth' against other kinds. This formative consciousness of competing media (not just of propaganda) may partly explain why Great War poetry maintains its cultural presence; even if *Blackadder Goes Forth* has become a trench-poet proxy. Politicians or historians rarely attack other poets. Yet we might compare the status of Yeats *vis-à-vis* the Easter Rising: a centenary more alive in contemporary politics. Historians argue with Yeats's 'Easter, 1916', but the poem has not gone away. The dying Yeats claimed: 'You can refute Hegel but not … the Song of Sixpence'.[4] What distinguishes poetic 'truth' from other kinds? To put the question another way: 'What is a war poem'? This chapter will touch on three broad ways of posing that question in relation to the Great War. The first adds the rider: 'as compared with war *verse*'. The second stresses the last word: 'What is a war *poem*?' That is, as compared with war-diaries, war-letters, memoirs, histories; Owen's 'Cinemas, cartoons, photographs, tales, plays'. Owen saw passages in his letters as akin to Sassoon's 'sketches': a seed of poems to come. But what differentiates those poems – or 'the Song of Sixpence' or Sassoon's 'Everyone Sang' – from the letters? Should all Great War 'texts' be read as a collective document that effaces literary markings? Or is the war now simply a Great Text? If not, thirdly, we might stress the question's first word: '*What* is a war poem?' That is, where should we draw any generic line? Or historical line: not, perhaps, in November 1918. The poetry itself runs, sometimes reflexively, to interrogative syntax: 'Who sent us forth? Who takes us home again?' 'Why do you lie with your legs ungainly huddled?' 'What in our lives is burnt/ In the fire of this?' 'How should we see our task/ But through his blunt and lashless eyes?' 'What matter makes my spade for tears or mirth?' 'What did they expect of our toil and extreme/ Hunger?' And perhaps 'what rough beast …?'[5] It may be intrinsic to Great War poetry, as to Great War history, that some element will always stay 'dark and chaotic in brain'.

1. POEMS AND CANONS

If Thomas's reputation grew rather slowly during the last century, one reason may be the generic elusiveness (multiplicity) of his lyric. Thus he has not always been reckoned a 'war poet'. William Cooke could write in *Edward Thomas: A Critical Biography* (1970): 'As a war poet Thomas is virtually ignored.'[6] Cooke and others have ensured that this is no longer so. Yet it's not just a question of squeezing Thomas into a category, but of how he opens it up. His belated admission to the Great War canon means that he has barely influenced its terms, especially its aesthetic terms – or lack of such. Although the 'trench life sketch' has become less normative, an overly thematic bias can show itself in other ways. It surely matters that Thomas is one of four 'war poets' who have significantly influenced later poetry: the others being Owen, Rosenberg and Robert Graves. Thomas was the oldest of these poets; he brought a rich literary hinterland to bear on the war; he had time to think before he reached the trenches. A Thomas-based concept of Great War poetry might challenge several – or all – canonical templates. It might both move aesthetic questions into the foreground and show the poetry in a more holistic light.

Like Matthew Hollis's book, Cooke's chapter 'Roads to France' takes its title from Robert Frost's tribute to Thomas:

His poetry is so very brave – so unconsciously brave. He didn't think of it for a moment as war poetry, though that is what it is. It ought to be called Roads to France.[7]

Frost's point is that 'Now all roads lead to France', a line from Thomas's poem 'Roads', covers 'all' his poetry. But if Thomas's poetry is indeed a 'journey to a war', if this journey is its path of paths, individual poems cannot properly represent him as 'war poet'. While anthologies of Great War poetry (central to canon-making) no longer ignore Thomas, he has little effect on principles of selection, and the chosen poems always 'mention the war'. That they mention it in different ways, illustrates the problem. Thus 'The sun used to shine' sets the war on an elegiac horizon of friendship and poetry; 'Man and Dog' places it in a historical vista of work and exploitation; 'Rain' draws it into a larger 'melancholic' scenario. And a poem that doesn't mention the war can be especially steeped in it.

Yet to plead that Thomas highlights the holistic nature of Great War poetry may push a door already wide open. This is a key finding of Santanu Das's overview 'Reframing First World War Poetry' in *The Cambridge Companion to the Poetry of the First World War* (2013). One way in which Das asks 'What is a war poem?' is by noting the tendency for *everything* to become a war poem: for the category 'Great War poetry' to expand to the point of dissolution. It's a sign of category-creep that Das should reach for catalogue: 'The recovery in recent years of poetry by women, civilians, dissenters, working-class and non-English (particularly Irish, Scottish, Welsh and American) writers'; 'the anonymous contributors to … the *Wipers Times*; non-combatants and civilians … jingo-imperialists and conscientious objectors …'.[8] Das's lists reflect the rise of the Great War anthology as social and cultural history or identity politics (in fact, some

'English' war poets might equally be Irish, Scottish or Welsh).
Anthologies like Catherine Reilly's *Scars Upon My Heart: Women's
Poetry and Verse of the First World War* (1981) and Vivien Noakes's
Alternative Book of First World War Poetry (2006) have undoubtedly
refreshed the field; as did Martin Stephen's *Poems of the First World
War* (1993), which sought to show that Owen's and Sassoon's 'truth'
is neither 'typical or representative'.[9] Yet, by what measure does
quantity outweigh quality? The 'typical or representative', however
construed, is about context rather than art. Dominic Hibberd and
John Onions organise *The Winter of the World* (2007) war-year by
war-year. But poetry may be what eludes context (including its
date) along with category. Stephen places Owen's 'The Send-Off'
in his 'Home Front' section; Thomas's 'As the team's head-brass' in
'Romantic Tradition: Animals and Nature'. Kenneth Baker's *Faber
Book of War Poetry* files 'Insensibility' under 'Useful Tips', with the
gloss: 'It was a positive disadvantage, as Wilfred Owen points out, to
be imaginative' – particularly if you are a Tory politician, perhaps.[10]
Tim Kendall's anthology *Poetry of the First World War* (2013) was a
notable attempt to resist or turn the contextual tide by 'arranging
the best poems in the best order'.[11] To stress the aesthetics of Great
War poetry is not to ignore politics or sociology. Poetry – lyric –
interweaves, and mutually complicates, elements that other writing
segregates. And Thomas's conjectural poems, which 'may retain
hardly any colour from … 1914', are not the same thing as works
shallowly linked with the war. *What* is a war poem? Perhaps Great
War poetry, as a category, should be neither too exclusive nor inclu-
sive to the point of meaninglessness. As it would prove – as Thomas
exemplifies – the whole aesthetic of certain poets was formed or
transformed by the Great War. Their poetry belongs to the epicentre
of an earthquake. But other poets and poems were shocked or
shaken, and seismic ripples continue into poetry today. It was crucial
that 'true Poets' shared in a wider cultural articulation: that many
'voices', many visual records, represent the war. Yet this can obscure
the unique complexity of voice and image in poetry.

By 'typical or representative' Stephen means patriotic. One canonical motif, which Thomas helps to complicate, is the opposition between patriotism and protest, 'Visions of Glory' and 'The Bitter Truth'.[12] In 2014 some historians and politicians revisited this opposition, and visited it upon poets. Max Hastings's *Catastrophe* (2014) was marketed as countering 'the poets' view of the war' – as if all poets or poems had a single view. Evidently, patriotism can include protest, and *vice versa*: witness Owen's 'Smile, Smile, Smile', where 'Nation' is followed by a question-mark and 'England', its virtue now monopolised by trench-soldiers, has 'fled to France'.[13] But Thomas underlines the point because no other poet approaches the war so dialectically. He refers to his enlistment (in July 1915) as 'the natural culmination of a long series of moods & thoughts'.[14] Some 'moods & thoughts' took shape as poems, and Thomas's poetic dialectics did not end with a decision, which, at root, turned on the question of duty to a national collective.

Thomas's 'War Poetry' notes call the war 'national'. But what nation? Britain? England? Wales? The UK – which then included Ireland? He had long distrusted patriotism, nationalism and even nationality: 'what with Great Britain, the British Empire, Britons, Britishers, and the English-speaking world, the choice offered to whomsoever would be patriotic is embarrassing'. Yet he sometimes made an exception for Wales: in 1901 he told a friend that he never felt a 'spark' of patriotism 'unless it be to love a few acres in Wales'. A passage in his novel *The Happy-Go-Lucky Morgans* proposes 'Land of my Fathers' as the ideal national anthem because it is 'exulting without self-glorification or any other form of brutality', and hence 'breathes' the true 'spirit of patriotism'.[15] Nonetheless, Thomas said in September 1914: 'I am slowly growing into a conscious Englishman.'[16] Like 'This England', his essay 'England' is a quasi-manifesto on the road to poetry. It probes the affiliations to country that war brings to the surface and into question. The essay begins: 'In times of peace and tranquillity the vocabulary of patriotism is not much used.' Thomas proceeds to anatomise the use and abuse

('ignorant, blatant, jingoism') of patriotic language, before suggest-
ing what England 'means … to most of us'. Having quoted from
Izaak Walton's *Compleat Angler*, he says:

> I believe … that all ideas of England are developed, spun
> out, from such a centre into something large or infinite, solid
> or aery … that England is a system of vast circumferences
> circling round the minute neighbouring points of home.[17]

Andrew Webb argues that Thomas's poetry, in fact, records 'the fail-
ure of English localist ideology as inherited from Burke, Wordsworth
and Ruskin'; that it proves the non-viability of 'locales' in which
'Englishness can be secured'.[18] But this assumes that localism (the
emotion inspired by 'a few acres' or 'minute … points') has no
meaning in and of itself. Similarly, when Thomas praises Irish poets
for 'sing[ing] of Ireland … with an intimate reality often missing
from British patriotic poetry', and calls Britannia 'a frigid personifi-
cation', he is not necessarily advocating Hibernia instead.[19] Perhaps
his underlying or unconscious concern is with 'locales' conducive
to poetry. Here, indeed, England-as-nation would prove as unwork-
able as Britannia. Thomas translates his 'system' into a co-ordinate
geometry for poems; his localism into poetic loci; his patriotism
into dialectics between those loci.

'The Manor Farm' and 'The Combe' are dialectically opposed
pre-enlistment poems. The former, which has links with Thomas's
'England' essay, ends by evoking an idealised past when 'This
England, Old already, was called Merry' (45). The latter ends with a
vista of intensifying darkness and violence:

> But far more ancient and dark
> The Combe looks since they killed the badger there,
> Dug him out and gave him to the hounds,
> That most ancient Briton of English beasts. (48)

Here some deeply indigenous contract with the 'English' (and pre-English) environment has been further violated by history. As contrasted with 'called Merry', the Combe's 'mouth … stopped with bramble, thorn, and briar' may conceal the unspeakable (48). 'The Manor Farm' and the post-enlistment 'This is no case of petty right or wrong' are the only poems in which Thomas effectively invokes England-as-nation. Elsewhere, England – like Wales – is geographical, if not neutrally so; and 'English' a mainly cultural epithet, as in 'Words' ('You English words') and 'Lob':

> '… Everybody has met one such man as he.
> Does he keep clear old paths that no one uses
> But once a life-time when he loves or muses?
> He is English as this gate, these flowers, this mire.
> And when at eight years old Lob-lie-by-the-fire
> Came in my books, this was the man I saw …' (77)

Lob's local, folkloric and earthly habitat sets Thomas's quirky personification of 'Englishness' against over-arching, imperial forms of patriotism. A quest-poem, like 'The Other' in a different sphere, 'Lob' pursues something elusive and multifarious rather than confirms something known. 'This is no case of petty right or wrong', where England-as-nation resurfaces, shows signs of internal strain (see below), and Thomas later wrote 'No one cares less than I':

> 'No one cares less than I,
> Nobody knows but God,
> Whether I am destined to lie
> Under a foreign clod,'
> Were the words I made to the bugle call in the morning.
>
> But laughing, storming, scorning,
> Only the bugles know
> What the bugles say in the morning,

And they do not care, when they blow
The call that I heard and made words to early this morning. (123)

The speaker represents himself as having written a poem (this poem) which contests the patriotic language of Rupert Brooke's sonnet-sequence 1914: 'Now, God be thanked Who has matched us with His hour', 'some corner of a foreign field/ That is for ever England', 'Blow out, you bugles, over the rich Dead!'[20] Thomas's long refrain-line and same-rhymed 'morning' contribute to an ominous open ending that contrasts with Brooke's ringing sonnet-closures. Thomas was not the only poet to attack Brooke's premises and heroic-Christian idiom: Brooke kick-started Great War poetry in English, however many kicks he may get himself. But Thomas's attack has special implications for poetic patriotism directed towards 'England'. It also implicates his enlistment. In June 1915 he told Frost that Brooke's 'sonnets about him enlisting are probably not very personal but a nervous attempt to connect with himself the very widespread idea that self sacrifice is the highest self indulgence', adding: 'I daren't say so, not having enlisted or fought the keeper'.[21] This alludes to an incident when an angry gamekeeper had threatened Thomas and Frost.[22] Because Thomas's reaction had been more pacific than Frost's, he accused himself of cowardice. Similarly, both as poetry critic and newborn poet, he evidently felt compromised by 'not having enlisted'. How dare he question Brooke's poems without matching his courage? 'No one cares less than I', a poem that strips war down to its naked arbitrary power, is Thomas's post-dated, now-validated critique of 1914. Further, given his own literary track-record, Thomas must have been provoked – perhaps creatively, perhaps fatefully – by how Brooke became associated with 'England'. Brooke, who volunteered in August 1914, may have influenced his self-rebuke in 'This England': 'either I had never loved England, or I had loved it foolishly, aesthetically, like a slave, not having realised that it was not mine unless I was willing and prepared to die rather than leave it …'.[23]

To look at Great War poetry through the lens of Thomas is to bring Ivor Gurney into sharper focus. The question of patriotism, Brooke and England is one zone where their poetry overlaps. Although they never met, Thomas was a Muse for Gurney. Gurney's poem 'The Mangel-Bury', which revisits the scenarios of Thomas's 'As the team's head-brass' and 'Swedes', begins: 'It was after war; Edward Thomas had fallen at Arras −/ I was walking by Gloucester musing on such things/ As fill his verse with goodness …'. Yet Gurney had begun by imitating Brooke, as in his sonnet 'To the Poet before Battle': 'Now, youth, the hour of thy dread passion comes;/ Thy lovely things must all be laid away'. The speaker seeks to 'make/ The name of poet terrible in just war'. Later, Gurney conceived his own 'Sonnets 1917' as: 'a sort of counterblast' against Brooke's ignorance of 'the grind of the war', 'the protest of the physical against the exalted spiritual'.[24] Even so, the sonnets are dedicated to Brooke's memory, and retain Brooke-like features: 'What better passing than to go out like men/ For England …?' Gurney would eventually call England 'only a hard and fast system which has sent so much of the flower of Englands artists to risk death, and a wrong materialistic system'.[25] But there remains the job of distinguishing between England as political 'system' and England as other things. Besides translating his own 'system' into poetic structure, Thomas represents the 'neighbouring points' as those of 'home': a dialectical variable in his poems. Some of Gurney's poems find an unexpected French home-from-home: among fellow-soldiers in billets and estaminets (Gloucestershire becomes the Gloucesters); or where the landscape evokes 'Cotswold' − which replaces 'England'. 'Home-Sickness' substitutes 'Earth's familiar lovely places' for an abstract nation by naming 'Blackbird, bluebell, hedge-sparrow, tiny daisies'.[26] The effect parallels Thomas's lists of particulars; as in 'If I were to own', which bequeaths to his son 'copses, ponds, roads and ruts,/ Fields where plough-horses steam and plovers/ Fling and whimper …' (115).

Yet Thomas does more than list. This testament, like similar poems for his daughters, invokes place-names (of Essex parishes) as both place and name, and as the chemistry between the two: 'Martins, Lambkins, and Lillyputs'. Rather than constituting minia-ture 'Englands', the place-names symbolise cultural and spiritual goods that attach us to the earth. They represent 'home' in a further sense; as does 'Home':

Often I had gone this way before:
But now it seemed I never could be
And never had been anywhere else;
'Twas home; one nationality
We had, I and the birds that sang,
One memory … (81)

This poem takes its bearings, as do other poems (see p. 278), from Steep: after nine years, suddenly recognised as 'home'. But, in applying 'one nationality' and 'One memory' to a local-ecological microcosm, Thomas conceives 'habitation' in a way that exceeds Gurney's object in *Severn & Somme* (1917): 'To say out what Gloucester is, and is to me'. The speaker of 'Crickley Hill' is thinking of Gloucestershire as he walks with another soldier at Buire-au-Bois: 'When on a sudden, "Crickley" he said. How I started/ At that old darling name of home!'[27] For Thomas, 'home', like other names, is more 'perplexed'. In '"Home"' it acquires inverted commas. Three soldiers, returning to army camp, realise that the word estranges them; and that 'union', in whatever sense, is contingent:

…'How quick' to someone's lip
The words came, 'will the beaten horse run home.'

The word 'home' raised a smile in us all three,
And one repeated it, smiling just so
That all knew what he meant and none would say.
Between three counties far apart that lay

We were divided and looked strangely each
At the other, and we knew we were not friends
But fellows in a union that ends
With the necessity for it, as it ought ... (114)

Here the 'points of home' are hardly neighbourly, let alone add up to 'England'. As in his testamentary poems, Thomas continued to channel patriotism mainly through 'a few acres' and their ramifications. Thomas and Gurney exemplify how radically Great War poetry tests 'the vocabulary of patriotism', the 'name of home', 'the word "home"'. In Owen's 'Exposure': 'Slowly our ghosts drag home ...'.[28]

Thomas's 'home' has a mythic dimension. 'The Brook', with its prehistoric horseman as well as eco-historical butterfly, is a home-poem partly in this sense (see p. 102). 'Home' appears in a related pre-war literary context, when Thomas writes of Charles M. Doughty's long poem *The Dawn in Britain*: 'I had no worthy sense of the rich great age of this home of my race until I found it here'. Thomas sums up Doughty's six volumes as 'a blank verse epic of Early Britain in which [are] combined elements from Geoffrey of Monmouth, the Roman historians, legend, and archaeology, so as to make a poem full of a massive national dignity and an exquisite human and natural beauty'. Of all Thomas's enthusiasms for new poetry, Doughty is one place where posterity has usually not followed him. Doughty's stiffly archaised language seems particularly remote from speech. Yet Thomas praises the 'fine simplicity' of these lines: 'Grey deep, how wholesome, to a shipman's eye!/ And who is 'scaped, from ape-faced world, not joys/ Look forth, o'er thy vast wandering breast, abroad ...'. Doughty (1843–1926) is now chiefly known for his influential travel book *Arabia Deserta*. Thomas admitted to Gordon Bottomley that 'positively Doughty is an antiquarian' and that 'he may turn out a [Robert] Southey after all'. Yet he still rhapsodised: 'Doughty is great. I see his men & women whenever I see noble beeches, as in Savernake Forest, or tumuli or old encampments, or the line of the Downs ... or a few firs on a hilltop'. This seems to be a case of myth-hunger. Thomas compares Doughty with Milton, Blake and William Morris, and finds in *The Dawn in Britain* 'a strange and dark intertexture which was only to be expected, both from the character of our age and from the nature of early history, to which the mythopoeic spirit no longer can, and science will not yet, give any clear unity'.[29] Thomas was not attracted to Doughty's imperial and paranoid politics as evinced by *The Cliffs* (1909), which warns that England is unprepared for a likely German invasion. But *The Dawn in Britain* may have infused him with a 'mythopoeic spirit' to be more lightly manifested by 'Lob'. Thomas's Wiltshire-based folk-hero belongs to 'village England' rather than to legendary Celtic Britain; the poem rejects antiquarian dependence on 'bits of barrows'; and, as elsewhere in Thomas, English literature moves between past and present not as pastiche but as 'intertextural' currents.

Lob – namer of birds, flowers and places – is ultimately poetry:

'... He has been in England as long as dove and daw,
Calling the wild cherry tree the merry tree,
The rose campion Bridget-in-her-bravery [...]
For reasons of his own to him the wren
Is Jenny Pooter. Before all other men
'Twas he first called the Hog's Back the Hog's Back [...]
             This is tall Tom that bore
The logs in, and with Shakespeare in the hall
Once talked, when icicles hung by the wall ...' (77-8)

Thomas brings the aesthetics of Great War poetry into focus because poetry is intrinsic to his war-Muse: the first and last refuge of his patriotism. He finds Walton inspirational because he conjures up 'English fields, English people, English poetry, all together'. It's as if 'English poetry' has mobilised Thomas for war-service or blocked the alternative future of joining Frost in America. It has also mobilised him as a pre-emptive canon-maker. Poetry governs the principles of his wartime anthology *This England*, built 'round a few most English poems like "When icicles hang by the wall" – excluding professedly patriotic writing because it is generally bad and because indirect praise is sweeter and more profound …'. *This England* is the polar opposite of the anthology *Lyra Britannica*, which Thomas had reviewed in 1906. He condemns its editor for promoting 'rhetorical verse' ('a bastard artifice, likely to give a fatally false notion of poetry itself') and for subordinating poetry to 'the realisation of the responsibility of every boy and girl born to the heritage of the glory of Britain'.[30] Reviewing two contributions to the wartime anthological *Kulturkampf*, Thomas calls *Patriotic Poems* 'just a sound collection of what people expect under such a title'; and says of the poets featured in *Poems of the Great War*: 'the war has not done anything for them, and they … have not done anything for the war which newspapers and street talk have not done as well'. Another review dismisses poetry that resembles 'the shouting of rhetorician, reciter, or politician' rather than 'the talk of friends and lovers'.[31] Thomas's endeavour to rescue patriotism from jingoism redefines 'England' not only as poetic loci but also as 'English poems'. This is poetry as cultural defence. Similarly, in December 1914, Owen wrote to his mother: 'Do you know what would hold me together on a battlefield?: The sense that I was perpetuating the language in which Keats and the rest of them wrote!'[32] 'Lob', which condenses materials from *This England*, brings cultural defence to the poetic surface: 'He never will admit he is dead/ Till millers cease to grind men's bones for bread' (79). That Lob 'Once talked' with Shakespeare places poetry at the apex of the intercourse between people and landscape which has fertilised folk-culture, shaped the English language, and founded poetry on speech:

> Poetry … has roots deep in a substantial past. It springs apparently from an occupation of the land, from long, busy, and quiet tracts of time, wherein a man or a nation may find its own soul. To have a future, it must have had a past.[33]

'Lob' prepares the ground for the complementary *ars poetica* poems: 'Words' and 'The Word' (see p. 32). Thomas's deepest mode of cultural defence, so deep as to leave cultural defence behind, is his creative engagement with 'the English lyric'. That he activates such a range of forms and genres seems a benchmark for the war's aesthetic repercussions elsewhere.

In their different kinds, 'War Poetry', *This England* and 'Lob' are critical summations. Thomas was best placed of the Great War poets to gauge the war's initial impact on poetry, the war's meaning for poetry. He had long reviewed the Kipling school more or less unfavourably. In 'War Poetry' he singles out Kipling and Henry Newbolt as 'belonging to a professional class apart', saying drily: 'It was their hour, and they have not been silent.' He also remarks that Kipling 'has hardly done more than speak in echoes of himself'. Thomas was equally ready for the new or aggravated patriotic guises assumed by 'imbecilic' verse. In 1900 he had complained that Harold Begbie's Boer War poems were 'full of blood and thunder' and that Begbie seemed 'to have used a sword (or a shovel) instead of a pen'.[34] Now Begbie crops up again:

> The public, crammed with mighty facts and ideas it will never digest, must look coldly on poetry where already those mighty things have sunk away far into 'The still sad music of humanity'. For his insults to their feelings, the newspapers, history, they might call the poet a pro-Boer. They want something raw and solid, or vague and lofty or sentimental. They must have Mr Begbie to express their thoughts, or 'Tipperary' to drown them.

This anticipates 'The Word': 'I have forgot, too, names of the mighty men/ That fought and lost or won in the old wars' (93). For Thomas, a poem's relation to any public event, like the other traces it carries, cannot be absolutely determined at the moment of composition, and is incalculable in the future. He judges that older 'true poets' have not necessarily responded to the war with true poems, and notes that 'few younger men who had been moved to any purpose could be expected to crystallise their thoughts with speed'. 'War Poetry', which pre-empts canons and categories, is the foundational study of Great War poetry. That is so, even if it seems an unwitting draft-aesthetic for Thomas himself as 'war poet', and he mainly takes 'war poetry' to mean patriotic poetry (this is December 1914). Thomas's open premises remain open. 'War Poetry' concludes with a prophecy underpinned by accurate praise for Hardy's 'Men Who March Away':

> Mr Hardy has written an impersonal song which seems to be the best of the time, as it is the least particular and occasional. He may write even better yet. I should also expect the work of other real poets to improve as the war advances, perhaps after it is over, as they understand it and themselves more completely.

2. VERSE AND PROSE

In 1903 Thomas wrote: 'Perfect verse is the brazen image of poetry which clever men are permitted to make.'[35] Verse is by definition 'particular and occasional': its theme or attitude carried rather than complicated by form. In 'War Poetry' Thomas stresses that, not poems, but *'verses'* [my italics] are 'written for occasions, great or small' and allows that 'they may be excellent'. He probably has less excellent 'jingo-imperialist' versifiers in mind when his notes scorn 'all sorts of <u>views</u>' and 'old canting catchwords'; when the article itself targets the 'bombastic, hypocritical, or senseless'. Yet he equally speaks as a weary poetry critic in hinting that established poets need to do more than write from 'a powerful social sense genuinely aroused': that is, do more than write verse. Most anthologies of Great War poetry mingle verse and poetry. For instance, the 1916 section of *The Winter of the World* juxtaposes verse (satirical as well as jingoistic) with poems by Sassoon, Thomas, Graves, Gurney and Rosenberg, which manifest an emergent 'war poetry'. The section contains twelve sonnets: tip of the annual sonnet-iceberg. Among these are Thomas's 'February Afternoon' and W. N. Ewer's 'To Any Diplomatist', which accuses: 'Engrossed, you never cared to realise/ The folly of the things for which you fought'. 'February Afternoon', too, has an accusatory thrust, but has other thrusts as well (see below). *The Winter of the World* contextualises the matrix that engendered 'war poetry'. Yet bad writing is a great deadener, as when its clichés harmonise divergent sonnet-endings: 'And go to death, calmly, triumphantly'; 'For others' sake strong men are crucified'.[36]

The Great War may be the supreme instance of an occasion that impelled poetry as well as verse to 'express views' or transfigure them into 'truth to this occasion alone'. But when poetry becomes 'viewy' (a negative term in Thomas's critical vocabulary) it must negotiate with verse. Thus in 'Easter, 1916' Yeats negotiates with the tradition of the Irish political ballad, and with 'views' or 'opinion': defined by the poem as 'Hearts with one purpose alone'. For Yeats, opinion is an internal temptation as well as external threat. The 1916 section of *The Winter of the World* should have included 'Easter, 1916'. It does include Thomas's 'This is no case of petty right or wrong', which also skirts verse/opinion by putting a 'case' for war:

This is no case of petty right or wrong
That politicians or philosophers
Can judge. I hate not Germans, nor grow hot
With love of Englishmen, to please newspapers.
Beside my hate for one fat patriot
My hatred of the Kaiser is love true […]
                                        Dinned
With war and argument I read no more
Than in the storm smoking along the wind
Athwart the wood. Two witches' cauldrons roar.
From one the weather shall rise clear and gay;

Out of the other an England beautiful
And like her mother that died yesterday.
Little I know or care if, being dull,
I shall miss something that historians
Can rake out of the ashes when perchance
The phoenix broods serene above their ken.
But with the best and meanest Englishmen
I am one in crying, God save England, lest
We lose what never slaves and cattle blessed.
The ages made her that made us from the dust:
She is all we know and live by, and we trust
She is good and must endure, loving her so:
And as we love ourselves we hate her foe. (104)

Thomas's pacifist-philosopher is Bertrand Russell; his patriot-politician, Horatio Bottomley. There's a parallel with Owen saying: 'I hate washy pacifists as temperamentally as I hate whiskied prussianists.'[37] The parallel suggests how, for both poets, being 'in' the war validates their views. It also suggests the need for something more complex than views. 'This is no case …', half-snared by the rhetoric it repudiates, shows Thomas less sure of the border between verse and poetry. The poem short-circuits the motives for his enlistment, simplifies his critical stance, and almost compromises the redemption of patriotism from jingoism. The gendered personification, the Phoenix-image, words like 'perchance', the oddly inadvertent allusion to Keats ('On First Looking into Chapman's Homer') betray the strains of being 'one in crying' anything. Rather too pat a trope, rhythm and rhyme ultimately license 'hate': the poem ends as (Brooke-like) verse. Yet a modal crisis lurks in the more complex movement of 'Dinned/ With war and argument I read no more/ Than in the storm smoking along the wind/ Athwart the wood'. At one level, this cognitive hiatus may repress residual unease about enlisting. But, at a rhythmic and reflexive level, it involves a clash between verse and poetry, 'argument' and symbol. The 'Dinned' poet-speaker is overwhelmed by the public noise with which he has tried to compete (in 'War Poetry' Thomas calls patriotic verse 'the noisy stuff'). The *Macbeth*-like 'witches' cauldrons', perhaps symbolising the 'dark and chaotic in brain', give way to the wishful rebirth of 'an England beautiful'. Love-talk's superiority to 'the shouting of rhetorician, reciter, or politician' is asserted rather than manifested. Perhaps Thomas thought 'This is no case …' too 'viewy': he did not include it in his *Poems* (1917). His larger reflexive dialectics develop the critique of 'War Poetry'. The next poem he wrote was 'Rain' – a 'bleak' reversion to interiority.

Siegfried Sassoon occupies the war-blurred border between poetry and verse. His poem 'The Poet as Hero' is an *ars poetica* that makes no bones about its 'view': 'Mocking and loathing War'. For Sarah Cole, Sassoon's 'Soldier's Declaration' is a poetic-political manifesto: 'a prism for reading … a body of verse that installs dissent against the war at its centre – at the level of word, line, image and voice'. Rupert Hart-Davis wrote that the war 'turned [Sassoon] from a versifier into a poet'.[38] We might say, rather, that he continued to veer between those dispositions; or that his satires of war-circumstance somehow dissolve the poem-verse distinction; or that extraordinary lines can redeem an uneven poem, as when 'The Rear-Guard' ends: 'Unloading hell behind him step by step'. 'Step by step': distinctive rhythm is the criterion. Sassoon's rhythms are not always those of mockery and loathing, nor does every poem end with a satirical punch-line. 'Everyone Sang' sings its crescendo: 'O, but Everyone/ Was a bird; and the song was wordless; the singing will never be done.' And the movement of 'The Dug-Out' unfolds as a huge gesture of tenderness, textured by assonance and repetition:

> Why do you lie with your legs ungainly huddled,
> And one arm bent across your sullen, cold,
> Exhausted face? It hurts my heart to watch you,
> Deep-shadow'd from the candle's guttering gold;
> And you wonder why I shake you by the shoulder;

Drowsy, you mumble and sigh and turn your head …
You are too young to fall asleep for ever;
And when you sleep you remind me of the dead.[39]

'Ungainly huddled' is itself an ungainly huddled phrase, then the line-break reaches across to spotlight 'Exhausted face'. The italicised ending at once interprets and condenses the previous movement. 'The Dug-Out' is 'trench life sketch' heightened into symbol: a feat Sassoon does not always manage. Like 'declaration', reportage is a staging-post on the border between poetry and verse. If Owen sometimes lays it on too thick and Keatsian, Sassoon can lay it on too thin: recycling 'descriptive' nouns, adjectives and verbs. Insofar as 'Declaration' is integral to *his* war-Muse, Sassoon can never jettison verse. None of his poems quite matches how 'Dulce et Decorum Est' transmutes outrage and reportage into form, psychodrama and symbol. That's why, like 'Easter, 1916', the poem is hard to argue with. Its structural complexity, what Das calls its 'pulse of pain', render it irreducible to the declaration that the Latin tag is an 'old Lie'. Das notes how this double sonnet moves 'from sounds produced between the body and the world … to sounds within the body'.[40] 'Pulse', as sound and rhythm, is one means whereby the 'I-speaker' engages 'you'. The last two lines do not stand alone (as those hostile to 'the poets' view' seem to think), but are generated by a conditional dynamic which requires 'you too' to absorb the whole poem:

… In all my dreams, before my helpless sight,
He plunges at me, guttering, choking, drowning.

If in some smothering dreams you too could pace
Behind the wagon that we flung him in […]
If you could hear, at every jolt, the blood
Come gargling from the froth-corrupted lungs […]
My friend, you would not tell with such high zest
To children ardent for some desperate glory,

The old Lie: Dulce et decorum est
Pro patria mori.[41]

View/vision is another borderline. Perhaps 'This is no case of petty right or wrong' gets stuck between view and vision.

Symbol and rhythm differentiate poetry from prose as well as from verse. 'What is a war *poem*?' Approaches to Great War poetry which stress reportage – both positively and negatively – can imply that it aspires to the condition of prose. But perhaps nothing could be further from 'the truth'. Thomas's 'real truth' does not invoke realism. The war detached him from prose. It helped to awaken his poetry. 'The sun used to shine' says more than 'This England'. Certainly Thomas did not go down the path opened up by the vivid documentary of the 'home front' reports he wrote for the *English Review* in Autumn 1914. Rather, he absorbed such reportage into the fabric of poems like 'Man and Dog' and 'As the team's head-brass'. Again, the war made Sassoon less of a versifier, not a British Barbusse.[42] It made Owen a better poet. Perhaps we should ask, not how poetry coped with the Great War, but why the war demanded poetry, *what* it demanded from poetry. In *Poetry and Its Others* (2014) Jahan Ramazani argues for a 'more interactive view of poetry's interplay with nonpoetry'. One of the 'others' he discusses is 'the news': newspapers, journalism. Perhaps because he has already done so much to illuminate Great War poetry, Ramazani does not directly broach this special case of 'news that stays news'. But it's relevant to what he writes of contemporary Irish poets: themselves alert to the poetry of 1914-16-18: 'News discourse has been … a shadow self, a shaping counter-force. It has pushed poetry to define itself in its difference from the newspapers and other media forms'.[43] We have seen Owen asserting poetry's superiority to 'other media forms'. Thomas's 'This is no case …' attacks 'newspapers' in the transposed terms of an angry letter to *The Times*. The poem also disparages other 'others' by implying that poetry is better fitted to 'judge' the war than are 'politicians or philosophers' or future 'historians'. In some Great War anthologies, poems sit alongside multi-generic prose 'others', including prose by poets. Thus (as with Thomas) we have ample scope for comparing their poems with prose written before or after the poetic event.

Across this comparative field, there are different kinds of difference. But, like the contrast between 'This England' and 'The sun used to shine', the contrast between Owen's poems and the poem-seeds in his letters suggests how far 'war poetry' aspires beyond prose. Owen told his mother: 'You must be prepared for a long period of Post Cards! I find I have put some poetic material on p. 3 for instance which ought to have been economised for my serious workshop.'[44] An earlier letter had contained the proto-poetic 'material', the war news, on which he based 'Exposure':

> The marvel is that we did not all die of cold. As a matter of fact, only one of my party actually froze to death before he could be got back, but I am not able to tell how many have ended in hospital … My feet ached until they could ache no more, and so they temporarily died. I was kept warm by the ardour of Life within me. I forgot hunger in the hunger for Life. The intensity of your Love reached me and kept me living … We were all half-crazed by the buffeting of the High Explosives … We were marooned on a frozen desert.

> Our brains ache, in the merciless iced east winds that knive us …
> Wearied we keep awake because the night is silent …
> Low, drooping flares confuse our memory of the salient …
> Worried by silence, sentries whisper, curious, nervous,
> But nothing happens.

> Watching, we hear the mad gusts tugging on the wire,
> Like twitching agonies of men among its brambles.
> Northward, incessantly, the flickering gunnery rumbles,
> Far off, like a dull rumour of some other war,
> What are we doing here? […]

Pale flakes with fingering stealth come feeling for our faces –
We cringe in holes, back on forgotten dreams, and stare,
    snow-dazed,
Deep into grassier ditches. So we drowse, sun-dozed,
Littered with blossoms trickling where the blackbird fusses,
        – Is it that we are dying?

Slowly our ghosts drag home: glimpsing the sunk fires, glozed
With crusted dark-red jewels; crickets jingle there;
For hours the innocent mice rejoice: the house is theirs;
Shutters and doors, all closed: on us the doors are closed, –
        We turn back to our dying [...]

Tonight, this frost will fasten on this mud and us,
Shrivelling many hands, puckering foreheads crisp.
The burying-party, picks and shovels in shaking grasp,
Pause over half-known faces. All their eyes are ice,
        But nothing happens.[45]

Some terms in the letter ('intensity', 'hunger for Life') become quali-
ties of a poem that symbolises war as 'a frozen desert' shutting down
all experience. Psychologically as well as physically, synaesthesia
underscores anaesthesia. Feet-ache fuses with brain-ache. Keats's
sensory immersion has given Owen a holistic means of representing
war: a means that both verse and prose lack. The practical problem
of getting bearings, while 'half-crazed' by explosives, becomes
total cognitive 'confusion', a phantasmagoria that distorts space and
time, and dissolves the boundary between inner and outer states:
gunnery 'like a dull rumour of some other war', 'mad gusts' like
human 'agonies'. The speakers' delusions, their proleptic 'ghostli-
ness', also anticipate post-traumatic stress and the post-war world.
For Ramazani, poetry differs from news because, as in MacNeice's
Autumn Journal: 'the present is multiplied, echoed, and stretched
into the past and future by poetic form and memory'.[46] Owen, like

Thomas, had profoundly absorbed poetry's memory-bank. In 'Exposure' Keats and the Bible – 'wars and rumours of wars' – connect the present with deep time. So does form: all the structures that summon what Ramazani calls poetry's 'memory of itself'. The poem's movement is integral to its icy symbolism. The present-tense quatrains, long lines further slowed by end-stopping, by consonantal rhyme and consonantal density, by irregular refrain, seem to doubt whether the poem itself is going anywhere. Two refrains are again huge questions: 'What are we doing here?' 'Is it that we are dying?' But 'Exposure' does go somewhere when its gaze shifts and 'ice' returns as an internal rhyme with 'eyes'. Here rhyme matters.

3. 'SERIOUS WORKSHOPS'

Compared with Owen's letter, 'Exposure' might be said to multi-task. But what idea of poetry shapes their difference? 'My serious workshop', says Owen. It's now more widely recognised that few soldier-poets were so cannon-stunned as to stand outside contemporary aesthetic debates and dynamics. Owen believed he was helping Sassoon and Graves to 'revolutionise English Poetry'.[47] Thomas recast the English lyric in the dual context of war and Robert Frost's innovations. At one level, 'Lob' is about 'tradition and the individual talent'. The Western Front's entanglement with literary life made all this poetry an interconnected *body* of work (whether poets knew one another or not) as compared to the more atomised war poetry of France, Italy or Germany. The expanded canon can conceal a unique poetic moment and movement. Once again, it's not only what poetry tells us about war. It's what the war tells us about poetry. A sign of 'reframing' (Das) here is that Randall Stevenson calls his poetry chapter in *Literature & the Great War* 'Unfamiliar Lines'; and that a 'contextual' chapter in the *Cambridge Companion* is Peter Howarth writing on 'Poetic Form and the First World War'. Yet both critics partly contravene Jay Winter's caveat in *Sites of Memory, Sites of Mourning* that 'the cultural history of the Great War' should not be seen as 'a phase in the onward ascent of modernism'.[48] War poetry as a 'site of memory' activates both poetry's 'memory of itself' and the memorial function of form. Further, its forms straddle the 'modernist/traditionalist divide' (questioned by Winter) because so-called 'traditional form' itself undergoes structural change. Stevenson urges us to value poets 'for the manner as well as the content of their witnessing', and shows how Owen's soundscapes match 'the shattered, nearly indescribable prospects he had to confront'. But there's a kind of 'waiting for modernism', or a sense that the war should have waited, when he praises Owen or Thomas for sometimes breaching 'conventional constraints of form' rather than appreciates their overall formal effort to make it new. Similarly, Howarth refers to 'the struggle of older forms with a reality which cannot be "contained" by them, and with which twentieth-century poetics spent much of its time trying to catch up'. Hence, he says: 'only modernist fragmentation can really convey the derangements of the war on the psyche, or the abandonment of any moral scheme of overall justification for war'.[49]

Howarth bases this judgment on an analysis of Thomas's 'February Afternoon':

Men heard this roar of parleying starlings, saw,
A thousand years ago even as now,
Black rooks with white gulls following the plough
So that the first are last until a caw
Commands that last are first again, – a law
Which was of old when one, like me, dreamed how
A thousand years might dust lie on his brow
Yet thus would birds do between hedge and shaw.

Time swims before me, making as a day
A thousand years, while the broad ploughland oak
Roars mill-like and men strike and bear the stroke
Of war as ever, audacious or resigned,

And God still sits aloft in the array
That we have wrought him, stone-deaf and stone-blind. (109)

Howarth says:

> The opening eight lines appear to be about the unchanging
> countryside, quietly ironising the self-importance of human
> scales of time. Only when the word 'war' enters in line 12 do
> we realise that this has been haunting the innocent 'shaw' and
> 'caw' all along, and has been there, too, in the sound of 'broad'
> and 'roar' … [But] the final two lines … articulate an anxiety
> that, by taking a God's-eye view … Thomas has been some-
> how deafening and blinding himself to the war, too … and
> the hint is that the neatness and antiquity of the sonnet form
> can only be part of that deflection [and] can only render the
> war less violent than it really is.[50]

Howarth seems right about the delayed entry of 'war', but fixed
assumptions about 'war poetry' and about form over-determine
his reading. The poem's initial focus is surely less the 'unchanging
countryside' than unchanging creaturely 'laws': the competition for
food and territory that shapes both human and animal behaviour.
War takes its place in a Darwinian vista. Words for sound – 'roar',
'parleying', commanding 'caw' – link bird-language, bird-strife, with
human politics and militarism. 'Roar', a word symbolically loaded
in Thomas's poetry, may cover noisy verse too. Disconcertingly,
'as ever' does not presume the present war to be more 'violent'
than any other. The poem's irony, cosmic rather than 'quiet' (except
by contrast), attacks a religious construct which denies sense-
experience: what men see, hear and 'do' in their earthly habitat.
Sonnet-form plays a part in that attack. As with Stevenson's
vocabulary of 'witness' and 'match', Howarth implicitly retains
a reportage-model, if one in which disjunctive verse would supply a
superior realism: 'really convey', what 'really is'. But, for all the

bad war-sonnets, did sonnet-form 'really' become 'antique' in 1914? Chapter 2 discussed its complex structural role throughout Thomas's poetry. In 'February Afternoon' he exploits the Petrarchan sonnet's recursive symmetries, its rhetorical and aphoristic resources, to lay down earthly 'law' against religious 'array': the poem's biblical 'shadow self' (as in the gyrations of 'first' and 'last'). Rather than 'constraining' or 'containing' something, sonnet-form helps to set up 'February Afternoon' as dramatic speech: the virtual same-rhyming of the octet; the repeated monosyllables that reinforce the rhythm (first, last, roar, strike/stroke, stone); the key-phrase 'A thousand years', which begins three lines in varied syntactical slots. As opposed to a weak protest poem, 'February Afternoon' seems a bleak metaphysical parable: a work of negative millenarianism that doubts the existence of any 'moral scheme'. 'Mill-like' echoes Blake as well as the proverbial 'mills of God'. The poem is also another rebuke to Brooke's God.

Critical assumptions about 'conventional' form or 'older forms' de-historicise all poetic form, and disallow the role of back-formation in aesthetics. The war led poets (including Yeats) to remake existing forms; while their quest for generic models took the European crisis into poetry's 'memory of itself' from Homer to Whitman's *Drum-Taps* to Hardy's Boer War poems. The most notable nineteenth-century conjunction between poetry and war had been the Romantic poets' relation to the Napoleonic wars: an era which Hardy's epic-drama *The Dynasts* had latterly revisited. In 'War Poetry' Thomas is highly conscious of that interface: 'But for the wars against Napoleon, English poetry would have been different'. And although he questions 'how many poems directly concerning [those wars]' are now read, he singles out Coleridge's 'Fears in Solitude: written in April 1798, during the alarm of an invasion'. 'Fears in Solitude' is Thomas's ideal 'patriotic poem' (perhaps this anticipates his Romantic remixings) because it internalises public events, because it criticises British 'tyranny' and popular clamour for 'bloodshed': 'no newspaper or magazine, then or now, would print such a poem, since a large part of it is humble'. Thomas calls Coleridge 'a solitary man who, if at all, only felt the national emotions weakly or spasmodically'. 'Solitary' situates this war poem not just literally in 'a quiet spirit-healing nook', but in the zone of Romantic lyric. 'This is no case of petty right or wrong' alludes to 'Fears in Solitude' which attacks newspapers for serving up war as the 'best amusement for our morning's meal'; features storm-imagery; and defines patriotism in terms of soul-landscape: 'there lives nor form nor feeling in my soul/ Unborrowed from my country!' This prefigures Brooke's 'dust whom England bore, shaped, made aware' and Thomas's 'The ages made her that made us from the dust'. But, as a template for Great War poetry, 'Fears in Solitude' also anticipates Owen's 'old Lie', and rebukes God's role in war-propaganda:

>   … forth,
> (Stuffed out with big preamble, holy names,
> And adjurations of the God in Heaven,)
> We send our mandates for the certain death
> Of thousands and ten thousands! …[51]

'Fears in Solitude' is less significant as directly influencing 'This is no case …' than as indirectly influencing Thomas's war pastoral and his 'home front' scenarios. It exemplifies how the Romantic presence in Great War poetry goes far beyond miscellaneous pastiche, allusion, revision or deconstruction. When war poets are said to abjure 'Romanticism', the word can slide between its literary meaning and 'romanticism' as sentimental glorification. It's true that 'Exposure' begins by redirecting Keats's 'My heart aches', and that in 'A Terre' Owen mocks Shelley's 'I shall be one with nature, herb, and stone': 'The dullest Tommy hugs that fancy now'.[52] But, even as versifiers travestied their legacy, the Romantic poets remained live models before and during the war. This was so for Rosenberg and Gurney as well as for Thomas and Owen. Rosenberg wrote in 1912 that he owed to Shelley 'some of the most wonderful sensations I have ever experienced'. Gurney wrote in 1917: 'One learns form and the true use of language' from 'classics like Milton, Keats and Shakespeare'.[53] Gurney and Owen read Thomas's *Keats*. The Romantic poets provide structural models, as with the different ways and contexts in which Thomas and Owen develop Keats's sensory immersion; generic models, as with the reconfiguration of Romantic 'Nature' by Great War pastoral; above all, perhaps, a model of belief in poetry: the idea that poetry matters as (to quote Owen's '1914') 'the Winter of the world/ With perishing great darkness closes in'. 'The Winter of the world' is a phrase from Shelley's *The Revolt of Islam*. Owen's draft Preface, however angry and ironical, is effectively 'concerned with Poetry' in the Messianic spirit of Shelley's *Defence of Poetry*. So is his 'Insensibility':

> … Happy are these who lose imagination;
> They have enough to carry with ammunition.
> Their spirit drags no pack.
> Their old wounds, save with cold, can not more ache.
> Having seen all things red,
> Their eyes are rid
> Of the hurt of the colour of blood for ever …[54]

Poetry's 'imagination' and 'spirit' carry the 'hurt'. Even if Thomas's defence of poetry takes more oblique forms, for him, too, the components of 'soldier-poet' cross the hyphen.

'Neo-Romantic' may be as apt and up-to-date a term for Great War poetry as 'proto-modernist'. Das's catalogue of poetic diversity includes 'Georgians and modernists',[55] but both labels are historically suspect. The 'modernist' critical paradigm has been retrospectively imposed on poetry of this period. And 'Georgian' is a doubly post-dated label: Thomas, with his more exact sense of literary history, wrote of Edward Marsh's first anthology: 'Not a few of these [poets] had developed their qualities under Victoria and Edward'. Even so, 'Georgian' still hangs in there as a term of critical attack and defence. Stephen says: 'by demanding that poets write only about what they knew and had witnessed ... Georgian poetry provided an admirable training ground for the poets of the First World War'. And Kendall, who rightly credits Wilfrid Gibson as a 'trench sketch' pioneer (Gibson based some poems on newspaper-bulletins), takes issue with critical modernism because it 'overlooks the Georgian origins of most surviving war poetry'.[56] Yet 'Georgian', like 'modernist', does not mark any coherent shared aesthetic around 1914. And to talk of 'writing only about what they knew' undersells some poets, oversells others, and again proves how a reportage-model persists. The literary history just behind Great War poetry includes the fall-out of the 1890s. As Thomas's reviews indicate, ideas of poetry derived from Symbolism and Aestheticism (both neo-Romantic) linger among the swirling cross-currents from which poets pick and mix at this complex literary-historical moment. Yeats, the arch neo-Romantic, dominated the pre-war poetic milieu. Owen, Thomas, Rosenberg and Gurney all greatly admired Yeats; and his wartime aesthetic trajectory, including its forms, appears relevant to theirs. In 1917 Gurney wrote of Yeats's *Responsibilities*: 'it is a most valuable book for a young poet, most stimulating, swift and high-hearted'.[57] As we have seen, a belief in lyric 'intensity', stripped of what belongs to verse or prose, governs Thomas's pre-war poetry criticism. Owen, Gurney and Rosenberg also invoke some kind of 'essence': Owen's 'truth untold ... the pity war distilled', his omission of proper names that 'the 'spirit' rather than 'letter' of his poetry might survive. For Gurney, 'immediate events ... must sink in to the very foundations and be absorbed'. Rosenberg hoped to 'approach' the war 'with less of the million feelings everybody feels; or all these should be concentrated in one distinguished emotion'.[58] It wasn't just about 'witness': poets reinvented the less tangible co-ordinates of the pre-war English lyric to engage with a crisis that soon took on metaphysical and episte-mological contours: 'Our brains ache'; 'dark and chaotic in brain'. Chaotic darkness continues into Thomas's poetic dialectics: all his cognitive roads lead to France. Causality or necessity or 'futility' is not only a political question 'Where death becomes absurd and life absurder', where poetry transmutes metaphysics into tragedy: 'O what made fatuous sunbeams toil …?'[59]. In fulfilling the unwitting prospectus of 'War Poetry', Thomas's poetry casts the symbolic dimension or character of 'Great War poetry' into relief – perhaps its most 'essential' difference from prose 'others'. Symbolism is another tricky term. But it represents dedication to something beyond the 'particular and occasional', dedication to a vision rather than a view: the gulf between Owen's letter and poem. Conversely, this 'most complex event of modern times'[60] may have demanded aesthetic intensity: 'compact essential real truth'.

The concentration of Rosenberg's 'Dead Man's Dump' meets that demand:

> … What fierce imaginings their dark souls lit
> Earth! Have they gone into you?
> Somewhere they must have gone,
> And flung on your hard back
> Is their soul's sack,
> Emptied of God-ancestralled essences.
> Who hurled them out? Who hurled?
>
> None saw their spirits' shadow shake the grass,
> Or stood aside for the half used life to pass
> Out of those doomed nostrils and the doomed mouth […]
>
> The drowning soul was sunk too deep
> For human tenderness …[61]

More questions there. In its very title 'Dead Man's Dump' confronts the newly perplexed relation between body and soul. But, at a reflexive level, phrases like 'fierce imaginings', 'soul's sack' and 'God-ancestralled essences' define the nexus between the physical and metaphysical in the poem's own make-up: hence its ability to speak for 'doomed' mouths. 'Dead Man's Dump' also marks how the war has simultaneously recharged ancient symbolism and introduced a grim new symbolic repertoire: 'The plunging limbers over the shattered track/ Racketed with their rusty freight,/ Stuck out like many crowns of thorns …'. 'Exposure', 'February Afternoon' and 'Dead Man's Dump' all mention 'God'. In Great War poetry, the 'death of God' ceases to be abstract. By the same token, poets renew poetry's *fin-de-siècle* role as spilt religion – not only in the obvious case of Owen's transposed evangelical zeal. Jay Winter's term 're-sacralisation'[62] fits the 'human tenderness' of 'Dead Man's Dump': the fiercely imagined symbolism constituted by all its formal elements. Rhythm is 'essential' to the way in which certain poems – even certain lines – seem to symbolise the entire war. In these instances, we hear one of Owen's elegiac slow movements; Thomas's earthly bio-rhythms; Rosenberg's prophetic resonance: 'Slowly our ghosts drag home … Shutters and doors, all closed: on us the doors are closed'; 'the broad ploughland oak/ Roars mill-like and men strike and bear the stroke/ Of war as ever'; 'None saw their spirits' shadow shake the grass,/ Or stood aside for the half used life to pass …'.

Reflexivity, another legacy from the 1890s, makes 'war poetry' a locus where poetry itself is now at stake: hence the revisiting and testing of Romantic credos. 'Dead Man's Dump', like 'Insensibility', turns 'doomed' soldiers into dying poets: the possible death of poetry along with God. And even if we believe that Romantic values like 'imagination', 'sensibility', 'soul' – and 'truth' – survive in the actual poems, poetry's 'memory of itself' is not necessarily taken for granted. Witness Thomas's sense that the tradition and forms of English poetry require (and constitute) defence: not by preserving them as 'old' but by 'wearing' them 'new'. 'Lob' stores poetry in cultural memory as cultural memory in poetry. When Thomas foresees poems that 'may retain hardly any colour from … 1914', he echoes his earlier recognition that only traces of 'things' 'endure in … written words': a reason why words themselves must endure.[63] 'The Green Roads' likens its poet-speaker to a thrush 'twiddling his song' at the edge of a forest of forgetting. Yet the twiddles of Thomas's unusually shaped couplets, with their internal rhyme and folk-echoing refrain, are hauntingly memorable:

> The green roads that end in the forest
> Are strewn with white goose feathers this June,
>
> Like marks left behind by someone gone to the forest
> To show his track. But he has never come back … (128)

The poems quoted above depend on various repetition-devices, and hence mnemonic devices, from the subtlest assonances to the rhetoric of closed/closed, strike/stroke, doomed/doomed.

The trace ('goose feathers') of what poetry commemorates depends upon its own memorability: Yeats's 'Song of Sixpence'. Thomas's adjective 'compact' correctly anticipates that lyric, at once intense and memorable, will be the dominant mode of Great War poetry. Lyric's kinship to letters or postcards makes it the most immediate poetic medium: the first draft of memory as newspapers of history. Epics are written later. Poetry's role in UK 'remembrance' of the Great War is unparalleled elsewhere, even if Laurence Binyon's 'We will remember them' fails to represent the problematics of either war or poetic memory. In 1914 Carol Ann Duffy published *1914: Poetry Remembers*: an anthology which marked the centenary by juxtaposing poems from 1914–18 with poems that contemporary poets had written in response to them. Yet Owen will hardly outlive *Blackadder* in a culture that does not, conversely, 'remember poetry' or understand its mnemonic origins and means. *Poetry Remembers* is a tautology. Some Great War poems concentrate 'essential real truth' into a single unforgettable lyric cadence: Sassoon's 'Everyone Sang', Owen's 'I saw his round mouth's crimson deepen as it fell', Thomas's quatrain 'In Memoriam (Easter, 1915)':

The flowers left thick at nightfall in the wood
This Eastertide call into mind the men,
Now far from home, who, with their sweethearts, should
Have gathered them and will do never again. (80)

This 'found' memorial (which anticipates the ceramic poppies) makes absence present. It condenses love and death, darkness descending on the countryside, a hint of crucifixion, 'home' distant or unlike itself: all culminating in the last line's halting and haunted rhythm. Critics who puzzle over the survival or revival of 'older forms' forget that those forms had a good war: that they can be integral to 'compact essential real truth' – far beyond 'this occasion alone'.

4. WAR AND LYRIC

Are the poems discussed here 'only' war poems? *What* is a war poem? No poem can be entirely composed of war. Thomas's remark (in 'War Poetry') about patriotic poems applies more generally: 'A patriotic poem pure and simple hardly exists, as a man who was a patriot pure and simple could not live outside a madhouse.' Great War poetry does not abandon poetry's habitual bases, even if it finds or renders them unstable. Owen wanted his poems to 'light the darkness of the world'.[64] War focuses more than its own 'truth': it potentially highlights or heightens other truths. The lyric remains 'myriad-minded'. Great War poetry holistically spans all the lyric genres in revised or hybrid guises. If those genres now seem magnetised by elegy, this itself heightens something fundamental to lyric; just as protest-elegy heightens something fundamental to elegy. For Louis MacNeice, the Second World War exposed 'the integral function of death' as regards life and poetry: 'Death is the opposite of decay; a stimulus, a necessary horizon'.[65] Death is certainly all that, if not always so positively, for Thomas and other Great War poets. Like 'The Dug-Out', Robert Graves's retrospective 'The Last Day of Leave (1916)' is a war-heightened love poem:

We five looked out over the moor
At rough hills blurred with haze, and a still sea:
Our tragic day, bountiful from the first.

We would spend it by the lily lake
(High in a fold beyond the farthest ridge),
Following the cart-track till it faded out.

The time of berries and bell-heather;
Yet all that morning nobody went by
But shepherds and one old man carting turfs.

We were in love: he with her, she with him,
And I, the youngest one, the odd man out,
As deep in love with a yet nameless muse […]

The basket had been nobly filled:
Wine and fresh rolls, chicken and pineapple –
Our braggadocio under threat of war […]

We spoke little, our minds in tune –
A sigh or laugh would settle any theme;
The sun so hot it made the rocks quiver.

But when it rolled down level with us,
Four pairs of eyes sought mine as if appealing
For a blind-fate-aversive afterword: –

'Do you remember the lily lake?
We were all there, all five of us in love,
Not one yet killed, widowed or broken-hearted.'[66]

As 'braggadocio under threat of war', this poem parallels other war pastorals that implicate love or friendship: Thomas's 'The sun used to shine', Margaret Postgate Cole's 'Afterwards': 'What use/ To have your body lying here/ In Sheer, underneath the larches?'[67] Graves intensifies war-pastoral tropes: the oxymoron 'tragic'/ 'bountiful'; soldiers idyllically bathing ('Diving like trout between the lily groves'); the extreme emotion and weather. 'The sun so hot it made the rocks quiver' apocalyptically echoes Burns. And the poet, speaking from the future, seems to condemn his friends to die. This intense love-and-death poem, also a poem of survivor-guilt, knows that it cannot be 'a blind-fate-aversive afterword'. But it can memorably ask: 'Do you remember the lily lake?'

Poems of love and war signal that this public occasion does not necessarily sideline Symbolist 'interiority', psychological as well as metaphysical: 'Rain, midnight rain, nothing but the wild rain/ On this bleak hut, and solitude and me …'. In 'War Books' Gurney asks if we expect 'the perfect drawing of a heart's dream'.[68] Yet, in another sense, his poetry's disturbed inner and outer worlds move between dream and nightmare. And what of Craiglockhart Hospital as a base for poetic coterie? Indeed, a key distinction between Owen and Sassoon is the degree to which Sassoon represses psycho-drama and phantasmagoria. Part of Owen's 'essential real truth' is that he identifies with 'Mental Cases'; presents quasi-Gothic night-mare scenarios, as in 'The Show'; and internalises the war as trauma: 'In all my dreams, before my helpless sight,/ He plunges at me …'. The Great War was not only a physical event: as Owen bears witness, it 'ravished' minds.[69] Jay Winter argues that the incidence of Post-Traumatic Stress Disorder has been grossly underestimated.[70] Owen's 'Strange Meeting', located in the unconscious as well as the underworld or after-world, is an even stranger poem than might appear. Besides trauma, war's strangeness induced crises of identity: Owen and Thomas both felt that becoming soldiers had made them 'other' than themselves. Self-estrangement informs the others, doubles and ghosts in their poems. At the end of 'The Show', Death exhibits 'a manner of worm', with 'the feet of many men,/ And the fresh-severed head of it, my head'.[71]

Since the inner journey of Thomas's poetry is inseparable from its journey to war, he opens up the whole psychological field. Here again, comparison with Gurney helps to suggest the dynamics at work. For both poets, 'home' is an elusive psychic locus too. Thomas's third poem called 'Home' contains this quatrain:

This is my grief. That land,
My home, I have never seen;
No traveller tells of it,
However far he has been. (64)

On reading Thomas's *Poems* (1917), Gurney noted: 'he had the same sickness of mind I have – the impossibility of serenity for any but the shortest space'.[72] Strictly speaking, they did not have 'the same sickness': 'paranoid schizophrenia' and 'bi-polarity' are possible names for Gurney's condition; 'depression', partly manifested by obsessive-compulsive 'self-consciousness', may be the best broad term for Thomas's. Confined to an asylum after the war, Gurney thought that electricity was persecuting him: 'And there is dreadful hell within me./ And nothing helps. Forced meals there have been and electricity …'. This poem, 'To God', includes the line: 'And I am praying for death, death, death'. Thomas, too, wrote death-wish poems. Yet there is a gulf between Thomas's structured psychodrama (see Chapter 5) and Gurney's inability to detach his darker poems from his mental state. Thomas's speaker switches roles between Self and Other, patient and analyst; whereas Gurney's often remains trapped in unresolved distress. 'To God' ends: 'Not often such evil guessed as between Man and Man.' Yet when Gurney aligns himself with Thomas as lacking 'serenity for any but the shortest space', he points to epiphany as a shared poetic trope. In this structural context, the nexus of mental turmoil and poetry sometimes maps onto war and peace. Thomas's 'Two Houses', set on the 'dusty' road to war, ironically splices an idyllic farmhouse scene with 'Dark echoes' from within and without (100). Gurney's roads *in* France have similar

twists. 'First March' represents a French landscape's 'sweet unex-
pected/ Balm' as easing inner 'chaos', and 'La Gorgue' celebrates
an estaminet as 'A mark in Time, a Peace, a Making-delay'. But 'Billet'
becomes a contrastingly negative epiphany: after waking to 'a golden
ratcheted/ Lovely web of blue seen and blue shut, and cobwebs
and tiles', the speaker hears a homesick Private speak 'the heart of
all of us' by saying: 'I get no good in France, getting killed, cleaning
off mud.'[73]

Indeed, war appears on both sides of the epiphanic or psychiatric
equation. Thomas's 'The Owl' dramatises not homesickness but
war-sickness: unease about 'what I escaped/ And others could not'
(65). Critics have long disputed the view that enlisting was all that
Thomas needed to 'snap out of' depression. Yet 'There was a time',
which ponders the paradox that a real crisis may resolve a (seem-
ingly) self-created one, assigns the war a therapeutic role:

There was a time when this poor frame was whole
And I had youth and never another care,
Or none that should have troubled a strong soul.
Yet, except sometimes in a frosty air
When my heels hammered out a melody
From pavements of a city left behind,
I never would acknowledge my own glee
Because it was less mighty than my mind
Had dreamed of. Since I could not boast of strength
Great as I wished, weakness was all my boast.
I sought yet hated pity till at length
I earned it. Oh, too heavy was the cost.
But now that there is something I could use
My youth and strength for, I deny the age,
The care and weakness that I know – refuse
To admit I am unworthy of the wage
Paid to a man who gives up eyes and breath
For what would neither ask nor heed his death. (128)

THE COMPACT ESSENTIAL REAL TRUTH

This poem, a Shakespearean sonnet with an extra quatrain, repeats words from Brooke's sonnets ('wage', 'gives up', 'breath'/ 'death'), while redirecting them towards a psychology, rather than rhetoric, of going to war. The last line, like 'No one cares less than I', renders war itself not a glorious cause but an impervious fate. Nonetheless, war speaks to some complex inner need. Even at their lowest ebb of commitment, this seems to be the case for both Thomas and Gurney. In Michael Hurd's summary: Gurney 'felt that the physical effort of army life would somehow cure his "neurasthenia" and that he would come to feel as other men: mind and body at peace with one another'. Hurd also suggests that Gurney 'had found the family he had always been looking for'.[74] Thomas wrote from the trenches: 'I have suffered more from January to March in other years than in this.' Gurney, who believed he had become 'saner', writes: 'It was a great time; full of fear of course, but not so bad as neurasthenia'; and again: 'my chief thought is that I have found myself unfitted for Life and Battle, and am gradually by hard necessity being strengthened and made fit for some high task'.[75] Although Thomas had practical skills that Gurney lacked, 'feeling as other men' and confronting life mattered to him too. He partly faces into war as a 'test': perhaps one set by Brooke, as 'There was a time' may imply. And perhaps – whether this would qualify as symptom or cure – he eventually felt compelled to test himself and his poetry to the uttermost: by joining the Royal Garrison Artillery; by volunteering for overseas service; by playing a form of Russian roulette. Yet in '"Home"' the speaker is split between accepting himself as 'Another man' and the possibility that his becoming the long-pursued 'Other' is a mirage; army life, 'only an evil dream'. All Thomas's dialectics continue to the end.

Both poets admit war into the most troubled recesses of the psyche. Like 'Rain', Gurney's 'Strange Hells' locates war in the mind – although 'unexpectedly' defeated by 'song':

There are strange Hells within the minds War made
Not so often, not so humiliatingly afraid

As one would have expected – the racket and fear guns made.
One Hell the Gloucester soldiers they quite put out:
Their first bombardment, when in combined black shout
Of fury, guns aligned, they ducked lower their heads –
And sang with diaphragms fixed beyond all dreads,
That tin and stretched-wire tinkle, that blither of tune:
'Après la guerre fini', till Hell all had come down …

The poem then asks: 'Where are they now, on State-doles, or showing shop-patterns', and ends: 'The heart burns – but has to keep out of face how heart burns'. At this point, war's 'dreads' appear less hellish than post-war ingratitude. The relation between Gurney's illness and the war is not neatly covered by actual or metaphorical 'shell-shock'. He became, rather, *peace*-shocked: that is, by society's disregard for him as soldier and 'war poet'. When the speaker of 'Riez Bailleul' recalls 'being sick of body and heart' in France, it is in order 'to hide this pain and work myself free / From present things'.[76] Disconcertingly, Thomas and Gurney internalise the enormity of the Great War as something recognisable. If their 'hell', like their 'home', is not always 'As one would have expected', it's because they configure war with the extent to which all life is 'strange' or *unheimlich*.

'War Poetry' ends by hoping that poets will come to 'understand [the war] *and themselves* more completely' (my italics). Graves's long blank-verse poem 'A Letter from Wales' (182 lines) might be read as a post-war counterpart to Thomas's 'The Other'.[77] Subtitled '*Richard Rolls to his friend, Captain Abel Wright*', this poem seems the best 'after-word' on war and the 'question of identity', including poetic identity:

This is a question of identity
Which I can't answer. Abel, I'll presume
On your good-nature, asking you to help me.
I hope you will, since you too are involved
As deeply in the problem as myself.
Who are we? …

More dramatic monologue than epistle, and including some sonnet-shaped passages, 'A Letter from Wales' remains just within the lyric zone – it may be partly *about* the lyric zone. The war is experienced by two dramatis personae, who keep getting killed and then resurrected as a series of 'substitutes' or 'representatives'. Rolls and Wright also double one another, partly in being 'war poets':

> So, these two friends, the second of the series,
> Came up to Wales pretending a wild joy
> That they had cheated Death: they stayed together
> At the same house and ate and drank and laughed
> And wrote each others' poems, much too lazy
> To write their own …

In their final (post-war) incarnation, 'I and you' are even more uneasily twinned:

> … there was a constraint in all our dealings,
> A doubt, unformulated, but quite heavy
> And not too well disguised. Something we guessed
> Arising from the War, and yet the War
> Was a forbidden ground of conversation …

'A Letter from Wales' is more than a clever riff on the fact that Graves had survived near-death and his own obituary; more than a version of his often-fraught relationship with Sassoon. It's another phantasmagoria that symbolises the entire war. 'Something we guessed/ Arising from the War' underlies all neuroses and metamorphoses. The soldier-poets' deaths and resurrections are intertwined with the changing vision of their poems, as from pastoral to war pastoral. Rolls recalls a Welsh sunset, amenable to Romantic 'Transfiguration', which inspires the poets to 'prophesy' and 'declaim' and to invoke a 'dragon'. Then he says:

And I remember that we looked and found
A region of the sky below the dragon
Where we could gaze behind all time and space
And see as it were the colour of pure thought,
The texture of emptiness, and at that sight
We came away, not daring to see more:
Death was the price, we knew, of such perfection …

This different transfiguration parallels the last two lines of Thomas's 'Rain'. The poets then meet death in the shape of 'Captain Todd', who babbles about Pater, Ruskin and the aesthetics of sunset. 'A Letter from Wales' tracks both the elusive self-in-war and the elusive course of 'war poetry'. It ends with an unaskable question:

What I'm asking really isn't 'Who am I?'
Or 'Who are you' (you see my difficulty?)
But a stage before that, '*How am I to put*
The question that I'm asking you to answer?'

Perhaps not only 'modernist fragmentation' conveys the war's psychic 'derangements'.

In 'A Letter from Wales' psychodrama and history intersect – as in Thomas's larger poetic journey. The means whereby Great War poetry negotiates history is another function of its holistic lyric scope. The poetry's truth-claims depend on how persuasively the lyric 'mind', in the lyric's terms, engages with the matter of war. Poems may even be first drafts of history as well as memory. Key factors are a poem's ability to symbolise history; to establish, rather than inhabit, its context; to render history structural. The historiography of the Great War has been called unparalleled in its 'sophistication and moral intensity'. It is said to be dedicated to 'total history', to involve 'reflexive history' and 'reflective space'.[78] Could poetry-envy be at work? 'This is no case of petty right or wrong' anticipates current controversies by pitting poetry's 'truth' (backed up by Coleridge) against what historians 'Can rake out of the ashes'. But Thomas's poetic 'history' usually takes more complex forms than insisting that felt experience trumps dispassionate hindsight. Chapter 2 suggested that his major departure from Wordsworth, a move conditioned by the war as well as by post-Darwinian 'Nature', is to historicise landscape and earth:

> What matter makes my spade for tears or mirth,
> Letting down two clay pipes into the earth?
> The one I smoked, the other a soldier
> Of Blenheim, Ramillies, and Malplaquet
> Perhaps. The dead man's immortality
> Lies represented lightly with my own … ('Digging', 99)

In *The South Country* Thomas claims to lack any 'historic sense', despite having read history at Oxford; although he allows that history may have 'got into my blood and is present in me in a form which defies evocation or analysis'.[79] This anticipates the history 'formed' by his poetry. In fact, a chapter in *The South Country*, 'History and the Parish', is where Thomas (innovatively) proposes reading landscape historically. Similarly, his *English Review* reports constitute 'history from below'. Again, his poetry is steeped in literary history; his very syntax loops back. In *The Great War in History* Jay Winter and Antoine Prost concede that 'Alongside and beyond what an historian can say, there remains unlimited space for poetry and meditation.'[80] But perhaps the poet also invades the historian's territory – hence their clash.

First, a poem as history carries traces that derive both from moments of experience and from the moment of composition. A poem's 'truth', its counterpart to the historian's 'evidence', is how effectively its structures mediate those traces. In 'Exposure' the poem itself is what 'happens', although it may convince us that other things happened too. Second, 'the symbolism of poetry' can 'compact' and interweave different modes of historical narrative.

Besides his personal history, Thomas's interwoven frameworks include eco-history, economic history, pre-history, local history, oral history, literary and cultural history, the micro-history of 'A Private', which concerns 'This ploughman dead in battle' (50), the macro-history of 'The Green Roads'. Poems also symbolise history by slowing down time, like 'Exposure'; by deepening it, like 'February Afternoon'; by contracting it, like 'Dead Man's Dump'. Third, as the war changed poets' horizons, so it changed poetry's own temporality: Owen's *annus mirabilis*; Thomas's accelerated poetic trajectory. Thomas's historical modalities are underpinned by how the war infiltrates his poetry's sources in memory (which includes forgetting). To read his poems is often to experience, as in 'It rains', 'The past hovering as it revisits the light' (121). His poem-palimpsests shuttle between long-term memory, short-term memory, and remembering the future; while the war dictates its own memorial imperative. All Thomas's poems are in some sense memoranda of the road, his notebook-habit in another guise. His foreword to France complements Graves's 'afterword'. 'As the team's head-brass', written as he was deliberating whether to seek an artillery commission, epitomises the complexity of poetic history:

> As the team's head-brass flashed out on the turn
> The lovers disappeared into the wood.
> I sat among the boughs of the fallen elm
> That strewed an angle of the fallow, and
> Watched the plough narrowing a yellow square
> Of charlock. Every time the horses turned
> Instead of treading me down, the ploughman leaned
> Upon the handles to say or ask a word,
> About the weather, next about the war.
> Scraping the share he faced towards the wood,
> And screwed along the furrow till the brass flashed
> Once more.

>   The blizzard felled the elm whose crest
> I sat in, by a woodpecker's round hole,
> The ploughman said. 'When will they take it away?'
> 'When the war's over.' So the talk began –
> One minute and an interval of ten,
> A minute more and the same interval.
> 'Have you been out?' 'No.' 'And don't want to, perhaps?' … (123)

'As the team's head-brass' anticipates studies such as Caroline Dakers's *The Countryside at War* (1987) and Alan Howkins's *The Death of Rural England* (2003). But the poem's historical bearings go beyond the impact of economic change, compounded by war, on English rural life. Here Thomas presents himself as a soldier-poet perched on the cusp of history. Several histories intersect in a memorable moment that draws together the speaker about to 'go out', a ploughman, his 'mate' killed on 'The second day/ In France', plough-horses, a woodpecker, lovers. Timelines include the farm's history since the 'night of the blizzard'; the soldier's ominous prospects; the woodpecker creating and losing its home; the lovers' disappearance and reappearance, which brackets war with peace; the *longue durée* represented by ploughing. In the latter case, history is also reflexively at work. 'As the team's head-brass' is not only 'war pastoral' but *about* war pastoral: it revisits pastoral's ancient origins in the shadow of epic, the links between ploughed field and battlefield, the very origins of 'verse' in the ploughman's 'turn' (the word occurs at two line-endings). The blank verse itself concentrates history by reviving the oldest pulse of poetry even as talk 'about the war' disturbs its beat: the soldier says: 'I could spare an arm. I shouldn't want to lose/ A leg. If I should lose my head, why, so,/ I should want nothing more …'. All the poem's histories converge on its final lines:

>   Then
> The lovers came out of the wood again:
> The horses started and for the last time

I watched the clods crumble and topple over
After the ploughshare and the stumbling team.

'For the last time' covers the soldier-poet's fate, the fate of rural
England and its associated traditions, the end of the pre-war world.
The elegiac rhythms somehow carry an immense weary weight.
Progress 'stumbles' as the crumbling, toppling clods hint at the
trenches. This war-pastoral culminates in a verse-movement that
suggests the movement of history from the deep European past into
a problematic future.

Ultimately, by carrying their own history, poems enable poetry
to remember its war-self or war-selves. The reception-history of
Great War poetry, whether as poems or in criticism, might be as
telling as the historiographical 'debates and controversies' mapped
by Winter and Prost. And the poetry's posterity – the posterity of
Thomas or Graves or Owen – is not only to be found in poems that
'mention the war'; in overtly 'public' poems; or in the poetry of later
wars: much as all that matters. In 'The Last Day of Leave' Graves's
post-war Muse masks a homoerotic wartime scenario. But this
itself suggests how deeply the war *formed* his poetry: poetry that has
formed other poets. 'Something …/ Arising from the War' has been
fundamental to the modern lyric.

5. JOURNEY'S END

As a journey to war, rather than immersion in it, Thomas's poetry
takes a different metaphysical shape from Owen's. It's partly the
difference between earth as the habitat of history and earth as
the arena for a tragic theatre. Owen turns the 'trench life sketch' into
an eschatological drama which encompasses 'the last sea and the
hapless stars'.[81] Thomas follows or creates 'Many a road and track'
towards 'the unknown'. 'Lights Out' symbolises his entire trajectory,
including an ambiguous finale. The penultimate stanza lays out a
road that goes all the way:

There is not any book
Or face of dearest look
That I would not turn from now
To go into the unknown
I must enter and leave alone,
I know not how. (136)

Mapped onto the war, Thomas's poetic journey consists of several overlapping phases. His poems might be roughly grouped as pre-enlistment poems up to 'I built myself a house of glass' (25 June 1915); a sequence from 'Words' to 'Cock-Crow' linked with deciding to enlist (26 June – 23 July 1915); post-enlistment poems from 'October' to 'The Watchers' (October 1915 – April 1916); poems linked with joining the Artillery and preparing to go to France. 'I built myself a house of glass' and 'The Watchers' are critiques of psychological and aesthetic solipsism, which seem to herald decision. Thomas's final phase (which thinks of itself as such) is increasingly valedictory: 'The green roads that end in the forest …', 'Dark is the forest and deep …'. Like the goose feathers pointing into the forest, small signs also mark the way: cherry petals 'when there is none to wed', 'Tall reeds/ Like criss-cross bayonets', 'the swift's black bow'.

Yet Thomas's poetry has been taking leave since the beginning. From phase to phase, he reworks valedictory scenarios and genres. For instance, as pastoral and as a comment on pastoral, 'As the team's head-brass' completes a farm-sequence initiated by 'The Manor Farm' and continued by 'Haymaking', written a week before he enlisted. Like 'Words', 'Haymaking' places its cultural affiliations – perhaps defensively – in the foreground. It ends:

The men leaned on their rakes, about to begin,
But still. And all were silent. All was old,
This morning time, with a great age untold,
Older than Clare and Cobbett, Morland and Crome,
Than, at the field's far edge, the farmer's home,

A white house crouched at the foot of a great tree.
Under the heavens that know not what years be
The men, the beasts, the trees, the implements
Uttered even what they will in times far hence –
All of us gone out of the reach of change –
Immortal in a picture of an old grange. (95)

'Haymaking', a triple sonnet in couplets, obliquely invokes Keats as well as John Clare. Its final freeze-frame has parallels with 'Ode on a Grecian Urn'. There's an unusual sense (for Thomas) of the poet disappearing into his 'immortal' work. It's also unusual for him to write a partly ekphrastic poem: to couple literature with visual art for rhetorical emphasis. Such insistent framing sets the poem's cultural affirmation against a backdrop of flux. At once self-elegy and a possible memorial to English pastoral, 'Haymaking' introduces valediction into the 'Safe under tile and thatch' scenario of 'The Manor Farm'. Despite the timeless way in which 'age' merges with 'morning', ending with 'beginning', a tremor of history on the move prefigures 'As the team's head-brass'. Shortly afterwards, Thomas wrote 'Two Houses': a diptych that deconstructs his pastoral 'picture'. A 'smiling' sunlit farmhouse, accessible only to the aesthetic gaze, is juxtaposed with a house of the dead: 'as if above graves/ Still the turf heaves/ Above its stones' (100). While 'heaves' seems ominously active, the farmhouse is compared to a 'muslined peach': something sealed-off, possibly delusive, a mask for 'the hollow past'. This leave-taking poem questions what is being left.

Legacy-poems are integral to Thomas's valedictory repertoire. 'Lob' is his most elaborate cultural testament. 'Haymaking' offers itself as cultural memory. Still further along the road (Spring 1916), he wrote the 'will-and-testament' poems for his children. In 'If I were to own' place-names and nursery-rhyme idiom acquire undertones of war. The will-maker hypothetically 'shoots' the 'Essex blackbirds' bequeathed to his son, and 'puts them into a pie':

Then unless I could pay, for rent, a song
As sweet as a blackbird's, and as long –
No more – he should have the house, not I:
Margaretting or Wingle Tye,
Or it might be Skreens, Gooshays, or Cockerells … (116)

Here a war-tainted inheritance can only be redeemed by 'song', poetry. Other poems put love, marriage, family and friendship ('The sun used to shine') into valedictory order. In 'No one so much as you' and 'And you, Helen', Thomas apologises for his inadequacies as a husband. 'I may come near loving you' still refuses to love his father (see p. 242). 'It rains' appears to give up on romantic love: 'never, never again,// Unless alone, so happy shall I walk/ In the rain' (121). Some poems move valediction centre-stage, although 'What will they do?' doubts its audience. Having asked 'What will they do when I am gone?' the poem's tone slides towards paranoia: 'I have but seen them in the loud street pass;/ And I was naught to them' (133). In October 1916 the Thomas family left Hampshire for High Beech, Essex. 'When first' says goodbye to Steep: no longer 'home' as the unknown of futurity closes in: 'Perhaps … the future and the maps/ Hide something I was waiting for' (134). 'How at once' asks how the speaker can see the swift, strangely knowing that it's the last sighting – for this year, perhaps this life (see p. 209). 'It was upon', a sonnet, goes back to the future by revisiting 'an unaccomplished prophecy' made in the past. The speaker recalls a 'wandering man' met twenty years ago, when 'a second Spring' in July had presented the 'earth outspread,/ Like meadows of the future' (126). The man had said: 'The lattermath/ Will be a fine one'. The sonnet's sestet makes 'lattermath' (second mowing) a metaphor for how poetry and war have changed/ may change everything: 'What of the lattermath to this hoar Spring?' More often now, Thomas's poems are asking rhetorical or unanswerable questions.

His last poems also connect past and future in more fully symbolic terms (their 'house' symbolism is discussed below). Like

Thomas's early parable-poems, from the opposite end of his accelerated gyre, they compress the human lifespan. Some poems centre on the journeying 'I' ('Lights Out'); others are semi-detached. 'The Gallows' is a parable-poem, a signpost poem, in which the gamekeeper's gibbet figures mass-slaughter. The poem ends with a prospect of endings:

> And many other beasts
> And birds, skin, bone and feather,
> Have been taken from their feasts
> And hung up there together,
> To swing and have endless leisure
> In the sun and in the snow,
> Without pain, without pleasure,
> On the dead oak tree bough. (130)

'The Child in the Orchard' is a parable of beginning rather than ending. It's as if Thomas bequeaths his own childhood, his own life, to a symbolic heir. Here legacy is represented by the white horse, at once creature and cultural icon (and perhaps a reference back to 'Up in the Wind'): '"Out of all the white horses I know three,/ At the age of six …"'. The poem's refrain counters 'the dead oak tree bough' with live birds and the education of Nature: '"… The swift, the swallow, the hawk, and the hern./ There are millions of things for me to learn"' (135). Thomas is again grounding symbol in folk-structures. 'Early one morning', another ambiguous valediction, another epitome of the journey, resembles 'An Old Song II' in being tuned to folksong. But this rover does not face towards poetry: 'I'm bound away for ever,/ Away somewhere, away for ever' (126). As in Autumn 1915, mortality looms larger than history in Thomas's psychodrama. Yet history underlies everything:

> That girl's clear eyes utterly concealed all
> Except that there was something to reveal.

And what did mine say in the interval?
No more: no less. They are but as a seal
Not to be broken till after I am dead;
And then vainly. Every one of us
This morning at our tasks left nothing said,
In spite of many words. We were sealed thus,
Like tombs. Nor until now could I admit
That all I cared for was the pleasure and pain
I tasted in the stony square sunlit,
Or the dark cloisters, or shade of airy plane,
While music blazed and children, line after line,
Marched past, hiding the 'Seventeen Thirty-Nine'. (132)

This sonnet is set in Brunswick Square, London, where Thomas was training at the Royal Artillery School. Spoken by one of a company heading for war, the poem has parallels with Owen's 'The Send-Off': 'secretly, like wrongs hushed-up, they went'.[82] The mortal effects of history are emphasised by how the tomb-simile, marking the unexpressed and inexpressible, sits next to synaesthetic impressions. Having been delayed by the simile's eruption into the ninth line, the sestet presents those impressions as an oddly inconclusive epiphany. This is because, both 'now' and in retrospect, what the speaker can 'admit' seems a displacement-exercise. Like 'The Send-Off', 'That girl's clear eyes' turns on silence – a phenomenon not confined to veterans after the war – and how to read it. People in, and readers of, the poem must decode lacunae which simultaneously 'conceal' and 'reveal'. Thus the 'hiding' of 'the "Seventeen Thirty-Nine" (the year when a Foundlings' Hospital was established in the area) suggests that martial panoply is masking a grimmer date: 1916. Disjunction includes an edgy return to the existential oxymorons of 'Liberty': dark and light, 'pleasure and pain', 'stony square sunlit'. 'Pleasure and pain' also echoes 'The Gallows'; 'sunlit' and 'tasted' repeat 'tasted sunlight' in 'The Other'. The poems that Thomas wrote in summer-autumn 1916 add further twists to his motifs, structures and images. 'Truth' becomes more strangely compacted.

Thomas maintains formal, as generic, variety to the end. But, after 'As the team's head-brass', stanzaic shapes or versions of sonnet-form (including more actual sonnets than usual) predominate: perhaps an aspect of compaction. In 'Lights Out' (rhymed AABCCB) enjambement and varying line-length reprise the journey; sonnet-like enclosing rhymes confirm the arrival; and same-rhyming marks an end:

> I have come to the borders of sleep,
> The unfathomable deep
> Forest where all must lose
> Their way, however straight,
> Or winding, soon or late;
> They cannot choose.
>
> Many a road and track
> That, since the dawn's first crack,
> Up to the forest brink,
> Deceived the travellers
> Suddenly now blurs,
> And in they sink.
>
> Here love ends,
> Despair, ambition ends,
> All pleasure and all trouble … (135-6)

The contrasting rhythms of 'The long small room' retrace the journey in slow motion:

> The long small room that showed willows in the west
> Narrowed up to the end the fireplace filled,
> Although not wide. I liked it. No one guessed
> What need or accident made them so build.

Only the moon, the mouse and the sparrow peeped
In from the ivy round the casement thick.
Of all they saw and heard there they shall keep
The tale for the old ivy and older brick.

When I look back I am like moon, sparrow and mouse
That witnessed what they could never understand
Or alter or prevent in the dark house.
One thing remains the same – this my right hand

Crawling crab-like over the clean white page,
Resting awhile each morning on the pillow,
Then once more starting to crawl on towards age.
The hundred last leaves stream upon the willow. (136)

Here, not choice ('To go into the unknown') but some never-to-be-known entropic force seems to impel both poem and speaker. The latter is defined by his writing life, his life-writing: neither of which has arrived at 'understanding'. As the poem changes tense, we watch him and it 'crawl on'. Founded on present participles, the second-last sentence crosses between quatrains over an enigmatic space towards the future. This is a poem that tells a 'tale' while affecting not to (see p. 204). It places the speaker in a pre-determined narrative frame: laid down by 'need or accident', incapable of being 'altered or prevented', reinforced by the willows' reappearance in the semi-detached final line. 'Hundred' is terrifyingly exact. 'The Sheiling', based on a farewell visit to Gordon Bottomley in Cumbria, moves differently again:

It stands alone
Up in a land of stone
All worn like ancient stairs,
A land of rocks and trees
Nourished on wind and stone […]

Safe resting there
Men hear in the travelling air
But music, pictures see
In the same daily land
Painted by the wild air … (137)

The same-rhymed lines, including a repeated rhyme-word, contribute to an effect of marking time – like 'That girl's clear eyes' in a different mode. As they converge on the 'unknown', these formally various poems also reflect back on Thomas's poetic journey: its shifts of 'road and track', its propulsion by choice and necessity, its 'ambiguity' in every sense of the word.

Thomas takes leave partly as 'an inhabitant of the earth'. His last self-elegies rework the relations between 'road' and 'house' which have informed his poetic journey since 'Up in the Wind'. Thomas's symbolic houses veer between the earthly habitat, human constructions, and the self. The 'dark house' of 'The long small room' is the body and earth that have 'built' or mystified the speaker's existence, even as his mind splits from such anchors: witness the tense of 'witnessed'. 'That girl's clear eyes' juxtaposes organic and inorganic matter in ways that don't quite cohere: tombs and 'airy' plane trees, 'stony square sunlit'. 'Gone, gone again', a quatrain-poem with a depressively entropic trajectory, ends with the simile of a derelict London house: 'I am something like that:/ Not one pane to reflect the sun' (132). 'The Sheiling' constitutes both a psychological and cultural landscape. As psychology, this poem is again spoken from partly outside a stable house-self, from a locus closer now to 'wild air' (repeated from Thomas's early poem 'The Source'). As culture, the interchange between interior and an exterior, 'worn like ancient stairs', implies that 'arts' (poetry) and 'wild air' can sometimes reach an earthly accommodation.

Thomas greatly admired Keats's last sonnet, 'Bright star, would I were steadfast as thou art', which stands 'at the beginning of his "posthumous life"'. His own final poems connect with qualities he praises: 'a vision of sky and earth, immense in its grandeur and its calm; and in the midst of it a man troubled by the principal unrest of life cries out for that same calm, for the oblivion of "melting out his essence fine into the winds", for "soothest sleep that saves from curious conscience" …'.[83] Keats especially haunts 'The Lane' and 'Out in the dark', written in December 1916: poems of culminating valediction. An unrhymed quasi-sonnet, 'The Lane' scrambles elements from the mortality-conscious poems of autumn 1915. It also reads like last-minute note-taking:

> Some day, I think, there will be people enough
> In Froxfield to pick all the blackberries
> Out of the hedges of Green Lane, the straight
> Broad lane where now September hides herself
> In bracken and blackberry, harebell and dwarf gorse.
> Today, where yesterday a hundred sheep
> Were nibbling, halcyon bells shake to the sway
> Of waters that no vessel ever sailed …
> It is a kind of spring: the chaffinch tries
> His song. For heat it is like summer too.
> This might be winter's quiet. While the glint
> Of hollies dark in the swollen hedges lasts –
> One mile – and those bells ring, little I know
> Or heed if time be still the same, until
> The lane ends and once more all is the same. (138)

Here the seasons and sensations of earthly life are hectically enjoyed, as in a last quasi-sexual fling ('swollen'). 'Froxfield' and 'Green Lane', local Hampshire names, mark the last or best of 'England' and earth. But 'The lane ends', the rhythm flattens out as in 'There's nothing like the sun'. Similarly, in 'Lights Out', 'love ends,/ Despair, ambition ends'. The reflexive path-endings of Thomas's earlier poems appear to have reached a final reckoning. In accordance with the speeded-up clock of war, 'time' runs out. 'Out in the dark' counterpoints the synaesthetic and rhythmic variety of 'The Lane' by surpassing all Thomas's previous darkness. Wholly situated outside the house of life, monotonously rhymed as if by fate, this poem inhabits a monochrome 'universe'. The interior collapses into the exterior. The speaker seems homeless, a ghost:

> Out in the dark over the snow
> The fallow fawns invisible go
> With the fallow doe;
> And the winds blow
> Fast as the stars are slow [...]
>
> And star and I and wind and deer
> Are in the dark together, – near,
> Yet far, – and fear
> Drums on my ear
> In that sage company drear.
>
> How weak and little is the light,
> All the universe of sight,
> Love and delight,
> Before the might,
> If you love it not, of night. (139)

To 'love' night, like 'the love of death' in 'Rain', has an ironic dash of melancholy as 'an aesthetic emotion' (see p. 110). Yet 'Out in the dark' may partly embrace or accept the dark, as Thomas thinks Keats does. What he says of 'Bright star' anticipates his own ultimate landscape: 'The snow spreads like winter's grave-cloth over the earth. The star hangs vigilant and regardless.'[84] Thomas's 'War Diary' and war letters tantalisingly suggest the poems he might have written at the Western Front. But before he embarked for France, he wrote 'as if' he would 'never come back', to quote 'The Green Roads'. He provisionally ended his poetic journey 'at the beginning of his posthumous life'.

CHAPTER 4

An Atlantic Chasm? Thomas and Frost again

To begin on a personal note: thirty years ago, I went to the US to give a talk on Edward Thomas. I asked then: 'Why is Thomas's poetry not better known over here, especially given his closeness to Robert Frost?' In 2013, speaking at Vanderbilt University, I found myself asking the same question. Of course, Thomas has many individual American admirers, and all his readers are indebted to Matthew Spencer's Handsel Books edition of the letters between Thomas and Frost: *Elected Friends* (2003). Yet the poets' closeness – it was friend-ship at first sight when they met in London in October 1913 – should be a critical signpost rather than a biographical enclave. Christopher Ricks's Afterword to *Elected Friends* scarcely touches on the friend-ship's broader meaning for modern Anglophone poetry or for its Anglo-American axis, which he, like other critics, still tends to file 'Under the Sign of Eliot and Pound'.[1] As applied to Frost and Thomas, 'Anglo-American' is more than an over-arching category. There is much traffic across the hyphen.

The title of this chapter takes 'chasm' from Frost who took it from 'Kubla Khan'. In 'A Romantic Chasm', his preface to the UK edition of *A Masque of Reason* (1948), Frost reflects on the Atlantic Ocean and literary distance. While allowing that he 'should hate to miss the chance for exotic charm my distance overseas might lend me', he is equally ironical about the 'awesome reality' of the gulf, and 'begins to wonder if it is anything more than a "romantic chasm" of poetry and slang'. He also says: 'I wish Edward Thomas ... were here to ponder gulfs in general with me as in the days when he and I tired the sun down with talking on the footpaths and stiles of Ledington and Ryton.' Frost goes on to depict Atlantic distance as no more – and no less – than the strangeness intrinsic to poetry itself:

> The estrangement in language is pretty much due to the very word-shift by metaphor you do your best to take part in daily so as to hold your closest friend off where you can 'entertain her always as a stranger' – with the freshness of a stranger. It often looks dangerously like aberration into a new dialect. But it is mostly back and forth in the same place like the jumping of a grasshopper ...[2]

Romantic strangeness cuts both ways: Thomas writes of Frost: 'It is curious to have such good natural English with just that shade of foreignness in the people and the poet himself.'[3] Poetic criss-crossings continue, but Frost's grasshopper may have had to make ever-larger leaps. Introducing her *Faber Book of Contemporary American Poetry* (1985), Helen Vendler claimed that 'the American language' has become 'separate, in accent, intonation, discourse, and lexicon, from English':[4] so much for 'Varieties of English' on each side of the Atlantic; for common media; and, most importantly, for fertile 'strangeness'. In *Barrier of a Common Language* (2003) Dana Gioia also proposed that the poetic Atlantic had widened. But, rather than re-declaring literary independence, Gioia blamed 'simple ignorance' or insular 'triumphalism' in some American quarters. For Gioia, any barrier to recognising 'inextricable' links is only metaphorically 'linguistic'.[5] Certainly, a weakening of critical signals, as with the (quantitative and qualitative) decline of poetry reviewing, has not helped transatlantic traffic in either direction.

Distance can also widen inside national boundaries, especially where tradition and value have been atomised or factionalised into 'poetries': into theoretical or identitarian or campus-coterie subsets. Yet current poetry wars, both civil and international, have sources in the past, in perceptions of the past, in hegemonic literary-historical

narratives – especially those constructed 'under the sign' of 'modern-
ism'. It's relevant that, in 1913-14, Thomas and Frost were aesthetically
at odds with Pound: that they championed the ear, 'the audile
imagination', 'the infinite play of accents in the sound of sense',
against Imagist 'eye-writing'[6]. Frost never deviated from the princi-
ples he laid down at that time. 'Modernist' constructions of literary
history, which are founded on *The Waste Land* and 1920s London,
elide Imagism's pre-war dialectical context (Yeats and Wallace
Stevens attacked Pound's ideas too).[7] The encounter between Frost
and Thomas – a pivotal Anglo-American poetic moment – is thus
cast into shadow. Michael Hofmann's Foreword to *Elected Friends*
represents them as meeting in a literary limbo: a 'muddle', 'a sort
of soft interregnum', a 'brief abeyance'. Hofmann draws no wider
inferences from his perception that 'Poetry seems to come naturally
and variously out of the relationship.'[8] By the same unhistorical
token, 'Frost's [American] defenders … have instinctively supported
[his] major stature by finding ways to link his work to Modernism'.[9]
This reflex not only suppresses or distorts Frost's distinctive mode
of poetic modernity, but also assumes a self-contained national
canon. Such 'defence' (why should defence be necessary?) ignores
Frost's aesthetic links with Yeats and Hardy as well as with Thomas.
From one angle, 1914 was no 'interregnum' but the epoch-defining
year of Yeats's *Responsibilities* and Frost's *North of Boston*: both powered
by the interplay between syntax and footed line. Hardy's *Satires of
Circumstance* was published in 1914 too. It may be a hopeful straw in
the wind (or wishful thinking) that Mark Richardson, introducing
Robert Frost in Context (2014), claims: 'few in the academy still think of
[the early twentieth century] as The Pound Era, while Eliot's peculiar
influence, from 1922 down through the 1960s, has come to seem a
thing more institutional in force than definitive in character'.[10]

1. 'THE ROAD NOT TAKEN'

Frost said of Thomas and himself: 'The most our congeniality could do was confirm us both in what we were.'[11] Here he was partly guarding his own (American) poetic identity. But the remark covers the affinity-in-difference that touches every facet of their poetry, and which their poems for one another distil. Perhaps the story begins with Frost writing or conceiving Thomas's first poem; or even creating a template for his poetry. The immediate – satirical – impulse behind Frost's celebrated poem 'The Road Not Taken', originally called 'Two Roads', was Thomas's habit of regretting, after their walks together, that they had not followed a better route:

> Two roads diverged in a yellow wood,
> And sorry I could not travel both
> And be one traveller, long I stood
> And looked down one as far as I could
> To where it bent in the undergrowth;
>
> Then took the other, as just as fair,
> And having perhaps the better claim,
> Because it was grassy and wanted wear;
> Though as for that the passing there
> Had worn them really about the same,
>
> And both that morning equally lay
> In leaves no step had trodden black.
> Oh, I kept the first for another day!
> Yet knowing how way leads on to way,
> I doubted if I should ever come back.
>
> I shall be telling this with a sigh
> Somewhere ages and ages hence:
> Two roads diverged in a wood, and I –

I took the one less travelled by,
And that has made all the difference.[12]

Thomas's obsessive-compulsive behaviour always amused Frost. After he decided to enlist, Frost said (as if talking about a poem): 'I have never seen anything more exquisite than the pain you have made of it.' Frost based 'The Road Not Taken' on his walks with Thomas during Autumn 1914: hence 'yellow wood'. Frost either sent Thomas the poem in Spring 1915, or – more plausibly – reminded him of it then. Thomas had kept the hand-written text in an envelope of that date which contained 'nothing else'. Most commentators (Jean Moorcroft Wilson is an exception)[13] assume that this fixes his first sight of 'The Road Not Taken'; that Frost, aware of Thomas's indecision about the future, had prodded him by sending the poem without an accompanying letter. But the evidence suggests that the envelope may once have contained a now-lost letter from Frost, which mentioned the poem, and advised Thomas to look it up. Thomas then 'found' a copy he already possessed. He told Frost in June 1915: 'I have found "Two Roads". It is as I thought. Not then having begun to write I did not know that is how it would be done.' He also says: 'the simple words and unemphatic rhythms were not such as I was accustomed to expect great things, things I like, from'.[14] This proves that Thomas had read 'The Road Not Taken', or at least an early draft, before 'beginning to write' (poetry) in December 1914. The poem to which the letter refers is called 'Two Roads', and Thomas quotes from it an older version of lines 9–10.

Thomas's alternative to enlistment was joining Frost in America: both to 'farm' with him, and to seek his literary fortune there. If, in Spring 1915, Frost did not send Thomas 'The Road Not Taken' for the first time, but reminded him of its existence and genesis, this still seems an intervention in the decision-making process. Frost presumably wanted a decision, if not the one Thomas actually made – although his feelings may be as complex as 'The Road Not Taken' itself (see section 5 below). The letter quoted above belongs to a rather scratchy series of exchanges about the poem, not all of which survive. Frost evidently teased Thomas about his habit of 'going in after himself', and provoked a complicated response: 'It is all very well for you poets in a wood to say you choose, but you don't … And so I can't "leave off" going in after myself tho some day I may.' This reaction shows that Thomas did not (as some critics believe) miss the poem's application to himself, but thought he was being rebuked by a decisive Frost-persona who has no truck with vacillation: 'I took the one less travelled by'. Frost then scolded Thomas for supposing that the chosen road has indeed made 'all the difference'; for not seeing that the last stanza's 'sigh' is a 'mock sigh, hypo-critical for the fun of the thing'; for not realising that all roads end, as they start, 'really about the same' (perhaps not roads to war). According to Frost, 'what if' scenarios are always vain: 'I dont suppose I was ever sorry for anything I ever did'.[15]

One of Thomas's first poems was 'The Signpost': a parable that consorts with his riposte to Frost, and which may have been directly sparked by 'The Road Not Taken'. The poem concerns a traveller who never budges from 'the hilltop by the finger-post'; and whose future (posthumous) 'wish may be' to return to the earthly cross-roads where he now 'Stand[s] upright out in the air/ Wondering where he shall journey, O where?'(37) Similarly, Thomas's 'The Path' (March 1915) leads nowhere (see p. 82). This poem refers to children 'wearing' the path, and 'looking down' the 'long smooth steep' beneath it. Perhaps 'The Road Not Taken', as well as Frost's critical advice and creative practice, helped to start something. Thomas's earliest poems are particularly rich in roads and paths; even if this emergent symbolism, which extends to his syntactical gyrations, essentially derives from the intersection between his inner labyrinth and his travels in the English and Welsh countryside. Yet 'The Road Not Taken' – if a prophetic template – may know this. It may prefigure the psychological landscape of Thomas's poetry more generally. The speaker is a divided 'I': a self split both in the present, and between present and future incarnations. And the poem's very title stresses not the potentially 'taken' road, but the occluded road: and hence desire. Thomas's hankering for a 'better' route, for lost or foreclosed options, connects with the motive power of desire in his poetry.

Yet is 'The Road Not Taken' itself so clear-cut? Thomas admonished Frost: 'I doubt if you can get anybody to see the fun of the thing without showing them & advising them which kind of laugh they are to turn on'. Tim Kendall notes that other readers have also failed to pick up Frost's ironical signals, such as the 'ostentatiously performative' rhetoric of the last lines.[16] David Orr comments that if Thomas, 'one of the keenest literary thinkers of his time', could not interpret a poem based on his own character, Frost was in trouble. Certainly 'The Road Not Taken' is often read as a version of 'My Way', perhaps thereby made more American. Orr bears this out in his fascinating cultural study *The Road Not Taken: Finding America in the Poem Everyone Loves and Almost Everyone Gets Wrong* (2015). He demonstrates that the poem's conclusion, *contra* Frost's gloss, has been usually read as affirming the individualism of 'the extravagantly autonomous American self', and hence quoted in advertisements, songs, TV episode-titles: in 'everything from coffee mugs to refrigerator magnets to graduation speeches'. Clearly Frost had not *intended* to present the poem's speaker as a triumphal individualist, but as someone unduly given to retrospective brooding. Indeed, coupled with 'sigh', 'all the difference' might not signify a good 'difference': 'all' is one of Frost's unquantifiable quantities. 'The Most of It' ends: 'and that was all' (see below). And, as Orr says, the friendship that engendered the poem gives it a quality that 'allows us to feel affectionate compassion toward the speaker, whom it's … possible to view less as a boaster or a neurotic than as a person who is perhaps excessively critical of his own perceived failings' – a person who knows he will brood.[17] (In 'October' Thomas gives a positive twist to a future backward-looking 'I': 'Some day I shall think this a happy day'.) But Orr also argues that American popular culture may not be entirely wrong about 'The Road Not Taken'.

Equating Frost's public persona and his persona in the poem, he says: 'A role too artfully assumed ceases to become a role and instead becomes a species of identity'. He continues:

> The poem both is and isn't about individualism, and it both is and isn't about rationalisation. It isn't a wolf in sheep's clothing so much as a wolf that is somehow also a sheep, or a sheep that is also a wolf. It is a poem about the necessity of choosing that somehow … never makes a choice itself – that instead repeatedly returns us to the same enigmatic, leaf-shadowed crossroads.[18]

The last sentence brings 'The Road Not Taken' closer to 'The Signpost', although here Winter 1914–15 has succeeded Autumn 1914, and the cross-roads of choice has a darker aura ('skeleton'):

> The dim sea glints chill. The white sun is shy,
> And the skeleton weeds and the never-dry,
> Rough, long grasses keep white with frost
> At the hilltop by the finger-post;
> The smoke of the traveller's-joy is puffed
> Over hawthorn berry and hazel tuft.
>
> I read the sign. Which way shall I go? … (37)

Perhaps both Frost and Thomas misread 'The Road Not Taken' because they were too close to it, too 'clothed' by it. Thomas may be even more integral to this poetic enigma than Orr's analysis, itself 'American', appreciates. A role 'becoming a species of identity' applies as much to Frost imitating Thomas (thereby creating a hybrid wolf-sheep persona) as to his appearing to affirm 'can-do individualism', when he meant to commend acceptance of where a 'taken' road leads.[19] Perhaps the poem entangles the poets as 'one traveller' in ways which neither recognised. From a cultural angle, this is a truly 'Anglo-American' poem. From an aesthetic angle, it places 'ambiguity' – by reviving its literal meaning as different roads – at the very foundation of poetic 'congeniality'. And from a psychological angle, 'The Road Not Taken' figures psychic kinship or twinship. The ambiguous interchange includes Thomas enabling Frost to 'sigh' in self-divided retrospect; Frost enabling Thomas to 'choose' in decisive prospect. Is Thomas's 'Other' partly Frost? In a letter (as in 'To E.T.') Frost calls Thomas 'brother': 'Edward Thomas was the only brother I ever had.'[20] Spookily, the first seeds of 'The Road Not Taken' were sown before he met Thomas. Frost told a friend in February 1912:

> Two lonely cross-roads that themselves cross each other I have walked several times this winter without meeting or overtaking so much as a single person on foot or on runners. The practically unbroken condition of both for several days after a snow or a blow proves that neither is much travelled. Judge then how surprised I was the other evening to see a man, who to my own unfamiliar eyes and in the dusk looked for all the world like myself, coming down the other ... I felt as if I was going to meet my own image in a slanting mirror.[21]

2. DIFFRACTED LIGHT

Thomas and Frost did meet, and part, 'in a slanting mirror'. Like 'The sun used to shine', Frost's elegies for Thomas involve self-elegy ('To E.T.' does so in a peculiarly graphic way) and poetry. In 'Iris by Night', 'We two' again walk under a Muse-like moon:

> One misty evening, one another's guide,
> We two were groping down a Malvern side
> The last wet fields and dripping hedges home [...]
> And then there was a moon and then a scene
> So watery as to seem submarine;

In which we two stood saturated, drowned [...]
Then a small rainbow like a trellis gate,
A very small moon-made prismatic bow,
Stood closely over us through which to go.
And then we were vouchsafed the miracle
That never yet to other two befell
And I alone of us have lived to tell.
A wonder! Bow and rainbow as it bent,
Instead of moving with us as we went,
(To keep the pots of gold from being found),
It lifted from its dewy pediment
Its two mote-swimming many-coloured ends,
And gathered them together in a ring.
And we stood in it softly circled round
From all division time or foe can bring
In a relation of elected friends.[22]

Frost creates a 'watery' quasi-baptismal atmosphere that consorts with the religious vocabulary: 'miracle', 'elected'. This phenomenon of the encircling rainbow is sometimes called a 'Brocken spectre' owing to its frequency on the highest peak of the Harz Mountains. A combination of low sun and 'saturated' air causes someone's shadow, haloed by a ring of light, to be cast on a misty surface. Since the moon more rarely causes such an effect, the 'moon-made prismatic bow' renders the poets' 'relation' all the more 'elected'. The illusion is produced by 'diffraction': a beam of light, broken up by passing through a narrow aperture, spreads out. In the poem this 'wonder' is preceded by 'confusing lights', which Frost links with those that, 'according to belief in Rome', presaged how 'the fragments of a former sun/ Could concentrate anew and rise as one'. 'A former sun' may again allude to 'The sun used to shine'. The symbol certainly reaffirms the poets' 'oneness', and implies the ever-renewed power of their shared 'concentration'. Yet, since diffraction fragments light, the climactic Iris-symbolism might be read as simultaneously centripetal and centrifugal: as radiating prismatic poetics into the future. With regard to literary reception, however, Frost was wrong about 'all division time or foe can bring'.

As for literary inception: Thomas's critical reading of American poetry helped to prepare him for Frost. London being then the global publishing-hub (which is why American poets sought to make their reputations there, why Pound and Frost were first published there), he reviewed poetry from every part of the English-speaking world. An invigorating sense of 'foreignness' also informed his response to Yeats and Synge. But it's in a (fairly negative) review of the Australian 'bush poet' A. B. 'Banjo' Paterson that Thomas asserts: 'To have a future, [poetry] must have had a past' (see p. 134). Because poetry needs time – as his own poetry did – Thomas makes few concessions to 'colonial' verse that seems outdated or premature. 'Minor poets', wherever located, are minor poets. He writes of a (white) South African anthology:

> There is plenty of local colour; and yet even this is very often a matter rather of new words than of emotions coloured by new things ... Their verses do not spring out of South African life and its peculiar conditions, but out of discontent with it or a desire to gild it and make it other than it is; or, if there is an occasional attempt at facing the facts, it is in the nature of a journalistic *chose vue*.[23]

Thomas had similar reservations about the pace at which American poetry was becoming American. He contradicts Annie Russell Marble's claim, in *Heralds of American Literature*, that 'the dawn was "rugged sincerity"'. For Thomas, 'it was unskilful imitation that succeeded only in making ineffectual the real fires beneath it'. Elsewhere he writes that Madison Cawein 'introduced the Gods of Olympus into Kentucky some years ago ... with incense of many words'; and that Cawein's latest book has 'far too many lines that display very clearly the lack of a native-subject-matter and the lack of a native music'. In contrast, his review of Stewart Edward White's topographical work *The Forest* (1903) commends White for being among 'the three or four authors who have ... discovered America':

> We do not include among these the novelists who write about the Civil War; nor yet Emerson, Longfellow, Poe. Had North America been, in fact, as in many ways it is, a suburb of Europe, these writers would not have written otherwise. For them Columbus was in vain. Thoreau, Walt Whitman, Mr Jack London and a few others have alone proved, as far as literature is concerned, that America exists. Four centuries after the men of action came and saw and merely conquered, these authors have in a real sense discovered a new world.[24]

Thomas later wrote more coolly about White ('one of the less than half wild providers of wildness for a very tame public'),[25] but continued to praise Whitman's 'real fires'. His reviews of *North of Boston* invoke Whitman, alongside Wordsworth, as Frost's precursor/counterpart in 'going back through the paraphernalia of poetry into poetry again'. Yet in 1906 Thomas had qualified his praise of Whitman in a manner that, uncannily, seems to demand Frost:

> [T]wo of [Whitman's] ideas have diversely and effectually invaded the minds of living men, the idea of multitude, and the idea of the vastness of each human personality; a third idea, of the harmony between the other two ... has probably not been so effectual ...
>
> Each page is at first as complex and confusing as the pages of a daily newspaper, and yet in the end, in some degree, made intelligible and present, as the paper is not, by a benign human spirit – in some degree. That he has not entirely succeeded seems to me due to just that universality, that novel method ... He is a man who, denying the value of words, is yet forced into a situation of unequalled pathos by the necessity of using

them in his isolation. He possesses enough humanity to admit as an abstract idea and an emotion the greatness and sovereignty of the individual, but not enough humanity to use the poor medium of speech, as Shakespeare and Shelley and Wordsworth did, so as drench them with his ideas ...

He has, of course, hundreds of phrases which are those of a master, but he seems, in a thousand places, to rise from his paper and from the cunning manipulation of words, to shriek aloud the awful consciousness that he is filled with a knowledge which can bless mankind, but mankind can never know; and then he sits down and writes something incommunicable ...

Many of his lines are literary. They are not natural speech, but that speech corrupted by an imperfect understanding of poetic diction or rhythm. The whole is not literary enough ... He should have lived a thousand years, and not written until he was near death. He has made memoranda for the use of many generations, but only memoranda.

And to me, at least, the supreme value and fascination of his work lies in its ineffectiveness, in its sublime record of a great man crying unintelligible things, in the heart and face and limbs and deeds of a strong man cramped violently between the lines of a book ... It is as if the divine sun, in which he often read and wrote, had put out the little fires of the words, and yet left something of itself there instead.[26]

This judgment resembles Thomas's feelings about Byron, with America adding a further calculus to the incommensurability of man and work. Perhaps Whitman, like Byron, enters the *ars poetica* of 'Health', where the 'mighty' sun is associated with an overpowering poetry (see p. 78). In hailing *North of Boston* as 'revolutionary', Thomas may see Frost as the first American poet to get all the measures right: the first to 'drench' English words with an American sensibility and 'native music'.

When writing on Whitman or Frost, when gauging the fit between poetry and America, Thomas implicitly claims authority to speak for 'the English lyric'. Today, Atlantic power-shifts have reversed his and Frost's positions – thus 'bringing division'. From Frost's prominent metropolitan advocate, Thomas becomes his remote footnoted acolyte (Eliot has benefited from an academic version of the 'special relationship'). Had Thomas chosen America rather than war, perhaps 'Everything/ Would have been different', to quote 'As the team's head-brass'. Foreign writers who migrate to the US generally receive more attention there than those who don't: witness the continuing imbalance between the American reputations of W. H. Auden and Louis MacNeice. Hence, too, the sad possibility that, concerned for his own all-American credentials, Frost sometimes held back from proclaiming his 'brotherhood' with Thomas.[27] In US-published anthologies, at a rough count of poems and pages, Frost is four times more conspicuous than Thomas.[28] Similarly, the index to *The Cambridge Companion to Robert Frost* (2001) cites Thomas once; Eliot and Pound together, twenty-eight times. Thomas fares slightly better in *Robert Frost in Context*, which has chapters on 'Robert Frost in England' and 'Robert Frost and the First World War'. Yet he receives only two passing mentions in the chapters listed under 'Stylistic Contexts' and 'Literary-Historical Contexts'. All this consorts with Thomas's absence from most American studies of Frost. Even Volume I of Frost's *Letters* gets three of its scant facts about Thomas wrong.[29] Because Frost, so to speak, 'came first', it seems to be assumed that his literary relationship with Thomas had no consequences, or has no implications, for his own poetry. It's not just that Frost maintains a posthumous dialogue with Thomas in poems discussed here: Thomas's formative dialogue with Frost, wherever else his poetry came from or went to, marks a crucial and influential extension of Frostian poetics. When Frost laments: 'I hadn't a plan for the future that didn't include him',[30] he means literary plans too. Had Thomas lived, Frost might have felt less isolated; less marginalised by critical 'modernism'; less compelled to woo a wider public, sometimes thereby coarsening his poetry. Aesthetically, Frost and Thomas are indispensable 'contexts' for one other. Their encounter still resonates in British and Irish poetry, even if their critical thinking remains neglected. The rhythms of 'The sun used to shine' imply the larger aesthetic consensus, as well as specific aesthetic principles, behind the poem: 'We turned from men or poetry …'. Frost seemingly felt that Thomas, with his total absorption of English poetry, had brought him closer to its roots. What he learned or took from Thomas underlies his sense that T. S. Eliot may have talked of 'tradition', but lacked access to it: '[He] has left us and you know he's never really found them'.[31] Praising 'Lob' (finding 'them'), Frost told Thomas: 'I never saw anything like you for English.'[32] As regards contemporary poetry, Yeats and Hardy were shared touchstones. Like Thomas, Frost thought Yeats 'the man of the last twenty years of English poetry'; and he alludes to Thomas when he insists: 'it is of course as a poet that [Hardy] will be remembered: such is the best critical opinion in England'.[33]

An American critic calls 'Iris by Night' 'under-appreciated'.[34] Certainly its meaning for Frost's diffracted poetics has been under-appreciated: the poem virtually 'canonises' his congeniality with Thomas. In a sense his most religious poem, 'Iris by Night' also celebrates poetry itself as miraculous. Like the fields of 'The sun used to shine', 'a Malvern side' becomes poetry's microcosmic domain. Beyond aesthetics, Thomas and Frost agree in conceiving poetry as a mystery: a mystery the academy is liable to profane. Praising 'gifted readers', Thomas says: 'The supreme felicity of their criticism will probably be a quotation.' Frost again seems to invoke Thomas-as-critic when (in January 1915) he attacks 'the present ways of the professionally literary in American universities':

[L]iterature is the next thing to religion in which as you know or believe an ounce of faith is worth all the theology ever written. Sight and insight, give us those. I like the good old

English way of muddling along in these things that we cant
reduce to a science ... People make their great strides in
understanding literature at most unexpected times. I never
caught another man's emotion in it more than when some-
one drew his finger over some seven lines of blank verse –
beginning carefully and ending carefully – and said simply
'From there to – there.' He knew and I knew. We said no
more.[35]

Thomas's 'I never saw that land before' and Frost's 'Directive'
approach poetic mystery by different roads. 'Directive' lays out a
journey to find 'A broken drinking goblet like the Grail', deliberately
'hidden' by the speaker. This self-proclaimed 'guide' or conscious
auteur invites us to enter a parabolic landscape: not only the poem
itself but also Frost's entire poetic cosmos, richly encoded:

Back out of all this now too much for us,
Back in a time made simple by the loss
Of detail, burned, dissolved, and broken off
Like graveyard marble sculpture in the weather,
There is a house that is no more a house
Upon a farm that is no more a farm
And in a town that is no more a town ...[36]

'I never saw that land before' (written in a stanza which has links
with that of 'The Road Not Taken') appears to start from an actual
'land', but gradually suggests poetry's domain (see p. 84). This
domain includes a 'brook', and 'water' has a metrical aspect: 'tribu-
taries/ Descending at equal interval'. As in 'Aspens', the notion of
poetry as 'whispering' may invoke Frost's *ars poetica* sonnet 'Mowing'.
The poet-speaker here is not a guide but 'journeying', open to revela-
tion. Poetry lies before him rather than behind. Similarly, 'what [is]
hid' (whether poetic origin or poetic expression) exists both outside
and inside him. The poem ends:

I neither expected anything
Nor yet remembered: but some goal
I touched then; and if I could sing
What would not even whisper my soul
As I went on my journeying,

I should use, as the trees and birds did,
A language not to be betrayed;
And what was hid should still be hid
Excepting from those like me made
Who answer when such whispers bid. (120)

'Directive' ends with what also looks like an affirmation of poetry:

Your destination and your destiny's
A brook that was the water of the house,
Cold as a spring as yet so near its source,
Too lofty and original to rage.
(We know the valley streams that when aroused
Will leave their tatters hung on barb and thorn.)
I have kept hidden in the instep arch
Of an old cedar at the waterside
A broken drinking goblet like the Grail
Under a spell so the wrong ones can't find it,
So can't get saved, as Saint Mark says they mustn't.
(I stole the goblet from the children's playhouse.)
Here are your waters and your watering place.
Drink and be whole again beyond confusion.

For Frank Lentricchia, 'Directive' recovers 'the pristine moment of our childhood imagination … the embryo moment of our maturer imaginative faculty'. Yet not every critic takes the poem's conclusion straight; or as the reflexive counterpart to Frost saying (in 'The Figure a Poem Makes') that a poem ends 'in a momentary stay against confusion'. Thus, for Blanford Parker, 'Drink and be whole again' is the culminating irony of a 'journey … to show the raw facts of the inhuman world in which we struggle … the littleness of human hopes, the paltriness of the imagination'.[37] A master of *mis*-direction, Frost often has his poetic cake and eats it. Yet the parallels with Thomas may endorse this poem's self-image as 'no playhouse but a house in earnest'. It's interesting that Orr should connect 'Directive' with 'The Road Not Taken', and call it 'the poem in which Frost makes his way back to the crossroads – but as an approximation of himself, not as a version of Edward Thomas'.[38] Yet perhaps Thomas's ghost walks beside him. The poem may even contain 'hidden' allusions to Thomas's poetry, as to Frost's own work. Frost plays on ideas of finding/ losing the self, as does Thomas in 'And you, Helen' and 'Lights Out': 'And if you're lost enough to find yourself/ By now …'. The apple trees and brook in 'Directive' recall 'The sun used to shine' as well as Frost's 'After Apple-Picking' and 'Hyla Brook' (Thomas, indeed, may be quoting Frost). Again, 'Weep for what little things could make them glad' echoes Thomas portraying his younger daughter in 'What shall I give?' as 'Wanting a thousand little things/ That time without contentment brings' (116). It's unlikely that Frost considers 'the children's playhouse' to be 'paltry': what Parker sees as reduction (everything getting smaller) is surely mystery. And the poem's parabolic course through time and space – from a large-scale American landscape to a field 'no bigger than a harness gall' – may, in one dimension, travel back to Gloucestershire in 1914. The notion of something 'hidden' is a clear affinity, as is its disconcerting exclusion of some readers: Frost's 'wrong ones'; Thomas's 'Excepting from those like me made'. Is this poem-goblet (akin to the protected 'pots of gold' in 'Iris by Night') purely for an élite? Tim Kendall notes that, in quoting St Mark, Frost cites the mystery encrypted in 'parable' – to which only the converted have the key. Therefore 'wrong ones', it would seem, contradicts Frost's stated 'ambition to write for all sorts of readers' since 'those who miss the ulteriority of his parables "can't get saved"'. Yet, even if

Frost and Thomas share a secret, perhaps 'wrong' readers are not so much 'the common reader' as the 'professionally literary': who never 'lose' themselves in a poem or go where it 'directs' them, but hook it up to some abstraction like 'modernism'. Frost says in 'Poetry and School':

> Our instinct is to settle down like a revolving dog and make ourselves at home among the poems, completely at our ease as to how they should be taken. The same people will be apt to take poems right as know how to take a hint when there is one and not to take a hint when none is intended. Theirs is the ultimate refinement.[39]

'Directive' is a reader's guide not only to itself or to Frost but also to poetry. It is 'the figure a poem makes'. It hints how to follow 'hints', how to track the poet's own steps, how to share in a poem's self-discovery as it 'inclines to the impulse' or 'rides on its own melting'.[40] By playing hide and seek with us, 'Directive' and 'I never saw that land before' perennially test our receptivity to poetic mystery. At one level, 'Directive' ends by asking readers to absorb at least the poem itself as a 'whole'. The end of 'I never saw that land before' works the other way round. By defining itself as 'A language not to be betrayed', by proposing how it might be written or read, the poem returns us to the beginning. Yet, at another level, 'Directive' also returns to its own origins – to poetry's origins – in the inspirational Hippocrene 'spring'. ('Harness gall' may evoke the creation of 'Hippocrene' by Pegasus's hooves.) To whatever dark conclusions their poems may come, neither Frost nor Thomas ever doubts poetry. Its articles of faith seem as inscribed in the partly 'playful', partly 'earnest' tone of 'Directive' as in the credo of 'I never saw that land before'. 'The sun used to shine', 'Iris by Night', 'I never saw that land before' and 'Directive' are landscapes of poetry somewhere around Helicon. The 'you' of 'Directive' is slippery: reader merges into guide/poet. Thus Frost may tell himself, too, to 'drink' from poetry's 'lofty and original' source ('valley streams' are the 'wrong' kind of poet). Who says to whom: 'Here are your waters and your watering place'? Certainly this place resembles 'the brook's water glittering' in 'The sun used to shine', the 'watery scene' of 'Iris by Night'.

3. EARTH AND SONG

The mutual entanglement of 'The Road Not Taken' indicates that psychological likeness (and difference) contributed to poetic 'congeniality'. Like Thomas, Frost experienced near-suicidal depression: hence, in part, their common symbolism of dark forests and wild weather. But intellectual likeness (and difference) shaped this symbolism too. The triad of Hardy, Thomas and Frost exemplifies psycho-metaphysical complexities that play into poetic modernity. Each is a poet for whom God has died or never existed: a poet who, to quote Hardy's 'The Darkling Thrush', appears to 'fling his soul/ Upon the growing gloom'.

Thomas and Frost are (on the whole) less gloomy than Hardy – every poet is – but their pastoral similarly belongs to the post-Darwinian episteme. 'Earth' is as prominent a word in Frost as in Thomas: 'Earth's the right place for love' ('Birches'); 'As if the earth in one unlooked-for favour/ Had made them certain earth returned their love' ('Two Look at Two').[41] As a teenager, Thomas read, accepted and absorbed Darwin's *The Descent of Man*.[42] In *Robert Frost and the Challenge of Darwin* Robert Faggen makes a case for Darwin's continuous importance to Frost, especially as regards the idea of evolutionary competition. For Faggen, Frost's 'pastoralism [is] the creation and destruction of hierarchies by competing forces in a wilderness of matter'. He emphasises Frost's motifs of struggle and survival: 'a human enterprise of labour, struggle, and waste', which derives from the fact that 'we are products of a blind and wasteful creator'.[43] Perhaps Faggen brings Frost's Darwin rather too close to social Darwinism: to survival of the (economic) fittest; to a crisis in relations between American capitalism and American providential Protestantism. In 1936 Frost observed that 'Darwinian metaphors of evolution, survival values and the Devil take the hindmost' had been pressed too far: 'Life is like battle. But so is it also like shelter.'[44] If Frost, nonetheless, seems 'challenged' by Darwin, this suggests that the death of God, with its implications for human agency and humanity's special position, affected him as it did not affect Thomas. The 'two-pointed' ladder in 'After Apple-Picking', a ladder that perhaps only poetry can supply 'after' Eden or after Darwin, remains ambiguously tilted 'Toward heaven still'. The poem has reflexive parallels with 'The Circus Animals' Desertion', where Yeats's substitution of poetry for religion is an undercurrent. Frost's scepticism retains a religious tinge in that it can seem a form of mourning, as at the end of 'For Once, Then, Something': 'What was that whiteness?/ Truth? A pebble of quartz? For once, then, something.'[45] Thomas's quest for 'something … / To be contented with' is psychological rather than theological (see p. 108). Only in poems that mention the war ('February Afternoon', 'No one cares less than I') does Thomas put a 'blind' or 'bungling' creator in the dock.[46]

Both Frost and Thomas project an earth shared with other creatures. In Thomas's 'The Brook' man and butterfly 'have earth/ And sun together' (96). Frost's sonnet 'On a Bird Singing in Its Sleep' affirms evolutionary kinship with an unnamed bird, which has come 'On the long bead chain of repeated birth/ To be a bird while we are men on earth'. Perhaps Faggen over-determines the Darwinian point here, when he refers to Frost's 'uneasy' linking 'of the bird's continuing survival with human existence'.[47] 'To be a bird while we are men on earth' seems not such a gloomy vista. In 'Two Look at Two' it's a meeting with deer that raises the – much-hedged – possibility that earth 'returns [our] love'. 'The Most of It', although with further hedging, presents the opposite possibility. The speaker '[cries] out on life' for more than his 'own love back in copy speech': for 'counter-love, original response'. But nothing happens except the apparition of 'a great buck'. As contrasted with 'copy speech' (God in man's image), the buck is either a dusty or bracing Darwinian answer: 'and that was all'. Less bothered by humanity's isolation or irrelevance, Thomas's poems never seek a return for 'love' of earth: 'When gods were young/ This wind was old' (44). Perhaps this is to say that Thomas reads Darwin ecologically rather than in terms of evolutionary competition or the death of God. The latter, indeed, opens up new mysteries: 'How little do we know of the business of the earth, not to speak of the universe … this commonwealth of things that live in the sun, the air, the earth, the sea, now and through all time'.[48] Conceptually, Frost's pastoral is more that of a farmer or pioneer; Thomas's, more that of a naturalist. In Thomas's 'House and Man', trees darken and 'look upon' a house, thus absorbing man into Nature: '"Lonely!" he said, "I wish it were lonely"' (60). In Frost's 'An Old Man's Winter Night', possibly a response to Thomas's poem, an old man holds out even though 'All out-of-doors look[s] darkly in at him'. The poem ends:

> The log that shifted with a jolt
> Once in the stove, disturbed him and he shifted,
> And eased his heavy breathing, but still slept.
> One aged man – one man – can't keep a house,
> A farm, a countryside, or if he can,
> It's thus he does it of a winter night.[49]

Whereas Thomas 'inhabits', the more active verb 'keep' seems key to Frost's framing of our earthly situation. 'The Most of It' begins: 'He thought he kept the universe alone'. Another poem enjoins a young orchard, threatened by weather, birds and animals: 'Good-by and Keep Cold'. Frost likes to estimate 'Our Hold on the Planet': hence his ambiguous quantifying of 'most' and 'all'. As between farmer and naturalist, the post-Darwinian pastorals of Frost and Thomas belong to a spectrum rather than expose a chasm. But it's Thomas who positively welcomes 'a diminution of man's importance in the landscape'; who rejects 'the parochialism of humanity'; who desires us to understand 'our position, responsibilities and debts among the other inhabitants of the earth'. His poetry remains broadly true to what he wrote in 1908: 'Man seems to me a very little part of Nature and the part I enjoy least.'[50]

Post-Darwinian pastoral gives birdsong a further reflexive dimension: that is, as analogue or metaphor for poetry's intercourse with 'earth'. In Frost's poetry, too, 'song' links birds and humanity as 'parts of Nature'. His sleeping bird sings 'out of sleep and dream': that its song does not make it 'prey' implies that poetry is a genetic survivor. Frost's 'The Oven Bird' is another adaptive *ars poetica*. This bird 'knows in singing not to sing'; 'says' what 'Mid-summer' means for the cycle of the year and of life; and figures the making of poetry in a problematic universe: 'The question that he frames in all but words/ Is what to make of a diminished thing'.[51] (There may be a contrast between Frost's 'diminished thing' and Thomas's welcome for man's 'diminution'.) Thomas's bird-poems often involve a similar self-referential complex of 'knowing', 'singing' and 'saying'. The song of his 'Sedge-Warblers', which 'lacks all words, all melody,/ All sweetness almost' is celebrated as 'Wisely reiterating endlessly/ What no man learnt yet, in or out of school' (91). This is not sentimental: Thomas gives birds' own languages more status, and attributes to them a richer vocabulary, than does Frost: his 'pure thrush word' (said and sung) reverberates more widely than does the 'little inborn tune' of the sleeping bird (93). Yet, as it's 'we' who 'name the fall' in 'The Oven Bird', so Thomas asks in 'The Thrush':

> … is all your lore
> Not to call November November,
> And April April,
> And Winter Winter – no more?
>
> But I know the months all,
> And their sweet names … (103)

Neither poet can escape anthropomorphism. But perhaps Frost more overtly controls what birds 'say'; whereas 'The Thrush' takes shape as an inter-species conversation.

The following extracts are from Thomas's 'March' (written first) and Frost's 'Our Singing Strength':

… What did the thrushes know? Rain, snow, sleet, hail,
Had kept them quiet as the primroses.
They had but an hour to sing. On boughs they sang,
On gates, on ground; they sang while they changed perches
And while they fought, if they remembered to fight:
So earnest were they to pack into that hour
Their unwilling hoard of song before the moon
Grew brighter than the clouds. Then 'twas no time
For singing merely. So they could keep off silence
And night, they cared not what they sang or screamed … (35)

… In spring more mortal singers than belong
To any one place cover us with song […]
Now was seen how these liked belated snow.
The fields had nowhere left for them to go […]
The road became a channel running flocks
Of glossy birds like ripples over rocks.
I drove them under foot in bits of flight
That kept the ground, almost disputing right
Of way with me from apathy of wing,
A talking twitter all they had to sing […]

Well, something for a snowstorm to have shown
The country's singing strength thus brought together,
That though repressed and moody with the weather
Was none the less there ready to be freed
And sing the wildflowers up from root and seed.[52]

These poems have similar components: Spring delayed; the effect on birds; an implied link between birds and poet, poem and birdsong. In both poems, the birds make other noises besides 'singing'. This suggests that song cannot always be achieved, and that it draws variously on voice. Obviously Spring will come: the crux is song's demeanour towards its earthly habitat. Thomas's thrushes, however vocal and spirited, are engaged in a rearguard action against 'silence/ And night'. Frost's flock, although reduced to a 'talking twitter', seems endowed with greater agency: being poised to 'sing the wild-flowers up from root and seed'. This ultimate assertion of 'strength' is reinforced by how the assonance 'ready'/'freed'/'root' propels the final couplet. 'March' ends with a more tentative scenario. The speaker becomes 'aware of silence/ Stained with all that hour's songs, a silence/ Saying that Spring returns, perhaps tomorrow'. 'March' is another poem of knowing, singing, and saying. The approach-with-drawal of Spring is reflexively meshed with elusive bird-knowledge, Thomas's own 'unwilling hoard of song', and the self-qualifying course of his syntax. 'Our Singing Strength', too, represents song/ poetry as psychic release: from a 'repressed and moody' state. But the speaker's physical relation to the birds, as their 'drover' on the road, sets him slightly apart, and mirrors the poet's orchestrating role. In these instances, the Frost-speaker conducts the chorus; the Thomas-speaker leads from further back. It's not that reflexive Darwinian comparisons expose Thomas as having less 'singing strength' than Frost (just leaving a mysterious 'stain'). Nor should we see him as passively submitting to the earthly habitat; whereas Frost shows an American willingness to face its challenge, and Darwin's, with his own challenge as evolutionary actor. The 'earth' projected by each poet is dialectical: it depends on psychological and topo-graphical variables, on the tones and shades of particular poems. Yet, insofar as mutually defining dialectics are also at work, they turn on subtly different ideas of Gaia. The encounter between Thomas and Frost is, in one aspect, an encounter between English (or European) and American pastoral. It is also, as in this instance, an encounter between intellectual styles as much as substance: different or complementary modes of metaphysical enquiry. There are consequences for poetic form.

4. NARRATIVE, DRAMA, DISCOURSE, LYRIC …

In March 1915 Thomas looked back over his poems in a letter to his friend John Freeman:

> [S]ince the first take off, they haven't been Frosty very much or so I imagine and I have tried as often as possible to avoid the facilities offered by blank verse and I try not to be long – I even have an ambition to keep under 12 lines (but rarely succeed).

A year later, writing to Frost, he took a different tack – perhaps having been admonished: 'Your talking of epic & play rather stirred me. I shall be careful not to <u>indulge</u> in a spring run of lyrics. I had better try again to make other people speak.'[53] Yet Thomas did so 'indulge', and went on indulging. The poem '"Home"', in which another soldier speaks (see p. 131), dates from soon after that letter; but its thirty-five lines are hardly eclogue, let alone epic. From the outset, not being 'Frosty very much' seems correlated with brevity and with lyric, even if Frost himself can be both brief and lyrical. In part, this may be a matter of sibling-differentiation, conscious or unconscious. But it also confirms the aesthetic direction in which Thomas has been moving since he began to celebrate 'the myriad-minded lyric'.

Frost's first book *A Boy's Will* (1913) is a collection of lyric poems. *North of Boston* mainly consists of eclogues: dialogue-poems, generally between 100 and 200 lines, which may also involve a narrator. 'A Servant to Servants' is monologue, but cut from the same cloth. Reviewing Schelling's *The English Lyric*, Thomas had argued: 'Unless a lyric is any short poem in stanzas the name should not be used for what is mainly narrative or dramatic. It should be possible to see in the modern lyric a core like that in an old ode.' Yet, reviewing *North of Boston*, he called Frost's eclogues 'drama with a lyric intensity which often borders on magic'.[54] Perhaps it was the narrative, rather than dramatic, element in the eclogues that Thomas found 'uncongenial'. When he terms Masefield 'a lyric essayist' rather than a novelist,[55] he might be describing his own plotless *The Happy-Go-Lucky Morgans*, where mood also counts for more than character. Thomas's first poem, 'Up in the Wind', is his Frostiest (see p. 49). 'The White Horse', the prose-sketch from which the poem emerged, includes the notion of making 'a story' from the 'feeling' aroused by the inn's location. But both sketch and poem are more 'feeling' than 'story'. The first narrator of 'Up in the Wind' is an incipient poet-narrator, subjectively invested in his material, rather than the (usually) more detached narrator who sets up Frost's eclogues. The second narrator, the 'wild girl', confides her personal history, interwoven with the inn's history. But her character is not fleshed out by the kind of back-story told by the woman-speaker of 'A Servant to Servants': a story of family relationships and mental illness. The poems converge at their most symbolic (as do Thomas's two narrators): that is, where natural phenomena figure the psyche. The girl's obsession with 'roaring' wind-swept trees parallels a passage in 'A Servant to Servants' where the woman identifies with a wave-tossed lake, and speaks of 'tak[ing] the rising wind/ About my face and body and through my wrapper,/ When a storm threatened from the Dragon's Den'.[56] In 'Up in the Wind' the space vacated by narrative is occupied by landscape's greater prominence as actor: its eco-historical as well as psychological role: 'But the land is wild, and there's a spirit of wildness/ Much older, crying when the stone-curlew yodels/ His sea and mountain cry, high up in Spring ...' (31).

'Up in the Wind' is not the only poem by Thomas that, up to a point, tells a story. But only here does he approach the quasi short stories in *North of Boston*: epiphanic fictions which have something in common with Joyce's *Dubliners*. In 'The Other' and 'Lob', Thomas's

other two poems that exceed a hundred lines, 'story' assumes the
mythic shape of quest. Lob himself is both hero and teller of folk-
tales. In 'Man and Dog' narrative moves in the opposite direction,
taking the form of transfigured reportage: 'man' and poet-narrator
collaborate to tell a socially representative life-story (see below), as
the co-narrators of 'Up in the Wind' tell the land's story. Perhaps
Thomas, with his oral-historian instincts, is more inclined to
heighten remembered speech than to create a 'characterising'
speech. That may also apply to the 'wild girl' and to 'the different
people coming in and giving the tones of [rural] speech' in 'Lob' – to
quote Frost on the first part of the poem (which he preferred as
'offering something more like action').[57] Thomas's 'The Chalk-Pit' is
a dialogue-poem which problematises its own genre. One speaker
says of a 'haunting' overgrown pit: 'I prefer to make a tale,/ Or better
leave it like the end of a play'. The other speaker resists both tale-
making and drama. He recalls seeing lovers near the chalk-pit; and,
after the first speaker has rejected this fact as unbefitting his own
'fancies', ends the poem:

> 'You please yourself. I should prefer the truth
> Or nothing. Here, in fact, is nothing at all
> Except a silent place that once rang loud,
> And trees and us – imperfect friends, we men
> And trees since time began; and nevertheless
> Between us still we breed a mystery.' (89)

Both speakers build up 'mystery', but the speaker given the last word
confirms the poem's direction towards symbol rather than towards
fictional or factual 'truth'. 'A Tale' condenses the same trajectory:

> There once the walls
> Of the ruined cottage stood.
> The periwinkle crawls
> With flowers in its hair into the wood.

In flowerless hours
Never will the bank fail,
With everlasting flowers
On fragments of blue plates, to tell the tale. (73)

A brief image, a quintessence of memory-traces, suffices 'to tell the tale'. This sly *ars poetica* (from March 1915) marks lyric's power to compress narrative and make it 'everlasting', even if such 'flowers' are not the real deal. What image encodes in 'A Tale', sound encodes in 'The New House', which ends:

All was foretold me; naught
Could I foresee;
But I learnt how the wind would sound
After these things should be. (68)

Here narrative is wholly elided, wholly implied. Thomas's poems concentrate many stories into resonant images: wind and rain, trees, houses, paths, an ash grove, cherry-petals, 'flowers left thick at nightfall in the wood'.

Considered as 'a play', 'The Chalk-Pit' presents two perspectives rather than two characters. Thomas splits different sides of an aesthetic question between opposing voices or between aspects of his own (critical) voice. In fact, Frost does not fully characterise all his speakers. His poems, too, can be 'eclogue' in the Virgilian sense of rural figures debating aesthetic or philosophical issues (Virgil was a key model for *North of Boston*). Thus 'The Mountain' presents a conversation that goes round and round what may again be Helicon ('all the fun's in how you say a thing').[58] Like 'The Chalk-Pit', Thomas's 'Wind and Mist' is indebted to the conceptual mode of Frost's eclogue, although here the split between 'views' is psychological. A hilltop house, where Thomas had suffered a breakdown, becomes the object of contested perception in a more holistic sense than Frost's mountain or brook. The poem involves narrative – the story elided in 'The New House' – but is primarily symbolic. Thomas elaborates his symbolism of house and weather to dramatise a mind under siege. Two people meet 'inside the gateway that gives the view': a visiting stranger (as it appears) and the house's former inhabitant. To the stranger, to a saner Self perhaps, the house seems ideally situated: 'I never liked a new/ House better'. But the other speaker associates the house with inner dislocation and a testing of 'reality':

> … The flint was the one crop that never failed.
> The clay first broke my heart, and then my back;
> And the back heals not. There were other things
> Real, too. In that room at the gable a child
> Was born while the wind chilled a summer dawn:
> Never looked grey mind on a greyer one
> Than when the child's cry broke above the groans.'
> 'I hope they were both spared.' 'They were. Oh yes.
> But flint and clay and childbirth were too real
> For this cloud castle …' (74)

Perhaps, at one level, narrative 'reality' (the child's birth) and symbolic reality ('this cloud castle') mutually test one another. 'Wind and Mist' extraverts the disturbed 'I' of poems like 'Rain'. It brings the dramatic nucleus of Thomas's psychodrama into the foreground. Eclogue stages what lyric, by dispersing Self and Other among its structural elements, suggests. It's notable that Thomas never repeats the specific blends of narrative and drama in 'Up in the Wind', 'Man and Dog', 'The Chalk-Pit' and 'Wind and Mist'. And all these eclogues variously aspire to (and attain) the condition of lyric.

Frost did not necessarily give Thomas a template for lyric psychodrama – for 'going in after himself'. By 1914, Frost had written no lyrics strictly comparable to 'Beauty' and 'Rain'. At that point, his equally disturbed 'inner weather' was more likely to enter the dramatis personae of eclogues – perhaps he learned something from writing 'The Road Not Taken'. Indeed, critics often see 'Desert

Places', which Frost wrote in 1933 after a period of physical and mental illness, as a breakthrough:

> Snow falling and night falling fast, oh, fast
> In a field I looked into going past,
> And the ground almost covered smooth in snow,
> But a few weeds and stubble showing last.
>
> The woods around it have it – it is theirs.
> All animals are smothered in their lairs.
> I am too absent-spirited to count;
> The loneliness includes me unawares.
>
> And lonely as it is that loneliness
> Will be more lonely ere it will be less –
> A blanker whiteness of benighted snow
> With no expression, nothing to express.
>
> They cannot scare me with their empty spaces
> Between stars – on stars where no human race is.
> I have it in me so much nearer home
> To scare myself with my own desert places.[59]

Jay Parini comments: 'For equal severity, one would have to turn to Gerard Manley Hopkins's so-called Terrible Sonnets … Like Hopkins, Frost would sink into a bleak melancholy, then cast his thoughts upon the landscape around him, finding in that external reality a corresponding vision of bleakness.'[60] But there is 'equal severity' and 'bleakness' in a poem written seventeen years earlier, set at night in English rather than American weather, and possibly recalled:

> Rain, midnight rain, nothing but the wild rain
> On this bleak hut, and solitude, and me

Remembering again that I shall die
And neither hear the rain nor give it thanks
For washing me cleaner than I have been
Since I was born into this solitude ... (105)

The most fundamental likeness between the poems is how they dwell or brood on repeated words, starting from mantra-like, main-verbless opening lines: Frost's snow, falling, fast, night/benighted, lonely/loneliness, expression/express, scare; Thomas's rain, wild, midnight/tonight, solitude/solitary, die/dead/dying, 'broken reeds', love. The poems share 'nothing'. Word-sounds turn the sentence-sounds of both poems into an interior echo-chamber. But there are differences too. 'Rain', like other poems by Thomas, is close to Hamlet-like soliloquy. The 'I' broods on his entire life in a context that implicates dead soldiers. Frost's 'I' has been reduced to an equally depressive and solipsistic condition, figured by 'blank' snow rather than by 'dissolving' rain. Yet his situation, in several respects, is more contained. After the inner collapse of the middle stanzas ('The loneliness includes me unawares'), the last quatrain surfaces to comment on the preceding images. 'Inclusion' gives way to conclusion; whereas 'Rain' enfolds comment within soliloquy, within continuing psychodrama. The speaker's self-cancelling death-wish may leave him worse off than ever: 'If love it be towards what is perfect and/ Cannot, the tempest tells me, disappoint'.

'Desert Places' and 'Rain' differ in how they come to their dark conclusions. Frost raises existential questions; Thomas smuggles them in. Yet as (underrated) metaphysical poets, Frost and Thomas start from the same perplexing crossroads, where poetry assumes the guise of a journey or quest, where 'saying' plus 'singing' may enable 'knowing'. Richard Poirier, in *Robert Frost: The Work of Knowing* (1977), stresses Frost's 'closeness to certain aspects of twentieth-century philosophy', and shows that his 'strenuous kind of difficulty' works with, and through, every aspect of poetic structure: 'The poem manages to keep nearly everything to itself'.[61] This may be even truer of Thomas's poetry. Frost's later work can become conceptually simplified when he deviates from that principle: when he betrays the 'hidden', when saying overwhelms singing. But Frost is always readier than Thomas to heighten the speculative, and hence discursive, component of lyric structure. In severing prose-links, Thomas suppresses discourse as well as description. His poems tend to 'frame questions' as parable or as seemingly neutral imagery. They draw us gradually into their road:

> The green roads that end in the forest
> Are strewn with white goose feathers this June,
>
> Like marks left behind by someone gone to the forest
> To show his track. But he has never come back … (128)

The repeated 'forest', the internal rhyming of the second line, lay a 'track'. Frost's poems often begin with a proposition rather than an impression, or by pointing to a circumstance that the poem will unpack: 'Something there is that doesn't love a wall', 'Something inspires the only cow of late', 'There is a singer everyone has heard', 'When I see birches bend to left and right/… I like to think'.[62] But once again there is a spectrum. Thomas's 'Parting' begins by proposing: 'The Past is a strange land, most strange' (60). 'This is no case of petty right or wrong' is almost all statement; 'Old Man', almost all speculation. The first stanza of 'How at once' is a question:

> How at once should I know,
> When stretched in the harvest blue
> I saw the swift's black bow,
> That I would not have that view
> Another day
> Until next May
> Again it is due? (131)

Yet that question (a question about epistemology) looks inwards. Thomas has no real equivalent to the 'Frost-voice': a recognisably discursive voice sometimes heard beyond the play of intonation, and increasingly so as time went on.

Frost's 'A Boundless Moment' and Thomas's 'But these things also' are another pair of not-quite-Spring poems, walk/quest poems:

> He halted in the wind, and – what was that
> Far in the maples, pale, but not a ghost?
> He stood there bringing March against his thought,
> And yet too ready to believe the most.
>
> 'Oh, that's the Paradise-in-bloom,' I said;
> And truly it was fair enough for flowers
> Had we but in us to assume in March
> Such white luxuriance of May for ours.
>
> We stood a moment so in a strange world,
> Myself as one his own pretence deceives;
> And then I said the truth (and we moved on).
> A young beech clinging to its last year's leaves.[63]
>
> …
>
> But these things also are Spring's –
> On banks by the roadside the grass
> Long-dead that is greyer now
> Than all the Winter it was;
>
> The shell of a little snail bleached
> In the grass; chip of flint, and mite
> Of chalk; and the small birds' dung
> In splashes of purest white:

All the white things a man mistakes
For earliest violets
Who seeks through Winter's ruins
Something to pay Winter's debts,

While the North blows, and starling flocks
By chattering on and on
Keep their spirits up in the mist,
And Spring's here, Winter's not gone. (67)

Both poems pivot on error (illusion, deception, mistake), on mis-read signs, on failed or incomplete epiphany – Frost's title ironises epiphany. But they take different strategic approaches to error. 'A Boundless Moment' is built around an explicit question: 'and – what was that …?' The speaker (the Frost-voice in half-mischievous mode) evokes Eden only to expel it. 'But these things also' starts with 'But', and poses a question indirectly: by picking a quarrel with every Spring poem hitherto written. This poem is constructed as a journey from one 'thing' to another, rather than as an overall conceit. Similarly, the poems contrast in how they complicate relations between error and 'truth'. 'A Boundless Moment', like other poems by Frost, is interested in earthly and perceptual 'bounds': here again 'most' is a relative measurement. The poem registers the impulse to 'believe', to deceive and be self-deceived ('We stood a moment so in a strange world'), but pursues 'truth'. Thomas's deceptive 'white things', although not violets, seem half-valued in themselves: 'the small birds' dung/ In splashes of purest white'. Frost rounds out an emblematic tale, a miniature *Paradise Lost*. Thomas maintains a quest-ing ambiguity up to the semi-contradictory statements of the last line. Perhaps this is a variant on Thomas hesitating to choose, and Frost 'moving on'. These poems by no means exhaust either poet's approach to metaphysical questions. But, like other poems paired in this chapter, they point to differences that can seem more than struc-tural or strategic. At the same time, they exemplify the underlying 'congeniality' whereby both poets persistently seek cognitive bearings in the phenomenal world. To return to 'The Signpost': 'I read the sign. Which way shall I go?' 'A Boundless Moment' and 'But these things also' read the images of which they consist. What Poirier says about Frost covers Thomas too: 'his ultimate subject is the interpretive process itself'.[64]

Form is a means of seeking. Thomas's quatrains above are less regular than Frost's (both poems are rhymed ABCB): adapted to making or marking a series of discoveries. 'But these things also' is a single sentence; it has more run-on lines; rhyme is less pronounced; individual lines depart further from strict iambics: 'The shell of a little snail bleached'. These distinctions broadly apply across their quatrain-poems, of which both poets wrote a fair number. As quotations above show (see pp. 204–5), the movement of Thomas's quatrains is always distinctive: varying from line to line, from stanza to stanza, from poem to poem. Frost can render the quatrain, even in some of his best poems, partly a means to an end. The rhyme 'deceives'/ 'leaves' is an aphoristic clincher. Michael Schmidt, who made a comparative prosodic study of Frost and Thomas, remarks: 'I was struck by how in the end irritatingly regular the poems in Frost's first three or four books seemed to be, as against the much quieter and more subtle dynamic of Thomas's prosody.'[65] If Frost's forms can verge on the vehicular, this seems a function of how the Frost-voice sometimes takes discursive charge. If any notional Thomas-voice usually remains *sotto*, this seems correlated with more consistently 'organic' forms. And if 'The Road Not Taken' is 'misin-terpreted', one reason may be that Frost's wider audience expects ringing conclusions; or even that Frost himself has gone further in that direction than his irony intended. In Thomas, again, there is greater overlap between stanza-form and 'free blank verse' (see p. 54). Frost has no counterpart to how sentence overrides line and quatrain in 'The sun used to shine'. Thus, even as he affirms his debt to Frost, Thomas introduces sibling-differentiation. Thomas's syntax is also generally more involved, inverted and hence introverted –

getting away from prose again. In the first quatrain of 'But these things also' a prose order might be: 'the long-dead grass on banks by the wayside'. The poetic order stresses 'long dead' and 'grass', at the beginning and end of lines, and encapsulates the roadside's recent history by setting 'long dead' in rhetorical relation to 'all the winter'. Thomas's syntax often entangles past, present and future. The first stanza of 'How at once', with its intertwined moods and tenses, attaches 'knowledge' mysteriously gained in the past to 'next May'. By 'next May' Thomas would be dead, as the second stanza seems to forebode:

> The same year after year –
> But with the swift alone.
> With other things I but fear
> That they will be over and done
> Suddenly
> And I only see
> Them to know them gone. (131)

Here 'seeing' and 'knowing', reading signs, interpretation, are again in the foreground, as the syntax reaches into the future, and into a past within that future. The paradox of seeing something 'gone' makes knowledge, in this case, disturbingly terminal.

For both Thomas and Frost, every element of syntax is integral to the metaphysical 'work of knowing' as manifested by poetic form. Frost, too, can end a poem on a qualifying clause: 'For once, then, something.' He can also begin a poem – 'Directive' – with a prepositional phrase and a noun/adjectival phrase that seemingly go backwards: 'Back out of all this now too much for us'. Ellen Bryant Voigt notes that 'this' is both separate from and attached to 'now'.[66] Yet Thomas has many such effects. The ending of 'House and Man' (not only as compared with that of 'An Old Man's Winter Night') indicates how his syntactical roads are liable to double back or go an extra intricate mile. This is another shuttle between past and present, another stab at 'interpretation':

But why I call back man and house again
Is that now on a beech-tree's tip I see
As then I saw – I at the gate, and he
In the house darkness, – a magpie veering about,
A magpie like a weathercock in doubt. (60)

Present-tense 'see' and past-tense 'saw' are conjoined by the
proleptic 'on a beech-tree's tip'. Then parenthesis, emphasised by
the line-break, encloses and re-stages the past scene. Here, further
prepositional phrases delay the magpie's advent as object of 'see'
and 'saw', as the presence on the beech-tree tip. This 'weathercock'
sentence problematises 'why': the link between recalling 'man and
house', seeing two magpies, and the concluding simile. Thomas often
deconstructs the sentence, not by breaking syntax, but by creating
juxtapositions impossible to prose. The sentence-sound becomes
wholly poetic. Poetry allows Thomas's syntax to 'go in after itself'.
When he wrote 'Old Man', 'Mending Wall' was the closest specula-
tive model in *North of Boston*. 'Mending Wall' reflects on walls,
natural forces, boundaries and 'something'; as 'Old Man' on names,
sense-experience, memory and 'nothing':

Something there is that doesn't love a wall,
That sends the frozen ground-swell under it,
And spills the upper boulders in the sun ...[67]

Old Man, or Lad's-love, – in the name there's nothing
To one that knows not Lad's-love, or Old Man ... (36)

The movement of mind differs in these opening lines: the chiasmus
of plant-names contrasts with how 'Mending Wall' drives forward
from phrase to phrase. Once more, this is not an invariable differ-
ence: Thomas's syntax can drive forward too – as with the 'avenue' at
the end of 'Old Man'; Frost's syntax can tie itself in knots. Yet it may
be a root of difference that Frost tends to keep the sentence-sound

upfront; Thomas, to distribute its dynamic force by taking it back into other elements of poetic structure.

Affinity-in-difference covers the set forms of blank verse, sonnet and couplet, as well as quatrain. Thomas, a reviewer deluged by bad sonnets, had a long-standing hostility to sonnet-form as particularly 'set': 'mathematics' rather than art (see p. 103). This wariness led him to write only seven sonnets (four of them 'occasioned' by the war); whereas the sonnet became a regular part of Frost's repertoire. We have also seen that Thomas inserts skeletal sonnet-structure into couplets or blank verse. Frost has fewer of those concentrated, formally hybrid poems, so characteristic of Thomas, which hover in the sonnet's vicinity, and of which 'Rain' and 'House and Man' are different examples. Curiously, Frost wrote more couplet-poems after Thomas's death, but none that take the run-on liberties of 'House and Man' (where the last five lines are also a kind of sestet). Thomas also has more one-off forms. Yet, in *North of Boston*, 'After Apple-Picking' gave him a wonderful model of form and symbol uniquely meshed. Perhaps Frost's poems are most formally organic when most reflexive: often when their overt focus is some kind of work or journey or movement or all three together; when documentary or narrative is consumed by lyric. Frost is sometimes at his best when most 'like' Thomas. Witness the difference between the blank-verse sentence-sounds of 'Birches' and 'Directive'. In mimicking birch-swinging, in stressing its own rhythm, 'Birches' represents poetry as an impetus from line to line that subverts the metrical grid: 'When I see birches bend to left and right/ Across the lines of straighter darker trees …'. By blending imperative and narrative momentum with questing twists, the rhythms of 'Directive' represent poetry (writing and reading it) as both architectonic and discovery:

Make yourself up a cheering song of how
Someone's road home from work this once was,
Who may be just ahead of you on foot
Or creaking with a buggy load of grain.

The height of the adventure is the height
Of country where two village cultures faded
Into each other. Both of them are lost.
And if you're lost enough to find yourself
By now, pull in your ladder road behind you
And put a sign up CLOSED to all but me …[68]

This stage of the journey, which folds narrative into invention, into subordinate clauses, is a 'song' within a song: an epitome of the whole poem. The build-up from 'Make' to 'grain' can be sensed as both 'ladder' – a reference to 'After Apple-Picking' – and 'road'. It also engages poetry's origins in the body, in physical movement. The assonances 'work'/'creaking' and 'road'/'ahead'/'load' underline a process of 'making up' together with a progress from 'height' to 'height'. In some aspects, 'Directive' parallels 'Old Man' rather than 'I never saw that land before'. Like 'Old Man' it is a memory-oriented poem (unusual for Frost): a poem that attaches poetry's origins to memory, a poem that makes interior roads or paths as complicated as possible.

As lyric poets, Thomas and Frost do not 'fade/ Into each other'. Perhaps comparison brings out their distinctive, as well as best, qualities. Thomas's 'July' (1915) and Frost's 'Spring Pools' (1927) are written in the same stanza-form, with some common imagery:

Naught moves but clouds, and in the glassy lake
Their doubles and the shadow of my boat.
The boat itself stirs only when I break
This drowse of heat and solitude afloat
To prove if what I see be bird or mote,
Or learn if yet the shore woods be awake.

Long hours since dawn grew, – spread, – and passed on high
And deep below, – I have watched the cool reeds hung
Over images more cool in imaged sky:

Nothing there was worth thinking of so long;
All that the ring-doves say, far leaves among,
Brims my mind with content thus still to lie. (88)

…

These pools that, though in forests, still reflect
The total sky almost without defect,
And like the flowers beside them, chill and shiver,
Will like the flowers beside them soon be gone,
And yet not out by any brook or river,
But up by roots to bring dark foliage on.

The trees that have it in their pent-up buds
To darken nature and be summer woods –
Let them think twice before they use their powers
To blot out and drink up and sweep away
These flowery waters and these watery flowers
From snow that melted only yesterday.[69]

These poems share a Hippocrene-watery reflexive/ reflective dimension: Thomas's still lake; Frost snow-melt pools. Each poem represents a holistic environment. Yet 'Spring Pools' is constructed more as a conceit, 'July' more as impression-induced reverie. 'Spring Pools' asks that origins, perhaps the mind-pools of poetry too, should not be obscured by what they engender. 'July' more overtly shows the imagination at work – or pretending not to work. The speaker's receptivity turns natural phenomena into something else, images into 'imaged sky'. This is 'negative capability' in action (or inaction): it bypasses 'thinking'. The poem culminates as the mind reflexively 'brims'. What birds 'say' once again symbolises lyric. Frost and Thomas handle the six-line stanza in ways that correspond to the distinction between conceit and reverie. In 'Spring Pools', the coincidence of stanza and sentence drives a two-pronged rhetorical build-up whereby (to a degree) image serves statement. The movement of 'July' is more fully mimetic, as in reprising the coming of dawn. Frost's triad of verbs ('To blot out and drink up and sweep away') has less kinetic presence than Thomas's triad. The sensory force of 'Spring Pools' is concentrated into particular phrases, especially at the climax: 'These flowery waters and these watery flowers'; the delicate movement of 'snow that melted only yesterday'. In each poem, repetition reinforces the 'doubling' essential to their structures. But in 'July', as so pervasively in Thomas, assonance deepens the echoes ('stirs … drowse … solitude … shore woods', 'ring-doves … leaves among') rather than sharpens the point. Similarly, Frost employs a 'progressive' rhyme scheme (AABCBC), which once again exploits rhyme to emphatic and aphoristic effect. The two-rhyme scheme of 'July' (ABABBA) ends where it starts. Like the way in which each stanza covers the same ground, it is integral to the mirroring and brimming that constitute reverie as form.

'Spring Pools' has been read as a lament for evanescent beauty. Yet the imagery of both stanzas spans Frost's visionary spectrum. While the woods 'darken nature'; the pools and flowers 'chill and shiver'. The poem's thrust is, rather, to rebalance the perceived relation between its symbolic seasons. The agency attributed to the trees ('Let them think twice', 'powers') is actually invested in the poet-speaker. Here Frost may set his lyric core, its pools, its 'pent-up buds', against his larger constructions. He can 'think twice'. Perhaps 'Spring Pools' defends its own genre – a genre prominent in *West-Running Brook,* of which it is the first poem. If we read the poems as poems about poetry, 'July' affirms lyric self-sufficiency; 'Spring Pools' reaffirms lyric's ability to 'reflect' (almost) the 'total sky', but keeps further prospects in view.

5. DIVERGENT ROADS

In July 1915 Thomas chose to enlist rather than follow Frost to America. Going to America was not just a way of not going to war. Poetry was at stake in each alternative, and mutually so. Frost's letters indicate that he knew this: just as he knew it was not 'his' war, despite his indebtedness to 'the country that has made me a poet'.[70] Tim Kendall's chapter in *Robert Frost in Context* traces Frost's shifting attitude to the war across letters and poems. Kendall shows that his reactions encompassed guilt about being a non-combatant; ambivalence about America becoming a combatant; and regret that his poetry was not more engaged with the war. Such a complex of feelings suggests that we should discuss neither Frost nor Thomas in this connection without regard to their aesthetic, as well as personal, reciprocity. When Frost called Thomas's poetry 'Roads to France',[71] he was partly marking the spot where their poetic roads had diverged, a spot already marked by Thomas's sonnet 'A Dream':

Over known fields with an old friend in dream
I walked, but came sudden to a strange stream.
Its dark waters were bursting out most bright
From a great mountain's heart into the light.
They ran a short course under the sun, then back
Into a pit they plunged, once more as black
As at their birth; and I stood thinking there
How white, had the day shone on them, they were,
Heaving and coiling. So by the roar and hiss
And by the mighty motion of the abyss
I was bemused, that I forgot my friend
And neither saw nor sought him till the end,
When I awoke from waters unto men
Saying: 'I shall be here some day again.' (96)

Thomas wrote 'A Dream' a week before he joined the Artists Rifles. Coming between 'Haymaking' and 'The Brook', it belongs to his enlistment sequence in which sonnet and couplet interpenetrate. Based on a dream about himself and Frost, this (first) walking-together poem symbolises the quaking ground of their wartime relations. 'Strangeness' obliterates the 'known' world, including friendship. The ambiguous stream, which prophetically figures the war's course, seems to obsess or possess the dreamer. 'Bemused' fuses bewilderment with inspiration: Thomas implicitly meets, and chooses, his other 'muse'. The stream represents not only war but also its impact on the unconscious mind, from which a decision or poem may emerge 'into the light'. 'Heaving and coiling' invades sonnet-form itself.

Frost's possible (if not always direct or intentional) influence on Thomas's ultimate choice does not end with 'The Road Not Taken'. First, Frost was more belligerent towards Germany, instinctively pro-war. In September 1914 he wrote: 'Wilfrid [Gibson] hates the war, Lascelles [Abercrombie] hates the Germans. I hate the Germans but I must say I dont hate the war. Am I a jingo?' In his letter about the 'mock sigh' in 'The Road Not Taken' (26 June 1915), he criticised British conduct of the war, saying: 'Nothing will save you but Lloyd George and a good deal of him. You must quit slacking.' Jean Moorcroft Wilson comments: 'Thomas could have taken "You must quit slacking" to apply personally to him.'[72] In December 1916 Frost sent Thomas a not very good poem: 'Suggested by Talk of Peace at This Time'. The poem resists peace-talk, and hails 'France' (and possibly Thomas) as 'O Bravest'.[73] Second, there was the game-keeper incident, which made Thomas feel that Frost thought him a coward; and which, writing to Frost, he linked with enlistment and Rupert Brooke's poetry (see p. 129). Questions of 'bravery' and 'manliness' are in the mix. Frost told Thomas:

> I am within a hair of being precisely as sorry and as glad as you are. You are doing it for the self-same reason I shall hope to do it for if my time ever comes and I am brave enough, namely, because there seems nothing else for a man to do … Only the very bravest could come to the sacrifice in this way … For what has a man locomotion if it isnt to take him into things he is between barely and not quite standing … All belief is one. And this proves you are a believer.[74]

Writing to Helen Thomas after Thomas's death, Frost equated his bravery with his poetry: 'I have heard Edward doubt if he was as brave as the bravest. But who was ever so completely himself right up to the verge of destruction, so sure of his thought, so sure of his word?' In September 1916 Frost had been ironically pleased to get a 'black talk' letter from Thomas because he had begun 'to think our positions were reversed – you had got well-minded from having plunged into things and I had got soul-sick from having plunged out of them'.[75] That again defines Thomas as 'war poet' with reference to Frost's awareness of not being one. 'A Soldier' (in *West-Running Brook*) is Frost's most abstract elegy for Thomas. Picking up the emphasis of his letter to Helen, this sonnet celebrates a courage which survivors cannot comprehend. Frost compares the soldier to a 'fallen lance' that 'still lies pointed as it ploughed the dust', and assigns his 'spirit' (perhaps Thomas's poetry) a trajectory beyond the 'curve of earth':

> But this we know, the obstacle that checked
> And tripped the body, shot the spirit on
> Further than target ever showed or shone.[76]

Frost clearly wanted Thomas to join him in America, and this remained a post-war project. But perhaps another part of him, an aspect of their 'brotherhood' or mingled identity, wanted Thomas to take the road to France: a vicarious means of going to war himself: 'I am within a hair of being precisely as sorry and as glad as you are.' Frost's poem 'The Bonfire' (1916) suggests his desire, not just to bring the meaning of war home to America, but almost to 'plunge into' self-created conflagration. The main speaker tells children to light and face a symbolic bonfire, however scared they may be: '*War is for everyone, for children too.*' 'The Bonfire' continues a poetic dialogue between Frost and Thomas, which centres on firewood-images. In Frost's 'The Wood-Pile', firewood presents a metaphysical mystery; in Thomas's 'Fifty Faggots', it represents historical uncertainty. 'The

Wood-Pile' moves towards the speculation that 'only/ Someone who lived in turning to fresh tasks' could have abandoned a wood-pile to 'the slow smokeless burning of decay'. 'Fifty Faggots' tracks the metamorphoses of 'underwood', but inconclusively:

> There they stand, on their ends, the fifty faggots
> That once were underwood of hazel and ash
> In Jenny Pinks's Copse. Now, by the hedge
> Close packed, they make a thicket fancy alone
> Can creep through with the mouse and wren. Next Spring
> A blackbird or a robin will nest there,
> Accustomed to them, thinking they will remain
> Whatever is for ever to a bird […]
>   Before they are done,
> The war will have ended, many other things
> Have ended, maybe, that I can no more
> Foresee or more control than robin and wren. (90)

Like 'A Dream', this is a pre-enlistment 'ending' poem: the 'Close packed' faggots have a faintly military aspect. The speaker, unlike Frost's conjectural wood-pile builder, cannot determine the future. In similar contrast, 'The Bonfire' starts with the urge to seize 'control' from weather and history (Frost had read 'Fifty Faggots'): "'Oh, let's go up the hill and scare ourselves,/ … By setting fire to all the brush we piled/ With pitchy hands to wait for rain or snow…'".[77] Their wood-pile poems, like their Spring-singing poems, like the ways in which they take 'The Road Not Taken', show Frost and Thomas diverging as to the ratio between autonomy and necessity. Differences across the formal spectrum are bound up with meta-physical/cultural differences. These include different conceptions of history as regards the degree to which we 'control' events. 'A Dream' and 'Fifty Faggots' are expressly situated where all Thomas's poetry is situated: on the cusp, perhaps in the grip, of history: 'I stood thinking there'. In 'A Dream' the 'strange stream' adds war to poetry's watery source, and confirms history's 'mighty motion' as a rhythmic presence in Thomas's poems. This *ars poetica* 'forgets' Frost. The dialectics with Frost in these poems admit choice ('thinking'), but register the uncontrollable forces which condition that choice. Similarly, in 'The sun used to shine' the 'tide' of history adds a further formative dynamic to the kinetic charge constituted by 'we two' walking and talking.

Thomas historicises figures in the landscape, including himself, to a greater or deeper extent than Frost as well as Wordsworth. Frost's 'The Gum-Gatherer' (published in *Mountain Interval*, 1916) and Thomas's 'Man and Dog' (January 1915) involve conversation with a chance-met itinerant worker:

> There overtook me and drew me in
> To his down-hill, early-morning stride,
> And set me five miles on my road
> Better than if he had had me ride,
> A man with a swinging bag for load
> And half the bag wound round his hand.
> We talked like barking above the din
> Of water we walked along beside …[78]
>
> …
>
> ''Twill take some getting.' 'Sir, I think 'twill so.'
> The old man stared up at the mistletoe
> That hung too high in the poplar's crest for plunder
> Of any climber, though not for kissing under:
> Then he went on against the north-east wind –
> Straight but lame, leaning on a staff new-skinned,
> Carrying a brolly, flag-basket, and old coat … (56)

Both poems tighten the eclogue format by playing direct or indirect speech, and rhythms of walking and talking, across a grid of rhyme. Both model socio-economic relations, including the possibly problematic relation between itinerant and poet-speaker. But, whereas the 'gum-gatherer' seems an entrepreneurial self-starter (perhaps again making history rather than embedded in it), past and present interlock in 'Man and Dog'. The old man speaks of

>   … navvying on dock and line
> From Southampton to Newcastle-on-Tyne, –
> In 'seventy-four, a year of soldiering
> With the Berkshires, – hoeing and harvesting
> In half the shires where corn and couch will grow …

This CV is updated by the information that 'His sons, three sons, were fighting'. Here history is 'motion' as much as content, and in a more complex way than the forward 'stride' of 'The Gum-Gatherer'. The man's 'mind … running' on his past intersects with his present trek to find work and the unstable wartime context. Mental, physical and socio-political flux is felt as rhythm: 'They passed,/ The robin till next day, the man for good,/ Together in the twilight of the wood'. In that final couplet, the poem seems to enact the obsolescence of its own occasion. As with oral history, so with literary history: the deep literary-historical consciousness of Thomas's poetry, its function as cultural memory and cultural defence, is his ultimate divergence from Frost's aesthetic. 'Man and Dog' signals that pastoral becoming 'war pastoral' is part of this consciousness. In May 1916 'As the team's head-brass' would seal the transformation of the Frost eclogue into 'war poetry'.

Frost's poetic dialogue with Thomas, some of it about war and poetry, continued after Thomas's death. The dialogue takes an inevitably elegiac form in *New Hampshire* (1923) where 'To E.T.' belongs to a group of poems that seem to mourn Thomas more obliquely. 'To E.T.' begins with a strange tableau:

> I slumbered with your poems on my breast
> Spread open as I dropped them half-read through

Like dove wings on a figure on a tomb
To see, if in a dream they brought of you,

I might not have the chance I missed in life
Through some delay, and call you to your face
First soldier, and then poet, and then both,
Who died a soldier-poet of your race …[79]

Kendall finds a rare 'tonal instability' in this elegy. He calls it 'an example of poetry on its best behaviour, trying too hard to sound sincere, and straining for effect through that stuffy word "slumbered" and the all-too-poetical "breast"'. He sees the nuance of 'maternal nurturing' as incongruous, and notes that the opening lines have 'the curious effect of making Frost himself the "figure" adorning Thomas's tomb'.[80] Certainly, 'To E.T.' is inferior to the later 'Iris by Night'. But the poem may be 'sincere' in its very oddity: in that it so unconsciously enters Frost's unconscious ('slumber'); in that it presents his bond with Thomas as almost literally continuing into the grave. The hypothetical 'dream' would presumably give Thomas's 'A Dream' a happier 'end' by reuniting the war-severed friends. Given the poets' closeness, with its possible homoerotic tinge, the touches of *Liebestod* and death-*couvade* may be more than mock-heroic. The rest of the poem mostly, and rather conventionally, concerns the war, but the third stanza begins: 'I meant, you meant, that nothing should remain/ Unsaid between us, brother'. This sense of seamless affinity and profound conversation ('meaning', 'saying') adds to the impression that Frost is internalising Thomas's poems – as the poem that follows 'To E.T.' may prove. 'Nothing Gold Can Stay' reads like a covert elegy:

Nature's first green is gold,
Her hardest hue to hold.
Her early leaf's a flower;
But only so an hour.

Then leaf subsides to leaf.
So Eden sank to grief,
So dawn goes down to day.
Nothing gold can stay.

Something has prompted Frost to remake a poem, written years earlier, which begins: 'To start the world of old/ We had one age of gold'.[81] The poem's first five lines now echo Thomas's 'October': 'The green elm with the one great bough of gold/ Lets leaves into the grass slip, one by one' (101). Again Frost's 'Fragmentary Blue' may take off from 'fragments of blue plates' in Thomas's 'A Tale', which also consists of two quatrains (see above). Frost begins his poem with a question:

Why make so much of fragmentary blue
In here and there a bird, or butterfly,
Or flower, or wearing-stone, or open eye,
When heaven presents in sheets the solid hue?[82]

This question is answered by the idea that 'Since earth is earth' we need tokens of the vast but distant blue manifested by 'heaven' or 'sky'. ('A Soldier' similarly contrasts the speaker's earthly 'sphere' with the dead soldier's 'Further' reach.) Perhaps these two poems obliquely desire something characterised by brilliant 'hues' to be restored. Thomas had fair hair; his 'open eye' was blue. 'To Earthward' is another poem in *New Hampshire* that may have something to do with Thomas. Here Frost contrasts youthful love ('Love at the lips was touch/ As sweet as I could bear') with the 'salt', 'pain', 'tears' and bitter-sweetness 'now' attached to love. The poem ends:

When stiff and sore and scarred
I take away my hand
From leaning on it hard
In grass and sand,

The hurt is not enough:
I long for weight and strength
To feel the earth as rough
To all my length.[83]

Frost referred to 'To Earthward' as recording 'One of the greatest changes my nature has undergone': a change he never specified. He also found the poem too painful to read in public.[84] Does it end in another *Liebestod* posture? Does 'To Earthward' conceal 'To Edward'?

But the clearest dialogue, a more direct war-dialogue, is that between 'Lights Out' and Frost's 'Stopping by Woods on a Snowy Evening'. The key rhyme-words of Frost's celebrated last quatrain, 'deep' and 'sleep', are also Thomas's first rhyme words:

I have come to the borders of sleep,
The unfathomable deep
Forest where all must lose
Their way, however straight,
Or winding, soon or late;
They cannot choose … (135)

…

The woods are lovely, dark and deep,
But I have promises to keep,
And miles to go before I sleep,
And miles to go before I sleep.[85]

We are back to roads, woods, choice, necessity, endings: in 'Lights Out' 'love ends,/ Despair, ambition ends'. We may even be back to Frost seeing his 'own image in a slanting mirror' when walking in the snow at dusk. Both 'Lights Out' and 'Stopping by Woods' have been discussed as 'death-wish' poems. The multi-layered symbolism of 'Lights Out' mingles a death-choice with a life-choice: going to war, Thomas 'going in after himself' (see p. 182). As for the choice made in 'Stopping by Woods': we might factor Thomas's death into the impulse to 'stop' that puzzles 'My little horse' and critics alike. Resisting the woods' allure – with difficulty, the weary rhythm hints – again marks divergent roads: 'But I have promises to keep,/ And miles to go …'. Perhaps the poem's 'I' is stressed against an invisible 'You'. Perhaps the implied temptation is for Frost to go in after Thomas. Different perspectives on 'ending' affect how these poems end. 'Lights Out' ends with the forest's ambiguous invitation being accepted:

> The tall forest towers;
> Its cloudy foliage lowers
> Ahead, shelf above shelf;
> Its silence I hear and obey
> That I may lose my way
> And myself.

The rhythmic and syntactical contrast with Frost's repeated 'And miles to go before I sleep' implicates the ratio of 'straight,/ Or winding' in the poets' structural paths. But perhaps, in 'Lights Out', Thomas revisits the 'Road Not Taken' argument to concede that all roads 'end' in 'about the same' place; to repeat that we 'cannot choose' (being now still more aware that choices are made in un-chosen conditions); yet somehow to suggest that a particular road is being chosen and taken. Frost told a friend that Thomas 'wasn't in love with death. He went to death because he didn't like going.'[86] Frost is in 'Lights Out' as Thomas in 'The Road Not Taken' and 'Stopping by Woods'. And what Thomas learned from Frost made Frost part of English war poetry.

CHAPTER 5

Epistolary Psychotherapy:
The Letters and Lyrics of Thomas and Larkin

This chapter will concern lyric as psychology rather than lyric as genre, although the one melts into the other. Further comparison between Thomas and Frost might take us into this interior zone. But Thomas and Philip Larkin, who more intensively 'go in after themselves', bear special witness to the lyric's psychological origins, character and function. For both poets' work, the term 'psycho-drama' is peculiarly exact. As the literary utterance most closely indexed to its author's whole being, lyric seems essential to human self-understanding. To quote Thomas: 'Its appeal is to the central part of our nature, not to intelligence or experience merely.' And, to quote Yeats, lyric is where a poet's 'bundle of accident and inco-herence' becomes 'phantasmagoria' in which readers recognise their own being.[1] As Freud drew on literature, so the modern lyric has often been ahead of modern psychoanalysis. Thomas finds new names for 'melancholy'.

In 1970 Larkin reviewed William Cooke's *Edward Thomas: A Critical Biography*. For Larkin, Thomas's 'miserable' life – his fraught marriage and treadmill as a freelance writer – is his own nightmare come true. Larkin comments: 'the two sides of his life were intertwined, like swimmers dragging each other down: marriage meant children, children meant more hack work, hack work meant more domestic-ity'. The simile betrays Larkin's habitual fear of entanglement with another person, his sense of marriage as an assault on autonomy. His inverse identification with Thomas also betrays familiarity with psychic impasse, and with poetry's capacity to resolve it: 'from his mistaken and unlucky life there arose suddenly a serene and unquestionable climax'.[2] Yet, by his own account, Larkin's *modus vivendi* was correlated with a fair bit of misery too. His letters and poems suggest that *not* marrying and 'the toad *work*', in its salaried guise, can also drag a poet down: 'For Dockery a son, for me nothing,/ Nothing with all a son's harsh patronage'.[3] Larkin repeats the story of how a writer

> had an appointment in a London tea-shop with Edward Thomas, whom he did not know. On arrival he saw from the door the healthy, open-air Thomas sitting with an obvious and discontented-looking poet. Advancing to greet them, he discovered that the out-of-doors man was Ralph Hodgson: Edward Thomas was the other.[4]

Why does Larkin single out this anecdote? It may take one (a poet with his own misleading image) to know one. Anthony Thwaite and Andrew Motion have supplied a mass of materials that expose Larkin's dark side, although perhaps it was only necessary to read his poetry more attentively. Yet, as with Thomas's outdoorsy image, Larkin's shy-librarian image still disguises the neurotic whose lyric personae include the speaker of 'If, My Darling'. Both 'darling' and reader are introduced to a psychic interior, which contains 'fish grey' light, 'a string of infected circles' and 'Delusions' that 'sicken inclusively outwards'.[5] In effect, commentary on Larkin has unduly polarised between 'good' Larkin and 'bad' Larkin (misogynist, racist etc.), instead of engaging with the full psychological landscape signposted by 'If, My Darling'. There was a surprising feel-good factor in some responses to Larkin's *Letters to Monica* (2010); as when John Carey found 'the total effect' 'exhilarating', and Nicholas Lezard highlighted 'humanity, concern, tenderness'.[6] Certainly the letters can be tender as well as vivid, perceptive and witty. But relief at the comparative absence of blatantly illiberal remarks may have distracted reviewers from symptoms of illness. Larkin's lines about being 'fucked up' or 'One of those old-type *natural* fouled-up guys' are not just jokes.[7]

Similarly, Thomas's contribution to lyric psychodrama, especially to its darkest aspects, is not always recognised. Perhaps the nexus between his poems and his mental problems has been partially obscured by the war – not only by the old idea that enlisting 'cured' him. The symbolic seamlessness of Thomas's poetry disguises its different strands. Yet, if poetry itself cured or helped him, how did it do so? Larkin's 'suddenly' and 'serene' are overly transcendental. It's not just that Thomas's poems revisit the psychic conditions, including suicidal episodes, from which they emerged (or are emerging). Like Larkin's poems, they also suggest psychic conditions from which all poetry emerges. Again, both poets wrote self-analytical letters that form some kind of guide to their creative ground or underground: a guide this chapter will follow. Yet among the parallels between lyric and letter, as first-person exercises, is the fact that letters, too, may involve masks, performance, artful self-veiling, unreliable narrators. Jonathan Ellis warns: 'every letter, however authentic-seeming, is a mix of fact and fiction, self and other, storytelling and wish-fulfilment'.[8] The letters cited in this chapter are chiefly from *Letters to Monica* and from Thomas's letters to the poet Gordon Bottomley.

1. 'DUMB SOURCE'

For both Thomas and Larkin, poetry is a mystery. It depends on 'impulse'. Some, or all, of its origins are hidden. Larkin says: 'writing a poem is … not an act of the will'.[9] In her study of lyric, Mutlu Konuk Blasing rejects the term 'unconscious' as belonging to a particular historical context. She locates the lyric's 'virtual subjectivity' and its psychological matrix in language itself: the poet's primary relation to 'a mother tongue' invests poetry with 'the history that constitutes a speaking subject in a given language'. Blasing argues that poetry activates a holistic 'linguistic code' to which ordinary discourse has only partial access. Thus metre, for instance, is not a constraint but 'serves precisely to relax the discipline of referential use and set us free among the materials of language'.[10] Perhaps Thomas got there first with 'Fixed and free/ In a rhyme' (93). Yet 'unconscious' remains an apt adjective (if not necessarily noun) since 'the myriad-minded lyric' frees up aspects of the poet's mind or being, which only lyric itself brings into consciousness, into phantasmagoria. Donald Hall calls poems 'image-bursts from brain-depths'.[11] Synapses, and hence structures, are created where none formerly existed. Indeed, the context of Hall's remark is his sense that poetry has 'abandoned' him in old age, forcing him back on the shallower medium of prose. To quote Thomas: 'Poetry tends to be lyrical when it is furthest from prose, and most inexplicable.'[12] Indeed, his becoming a poet, the multi-layered memory-bank on which his poetry draws, exemplifies mysterious origins. Thomas's story may prove that poetry achieves cognitive access and cognitive interconnections denied to prose. This process (seemingly therapeutic) is symbolised by 'The Source', an early poem that reproduces its own genesis (see p. 23):

All day the air triumphs with its two voices
Of wind and rain:
As loud as if in anger it rejoices,
Drowning the sound of earth
That gulps and gulps in choked endeavour vain
To swallow the rain.

Half the night, too, only the wild air speaks
With wind and rain,
Till forth the dumb source of the river breaks
And drowns the rain and wind,
Bellows like a giant bathing in mighty mirth
The triumph of earth. (49)

'Wild air' represents uncontrollable interior forces that can only 'speak' incoherently or through a 'choked' medium. The 'dumb source' paradoxically takes control by 'breaking forth', by finding its own power. This resolves a split 'voice', as does the two-stanza poem. The crescendo of verbs (breaks/drowns/bellows), the strongly marked alliteration, the assonance of 'mighty mirth' with 'triumph', 'earth' finding its rhyme in the last short line: all enact a struggle whereby expression digs deep to overcome repression. The struggle has violent elements; it goes to oddly exaggerated extremes ('anger', 'mirth', 'triumph'). The 'triumph of earth' coincides with the hard-won triumph of poetry. This is a drama in which voice, speech, sound and rhythm seem agents as well as actors.

Thomas once believed that nothing could 'reopen the connection between [his] brain and the rest'.[13] As his poetry reopens connections, it inhabits as well as activates its 'dumb source'. It assumes the full scope of psychodrama. 'The Other' lays down a marker by beginning, 'The forest ended'; by presenting a conflict which engages conscious and unconscious, known and unknown, aspects of being. Thomas's psychodrama is pervasive: like his metaphysics, it works through every aspect of poetic structure. But 'The Other' and 'Wind and Mist' set the stage or the parameters. They do so in complementary ways, as their different genres (parable, eclogue) might suggest. 'The Other' encodes the psychological DNA that 'Wind and Mist' acts out. One common factor, a factor with an epistolary link, is that the poems' troubled protagonists try to explain themselves to uncomprehending auditors: 'dull boors' in 'The Other'; the stranger in 'Wind and Mist' who is told: 'You are all like that' (40, 75). These interlocutors partly represent, partly indict, the 'saner' world or self, which denies psychological pain. Thomas does not minimise pain. The psychodrama of 'The Other', despite phases of remission, is predicated on cyclical recurrence. The poem reflexively ends its interior journey by stressing that it doesn't end; that, for good and (mostly) ill, we are locked into our psychic habitat: 'no release/ Until he ceases. Then I also shall cease' (42). 'Wind and

Mist', which moves between interior and exterior worlds, presents a remarkable portrait of someone losing touch with a 'firmly grounded' self:

> … Doubtless the house was not to blame,
> But the eye watching from those windows saw,
> Many a day, day after day, mist – mist
> Like chaos surging back – and felt itself
> Alone in all the world, marooned alone.
> We lived in clouds, on a cliff's edge almost
> (You see), and if clouds went, the visible earth
> Lay too far off beneath and like a cloud.
> I did not know it was the earth I loved
> Until I tried to live there in the clouds
> And the earth turned to cloud …
>
>   I had forgot the wind.
> Pray do not let me get on to the wind.
> You would not understand about the wind.
> It is my subject, and compared with me
> Those who have always lived on the firm ground
> Are quite unreal in this matter of the wind.
> There were whole days and nights when the wind and I
> Between us shared the world, and the wind ruled … (74-5)

'Wind and Mist' exposes the roots of Thomas's house-and-weather symbolism. The house, eye-windows in the head, represents mental illness as a perceptual/cognitive phenomenon – and a tenacious one. Repetitions of mist/cloud/wind intensify the monosyllabic stresses of Frostian blank verse to make the protagonist's world-view dramatically present. He re-enters as well as recalls a depressive/obsessive state, which first distances ('mist') 'normal' reality, then substitutes an alternative reality ('wind'). His only release appears to be retrospect itself, the stuff of the psychoanalyst's couch, although he finally 'wants to admit/ That I would try the house once more'. This suggests that inner 'chaos' has left positive traces: perhaps the poem, which takes psychoanalysis into a new mode. Remission in 'The Other' implicates poetry (see p. 97). But so may the disease itself: one medical régime led Thomas to wonder 'whether for a person like myself whose most intense moments were those of depression a cure that destroys the depression may not destroy the intensity – a *desperate* remedy?'[14]

In Thomas's poetry 'wild air' symbolises psychic turbulence; forest or wood, a dark underlying zone. 'The Hollow Wood', like 'If, My Darling', enters that zone:

> Out in the sun the goldfinch flits
> Along the thistle-tops, flits and twits
> Above the hollow wood
> Where birds swim like fish –
> Fish that laugh and shriek –
> To and fro, far below
> In the pale hollow wood.
>
> Lichen, ivy, and moss
> Keep evergreen the trees
> That stand half-flayed and dying,
> And the dead trees on their knees
> In dog's-mercury and moss:
> And the bright twit of the goldfinch drops
> Down there as he flits on thistle-tops. (48)

This deathly ambience, with its weird discords and hints of a wrecked human body, parallels Larkin's 'unwholesome floor', 'creep of varying light', and 'incessant recital' that 'unpicks the world like a knot'.[15] Thomas's 'flitting' goldfinch, less powerful than the birds that 'laugh and shriek', is a self-image that places poetry in an uneasy relation to the 'wood'. 'If, My Darling' and 'The Hollow Wood' hover

over a dangerous brink. Although nearly a half-century separates Thomas's birth from Larkin's, the latter belongs in spirit, as the former more immediately, to the posterity of the *maudit* 1890s. They both admired Ernest Dowson, who exemplifies *fin-de-siècle* literary neurosis and alienation (see p. 110). In 'The Tragic Generation', his memoir of the 1890s, Yeats briefly entertains the idea that 'perhaps our form of lyric, our insistence upon emotion that has no relation to any public interest, gathered together overwrought, unstable men', but then posits that the matter may be more complex. As he rather briskly puts it: 'the first to go out of his mind had no lyrical gift'.[16] Indeed, Yeats's letters and journals, despite a few psychological wobbles (which made him fear madness), and despite his own intense lyric psychodrama, do not quite constitute the kind of case-history that Thomas and Larkin have left behind.

All we can say, perhaps, is that those case-histories locate 'instability' somewhere in the neighbourhood of poetic vocation and lyric intensity. Larkin tells Monica in 1966:

Our lives are so different from other people's, or have been, –
I feel I am landed on my 45th year as if washed up on a rock …
Of course my external surroundings have changed, but inside
I've been the same, trying to hold everything off in order to
'write'. Anyone wd think I was Tolstoy, the value I put on it.[17]

Larkin resisted marriage because it threatened the monastic solitude he thought crucial to creativity. Yet 'washed up on a rock' implies that resistance had psychological side-effects. Thomas, in contrast, had to fight for creative solitude. In 1905, overwhelmed by reviewing, by 'days and nights full of writing and reading', he tells Bottomley that he yet tries to keep alive 'my silly little deformed unpromising bantling of originality … the one thing in my life that resembles a hope – a desire, I mean'. As we see, Thomas thought that depression and artistic 'intensity' might be interdependent. Certainly, both he and Larkin clung to an almost masochistic sense of vocation.

Thomas was perhaps more disturbed than Larkin since, for so long, he had the sense without the vocation: 'There is no form that suits me, & I doubt if I can make a new form.'[18]

Walter Pater, a formative influence on both Yeats and Thomas, was the English guru to 'the religion of art'. Although Thomas reacted against Pater, he never lost what Pater calls 'the desire of beauty' – a desire that Pater associates with 'the poetic passion'.[19] 'Desire' and 'beauty' survive in Thomas's poetry, as in this case-history report from 'The Other':

> Many and many a day like this
> Aimed at the unseen moving goal
> And nothing found but remedies
> For all desire. These made not whole;
> They sowed a new desire, to kiss
> Desire's self beyond control,
> Desire of desire. And yet
> Life stayed on within my soul.
> One night in sheltering from the wet
> I quite forgot I could forget. (40-1)

That the object of 'desire' is unspecified makes desire foundational to the interior quest. (Thomas was stirred by Blake's mission to liberate those 'who are in some prison of spirit or stone for the imperishableness of their desire'.)[20] Mere 'remedies' would presumably destroy intensity, and the quester's 'goal' again seems to identify integration with (poetic) expression. The compressed 'made not whole' may or may not have an elided (syntactical) object. But, either way, 'wholeness' could signify a life or a work or both together: 'the one thing in my life that resembles … a desire'. The stanza has links with passages in Thomas's critical book *Feminine Influence on the Poets* (1910), which effectively explore the psychology of the lyric poet. Desire and love beget lyric:

[Women's] chief influence … has been exerted by the stimula-
tion of desire – desire to possess not only them but other
known and unknown things deemed necessary to that
perfection of beauty and happiness which love proposes. It is
a desire of impossible things which the poet alternately
assuages and rouses again by poetry. He may attempt to sate it
by violence in pleasure, in action, in wandering; but though
he can make it impotent he cannot sate it: or he may turn his
attempt inward upon himself. In either case he comes late or
soon to poetry.[21]

Thomas 'came late'. In 1945 Larkin is talking about his own desire
when he seeks a friend who 'consciously accepts mystery at the
bottom of things, a person who devotes themself to listening for this
mystery – an artist – the kind of artist who is perpetually *kneeling* in
his heart – who gives no fuck for anything except this mystery, and
for that gives every fuck there is'. This is the profane religion of art.
The cries for help in both poets' letters often issue from the gulf
between aesthetic desire and its fulfilment. Larkin tells Monica, who
has attempted to console him: 'I don't think you quite catch my
meaning about what-is-the-matter: I agree I can keep out of jug &
earn a living & enjoy myself – it's only writing, or not writing, that
irritates me.'[22] Thomas (the unwitting poet) thinks that a poet cannot
'sate' his desire by other means than poetry, and links unsatisfied
desire with psychic or actual suicide: 'he may turn his attempt inward
upon himself'.

All this raises chicken-and-egg questions. Does the original
impulse to write lyric poetry betoken (partly unconscious, 'dumb')
psychological complications that can be 'assuaged' by no other
means? Do those complications verge on instability? Or is it the
impulse itself, together with its frustration, which complicates or
destabilises the psyche? Or, as Thomas's assuage/rouse cycle implies,
are both the case? The letters of Thomas and Larkin seem relevant
to such questions; whether we read them as rehearsals for poetic

psychodrama (for Dickinsonian 'letters to the world') or as epistolary psychodrama behind the poetic scenes. 'Psychotherapy', in this chapter's title, signifies letters which seek relief from inner distress or which may, in the act of writing, relieve it. Sometimes explicit, sometimes implicit, that distress shapes epistolary relationships, and gives them a psychoanalytical character. Further questions are: What differentiates poetry from letters as a means of 'making whole'? Does (or how does) poetry's 'assuaging' role extend beyond the poet?

2. LETTERS AND POEMS

Thomas's early poem 'The Penny Whistle' contains the first of two references to letters in his poetry:

> The charcoal-burners are black, but their linen
> Blows white on the line;
> And white the letter the girl is reading
> Under that crescent fine … (50)

The crescent moon presides over a scene in which the 'black hollow voices' of wintry brooks represent an interior state, 'Betwixt rage and a moan', which 'hollowness' again renders ghostly or deathly. These voices implicitly yield to poetry when the girl's brother plays a 'melody' on his whistle: thereby attaching an inspirational folk-source to what the poem 'says' (see p. 22). The letter is an odd presence in this landscape of poetic origins, although all the sharp black-and-white contrasts under the moon have a dream-like character, and 'the girl' might be the Muse. Perhaps the letter (surrogate or prototype for the poem) adds writing and readership to melody and speech.

Ten years earlier, Thomas had drawn a firm line between letter and poem when he wrote of William Cowper's letters: 'Perfection is the constant dream of art. Letter-writing is innocent of that dream.

It relies more upon the capacity of its audience than true art ever does.' Yet he says elsewhere (not necessarily in contradiction): 'Poetry … should partake of the nature of an intimate correspondence, and, like that, should be braced by the endeavour to call forth a reply from the person, known or unknown, who is addressed.'[23] Certainly, both letters and poems 'address'. William Waters begins his study *Poetry's Touch: On Lyric Address* by asking: 'To whom does a poem speak? Do poems really communicate with those they address? Is reading poems like overhearing?' The third question alludes to John Stuart Mill's influential view that poems are 'distinguished by "the poet's utter unconsciousness of a listener"', and hence 'overheard'. Waters questions Mill's position by switching the emphasis from a poem's 'I' to 'specifically poetic ways of saying *you*'. His book brings (not just epistolary) poetry closer to letters because he focuses on poems that explicitly invoke a 'you', and argues that 'address' is integral to poetry – as to all utterance:

> Every coherent utterance aligns itself to, is coherent with respect to, some concept of its intelligibility, and intelligibility means uptake, receivability. Even self-address is modelled, as the term itself shows, on address in the more general sense. So address … is the fibre of language's use and being, inseparable from every word in every sentence.[24]

Perhaps this connects with Thomas's belief that literature 'must do all that a speaker can do by innumerable gestures and their innumerable shades'. In *Feminine Influence on the Poets* he both adopts and adapts Mill's view: 'Love poetry, like all other lyric poetry, is in a sense unintentionally overheard, and only by accident and in part understood, since it is written not for any one, far less for the public, but for the understanding spirit that is in the air round about or in the sky or somewhere.'[25] This 'understanding spirit' we might now term 'the implied reader'.

Waters neglects the dramatic character of the lyric 'I': all drama presumes a 'receiving' audience. About two-thirds of Thomas's poems involve 'I', but with greatly varying degrees of stage-presence. His remaining poems are mostly based in the third-person; only a few have the letter-like 'I-you' axis, which folds more specific response or reply into the notional audience. 'This is no case of petty right or wrong' does not address 'you', but takes a public letter as model (see p. 141). Three poems ('Will you come?', 'The clouds that are so light', 'After you speak') are covert love poems to unknown objects of desire or Muse-beauties. 'No one so much as you', 'And you, Helen' and 'I may come near loving you' are the very opposite. These anti-love poems, which address particular people, are overt instances of poetry as 'intimate correspondence'. 'No one so much as you', indeed, arose out of an exchange of letters between Thomas and his wife, during which he pretended that the poem addressed his mother rather than her. It's understandable why he should have done so: why he might have dropped, then retrieved, a hint:

> … My eyes scarce dare meet you
> Lest they should prove
> I but respond to you
> And do not love […]
>
> For I at most accept
> Your love, regretting
> That is all: I have kept
> Only a fretting
>
> That I could not return
> All that you gave
> And could not ever burn
> With the love you have,
>
> Till sometimes it did seem
> Better it were

Never to see you more
Than linger here

With only gratitude
Instead of love –
A pine in solitude
Cradling a dove. (111)

This poem partakes of epistolary distance by projecting the speaker's absence from 'here'. Its softer corollary 'And you, Helen', linked to the testamentary poems for their children (see p. 168), also semi-withdraws the speaker. Helen's final 'gift' will be 'myself, too, if I could find/ Where it lay hidden and it proved kind' (117). A blunter valedictory 'you' poem, a poetic 'Dear John' letter, is 'I may come near loving you'. Addressed to Thomas's father, the poem ends by invoking the addressee's rather than speaker's absence: 'not so long as you live/ Can I love you at all' (109). Thomas's 'I-you' poems tend to confirm that 'I' is a solitary, unstable and desirous condition.

Thomas was conscious of the letter's multivalency. When reviewing a writer's collected letters, he notices that some letters transmit a whole literary sensibility, whereas others serve as a waste-disposal unit. Thus he sees Ruskin's letters as of a piece with his published writings, in which he 'came more and more to weight – even, if that were possible, to overwhelm – his ideas with his personality, his moods, his processes of thought; everything, in fact, in his spiritual and mental life was crammed into the glowing, trembling page'. Contrariwise, Thomas calls Shelley's letters to Elizabeth Hitchener: 'an excellent outlet for those thronging crudities which were much better outside him than inside, where they might have festered and turned him into the worst type of fanatic, the stagnant'.[26] Letters would seem the textual and monologic mode that, apart from poems, most closely approximates to 'the postures which the voice assumes in the most expressive intimate speech'. Indeed, this phrase comes from Thomas's crisp defence of Frost's method in a letter to

Bottomley, and Frost's own major critical formulations of the 'sentence-sound' occur in letters that are themselves pithy models: 'You may string words together without a sentence-sound to string them on just as you may tie clothes together by the sleeves and stretch them without a clothesline between two trees, but – it is bad for the clothes.'[27] Thomas's letters, like his reviews, like his eventual autobiography, are spoken in a voice remote from the elaborations of his prose-style:

> An east wind or a wind from underground has swept over everything. Friends, Nature, books are like London pavements when an east wind has made them dry and harsh & pitiless. There is no joy in them … I have no idea what it means, but I crawl along on the very edge of life, wondering why I don't get over the edge.[28]

Thomas had no time or inclination to cultivate letter-writing as an art; nor does he always translate his distress into powerful metaphors. Nor (since he was not yet a poet) are his letters to Bottomley strictly the kind of inter-poet correspondence defined by Hugh Haughton: 'the exchange of poems and criticism … gets the reader closer to both the moment of writing and the moment of first textual release, the poet's voice and its echo in the ears of its first readers'.[29] Larkin's letters to Monica Jones, although she responds to his poems, do not really belong to this 'poets' letters' category either. Larkin had more leisure to write letters than had Thomas. Ellis notices the vividly 'memorable' detail in *Letters to Monica* – possibly an avoidance of writing poems – and Larkin's increasing eye on posterity (not so in Thomas's case).[30] But where Larkin and Thomas coincide is in their therapeutic use of, and need for, epistolary distance. Rather than establishing or invoking 'absent presence' (as letters are said to do), they depend on present absence. Here they resemble Cowper, for whom letters were 'a psychological necessity' as much as an art. To quote Bruce Redford: 'Cowper …

tries, through epistolary "Cordials" and geographical seclusion alike, to fortify himself against inner turmoil and outer disturbance.' A depressed letter from Cowper to Lady Hesketh resembles Thomas's 'east wind' letter: 'You describe delightful scenes, but you describe them to One, who if he even saw them, could receive no delight from them; who has a faint recollection, and so faint as to be like an almost forgotten dream, that once he was susceptible to pleasure from such causes.'[31] Revealingly, Thomas sees letters as affording Cowper 'the infinite relief of digression from customary good or evil', and says: 'Out of his very agony was wrought a sweet harmony.' He was interested in the nexus between Cowper's letters and poems ('a record of a man's life not easily to be paralleled'), as he was in Cowper's proto-Romantic sensibility: 'we are assisting at the growth of English poetry as we turn his pages'.[32] His poem 'Haymaking' initially mentioned Cowper, not Cobbett.

Letters to Monica and Thomas's letters to Gordon Bottomley are shaped by very different contexts of 'address'. An obvious difference is that Monica belongs to the context, whereas Bottomley remains outside the situation that leads Thomas to confide in him about his mental state. In part, this friendship was just a literary friendship. Thomas and Bottomley swapped views about books and writers. They gave each other creative and career advice. Bottomley corrected proofs of Thomas's works. Again, Bottomley was not Thomas's only confidant. He also shared his troubles with other friends, like Walter de la Mare. Thomas begins a letter to de la Mare: 'I am glad to hear from you though it is all about me.'[33] The letters to (and seemingly from) Bottomley are similarly 'me'-centred: we learn relatively little about Bottomley outside his literary life. In December 1912 Thomas apologised for this: 'I should have written except that my letters have been getting worse & worse. In fact for 3 months I have been advertising my sorrows & decimating my friends … My habit of introspection & self contempt has at last broken my spirit.' While Thomas did indeed 'advertise his sorrows' elsewhere, the fact that he and Bottomley rarely met made their relationship at once special and epistolary. An invalid, living in what is now Cumbria, Bottomley suffered from lung haemorrhages, and his physical illness complemented Thomas's psychological problems. Thomas told Bottomley's wife, Emily: 'It is a pity [Gordon] is not better fitted for the world & the world not better fitted for me.' Invalidism apart, Bottomley had the ideal writer's life: the peace and quiet that Thomas lacked. One way he helps is by keeping the possibility of such a life in view. Thomas signs off a letter: 'Oh Comforter, goodbye. It is in my mind today that you are alive & quite real & that – well, very few others are with whom I exchange talk & letters.'[34] In 'The Sheiling', which says thank-you as well as goodbye to Bottomley (see p. 173), Thomas aligns Bottomley's illness with his evident tact ('delicate'); his devotion to art with his 'kindliness' as 'Comforter'; perhaps poetry with psychotherapy:

… all within
Long delicate has been;
By arts and kindliness
Coloured, sweetened, and warmed
For many years has been.

Safe resting there
Men hear in the travelling air
But music, pictures see
In the same daily land
Painted by the wild air … (137)

'Safe resting' marks a sanctuary for all that 'wild air' represents. In Thomas's letters to Bottomley, epistolary distance opens up space beyond day-to-day relationships. Their interchange does resemble that between patient and psychiatrist – or counsellor or even priest: if Thomas calls Bottomley 'Comforter', Bottomley calls him 'Edward the Confessor'. Yet Thomas warns Bottomley that letters can prove slippery as diagnostic evidence: 'tho I am the Confessor, I can never confess everything to one man, even to you – I find I have uncon-sciously arranged my confessions according to the person & so each one of three or four is frequently surprised and put on a wrong scent'.[35] Larkin's letters to Monica Jones, however, are a worse mine-field. In her own footnoted letters – perhaps they should be more than footnoted – Monica gives comfort but also needs it. And, while both poets may don epistolary masks or veils, Larkin is often a *consciously* dishonest confessor, as Monica's discovery of various flirtations and affairs proves. In this correspondence, distance is more ambiguous. On Larkin's side, it is, first, defensive or self-protective, allied with delay and denial. In place of the lover's usual belief that a letter is a bridge to the other's presence (witness Robert Browning and Elizabeth Barrett), but a poor substitute for it, Larkin sometimes represents the letter as a superior medium of communication – no doubt, because he can control it. He says: 'I do to some extent seize up, automatically, when we meet'. Monica herself says, perhaps having learned her lesson: 'I'd *like* to be able to talk more. I think I could have, when we began, perhaps; but I never know what you are thinking, and thinking of me.' Larkin is honest enough to describe his elaborate epistolary analyses of their relationship as 'this almost-Russian verbiage, concealing I don't know what, probably nothing but funk'.[36]

If verbiage also conceals infidelities, Larkin's 'Talking in Bed' exposes a deeper problem with 'talk'. In a poem set 'At this unique distance from isolation', at the opposite pole to epistolary distance, the speaker confesses: 'It becomes still more difficult to find/ Words at once true and kind,/ Or not untrue and not unkind'.[37] Did Larkin recall the last lines of 'And you, Helen'? 'This unique distance from isolation' is an extreme periphrasis. It's as if an infinite gap can never finally close. And if 'isolation' maximises the 'true' and 'kind' words at Larkin's disposal, 'talking in letters' logically becomes preferable. Perhaps he would have loved Facebook, because not face to face. Viewed in this light, epistolary distance also protects Monica from mutual misery, from the 'unrest' figured by the poem's imagery of wind and cloud. At the same time, *Letters to Monica* hints that she may have destroyed some unkind letters. She writes: '[if] you don't like me enough to marry me; then it seems rather unkind for you to want to *tell* me so, & perhaps tell me the things that are wrong with me'. Later, Larkin says in response to another reproving letter:

> I'm not so confident about telling the truth as you: not so sure I can, not so sure I want to. I cling to pretence like the bathing steps at the deep end. You … interpret [this] as deliberate and hostile deceit. It doesn't seem like that to me, more like making life livable … at least I claim credit for trying to be nice.[38]

Besides being mutually protective, distance paradoxically closes some of the gap. That is, letters often seem Larkin's best approximation to married intimacy and domesticity. Long letters – Monica wrote some very long ones – circumvent, if they do not resolve, the impasse that 'Talking in Bed' presents. For instance, when Larkin is sub-librarian at Queen's University Belfast in the early 1950s, he goes into great detail about a change of lodgings. This is at a time when Monica herself is moving house in Leicester, but there is no suggestion that their 'rooms' might ever merge – except as shared epistolary detail. Larkin writes: 'I do think of you and sympathise through every day. A new place is always disastrous.' He enters into Monica's practical problems: 'Such things strike at the very root of life, of daily living & peace of mind.' He also involves her in his own new domestic arrangements or lack of them: 'what can I do with a Pyrex dish & top? Can I cook meat in it? It seems to get dry when I grill it. Why do my potatoes come to pieces?' Larkin sometimes provides almost minute-by-minute accounts of his 'daily living', as when he writes from Hull:

> Here am I, with nowhere to go & nothing to do. Outside the sun shines, the children shout … I'm lying on my bed. The

room is airless. Oh my dear! My life is all wrong. I have to go out to awful people tonight – this afternoon is the only time I have. And I do nothing … It would be such a beautiful day to be with you, and we're miles and miles apart.

Larkin's needs, not hers, call Monica up as a virtual presence in a shadowy vicarious epistolary marriage. Witness his horror at Thomas's actual marriage. He was significantly interested in another relationship, which largely depended on, or resided in, letters: that between Katherine Mansfield and John Middleton Murry. By a curious and tactless transference, he sides with Mansfield (whose writing he admired) against Murry's 'playing up to her all-for-love two-children-holding-hands line of talk', while being 'quite content to live apart from her & indeed [finding] actual cohabitation with her a bit of a strain'.[39]

Larkin's poems, as well as his *Selected Letters*, make it clear that letters are more generally so important to him as to be a surrogate mode of living: a way of living in writing. The speaker of 'At thirty-one, when some are rich' reflects that his 'letters to women' may be 'Stand-ins in each case simply for an act'. Larkin's letters are not just letters. Nor is getting letters just getting letters. In his introduction to the *Selected Letters*, Anthony Thwaite calls the reference to 'postmen' at the end of Larkin's poem 'Aubade' an 'image … of healing, of renewal, of … diurnal comfort': 'Postmen like doctors go from house to house' – epistolary psychotherapy indeed.[40] In Larkin's *juvenilia* letters are already a motif and metaphor. 'Letters unposted' mark the end of love; 'memories' of love are compared to 'letters that arrive addressed to someone/ Who left the house so many years ago'; 'the flicker of a letter' prompts an entire poem.[41] For the young Larkin, epistolary distance is evidently Romantic distance – desire – although, for Larkin, there will never be romance without distance: 'my Trouble is that I never like what I've got'. Unposted, unread or torn letters figure a fragmented psyche. Hence 'The eyelessness of days without a letter': 'eyelessness' evokes

Milton's blinded Samson: someone lost in the dark. In an earlier poem the Larkin-speaker says: 'I await a letter's flop/ To plait my ragged ends to formal shape'.[42] The idea that receiving a letter can turn neurosis into an artwork points to complications that only poetic formalising might truly assuage. For Thomas, letters themselves hold less mystique. Indeed, given his constant exchanges with editors, publishers and his literary agent, their absence can be a relief. Yet, like Larkin, he complains about friends who don't write; and his correspondence with Bottomley constitutes a vicarious literary, as opposed to domestic, life. The second reference to letters in his poetry again seems freighted with meaning:

> Early one morning in May I set out,
> And nobody I knew was about.
>> I'm bound away for ever,
>> Away somewhere, away for ever.
>
> There was no wind to trouble the weathercocks.
> I had burnt my letters and darned my socks […]
>
> A gate banged in a fence and banged in my head
> 'A fine morning, sir,' a shepherd said.
>
> I could not return from my liberty,
> To my youth and my love and my misery… (126)

Thomas indeed 'burnt his letters' when preparing to leave Steep and go to France – which is why we lack Bottomley's side of their correspondence. 'Darning socks', by ironic disproportion, underlines the huge step that 'burning letters' signifies. Although the trajectory of 'Early one morning' is ambiguous (see p. 170), this action, akin to burning boats or bridges, is correlated with moving on from 'misery' and burying 'the past': 'the only dead thing that smells sweet'. It appears that, however uncertain the future, one kind of pain is now in the past, along with the need for epistolary psychotherapy: 'A gate ... banged in my head'. Or perhaps the shock-therapy of war has taken over.

A relevant parallel between Thomas and Larkin is that both had contact with psychoanalysis. Thomas was splashed by the first wave of Freud's impact on England because, besides writing letters, he went from doctor to doctor. In 1912 he received treatment – essentially, counselling or a talking cure – from a doctor who was also a pioneering psychiatrist: the charismatic Helton Godwin Baynes, later Carl Jung's most prominent English disciple. Thomas told Bottomley that Baynes was 'working magic with my disordered intellects'.[43] Baynes gave Thomas some perspectives on his condition, and may have pointed him towards the autobiographical prose writings, such as *The Childhood of Edward Thomas*, which prepared the way for poetry. Thomas became disillusioned with Baynes, partly because his charisma was so widely diffused, but their encounter seems to linger in his poems. That is, he takes on the interpenetrating roles of patient and analyst; and (as when redefining 'melancholy') creates his own psychoanalytical language – language that includes image and syntax, and resists fixed diagnostic categories: 'what men call content', 'what I can have meant/ By happiness', 'what yet lives in me'. Even the near-suicidal speaker of 'Rain' dissects what he means by 'the love of death'. 'The Other' (which prefigures elements in Freud's essay on the '*Unheimlich*') is surely the first poetic outing for a modern version of the split self. Larkin's interest in psychoanalysis, as a means to self-knowledge, appears in his letters to J. B. (Jim) Sutton during the 1940s. These letters amount to a consciously self-analytical portrait of the young artist. At Oxford, Larkin attended seminars given by the Jungian psychologist John Layard, and he told Sutton: 'I am psycho-analysing myself by means of dreams'. Five years later, he wrote: 'I have gone on fuddling my head with psychology books'. In the 1940s, Larkin was also reading D. H. Lawrence 'like the Bible' and engaging with Lawrentian psychology.[44] The self-analysis in his poems and letters is alert to psychoanalytical concepts such as blockage, denial, arrested development and primary narcissism: 'the frosted artificially-sealed bivalve behaviour of my life … psychic cripplehood'; a 'monstrous infantile shell of egotism, inside which I quietly asphyxiate'. Larkin even suspects (psychoanalyses) his devotion to poetic mystery: 'if I am not going to produce anything in the literary line, the justification for my selfish life is removed – but since I go on living it, the suspicion arises that the writing existed to produce the life, & not *vice versa*'.[45] 'On Being Twenty-six' ends:

I kiss, I clutch,

Like a daft mother, putrid
     Infancy,
That can and will forbid
All grist to me
Except devaluing dichotomies:
     Nothing, and paradise.[46]

There are striking parallels between Thomas's and Larkin's epistolary self-analyses. Thomas asks: 'Why have I no energies like other men? I long for some hatred or indignation or even sharp despair, since love is impossible … Till then I must grind everything out, conscious at every moment of what the result is & so always dissatisfied.' This is what 'The Other' calls 'Desire of desire'. Larkin writes: 'My great trouble, as usual, is that I lack desires … In fact I feel as if the growing shoots of my character – though they must be more than shoots by now – had turned in on each other & were mutually neutralising each other.' Thomas writes: 'I … have attained a degree of selfconsciousness beyond the dreams of avarice (which makes me spend hours, when I ought to be reading or enjoying the interlacing flight of 3 kestrels, in thinking out my motives for this or that act or word in the past until I long for sleep).' Larkin writes: 'Lawrence wd describe me as all tangled up in the web of my self consciousness … & really if I could bring about some alteration in my mental state I think it would be for my self consciousness to be switched off. I don't mean any kind of shyness, but an inability to forget myself that quite inhibits any mental activity of the unconscious sort.'[47]

Such quotations might be multiplied. A key similarity is the sense that something is blocking the creative synaptic sparks between conscious and unconscious aspects of mind. Larkin says: 'One might as soon expect rabbits to come out & play in some glade lit by the glare of headlights.' Larkin, of course, is writing, or trying to write, poetry; whereas Thomas doesn't even know he isn't. But there is a likeness between this undiagnosed source of Thomas's trouble and Larkin's laments when not writing, or unable to complete, a poem. He attributes his lack of lyrical impulse to 'something cold & heavy sitting on me somewhere', adding: 'Will power can do nothing unless the impulse is there first.'[48] This again raises the chicken-and-egg riddle: does a psychological block cause writer's block or vice versa? Or are they interdependent? The disproportion between the sheer mass of Thomas's and Larkin's 'writing' and the concentration of their lyric art strengthens the view that a poet is not quite the same thing as a 'writer'. If Thomas's letters take up less space than Larkin's, this is because he wrote so much other prose: prose which conceals not writer's, but poet's, block. A problem with the publication of Larkin's letters, poetic juvenilia and poetic misfires – however fascinating – is that they might clutter the lyric core of his achievement. Mark Lawson once observed on the BBC Radio 4 arts programme *Front Row* that Larkin was no longer just the author of a few slim vols. But actually he is just that, and that's what matters.

By 1913, perhaps partly thanks to epistolary psychotherapy, Thomas had the analysis if not the cure. He told a new epistolary friend, Eleanor Farjeon: 'You see the central evil is self-consciousness carried as far beyond selfishness as selfishness is beyond self denial … and now amounting to a disease, and all I have to fight it with is the knowledge that that in truth I am not the isolated selfconsidering brain which I have come to seem – the *knowledge* that I am something more, but not the belief that I can reopen the connection between the brain and the rest.'[49] Yet eighteen months later, Thomas wrote his first poem. 'There was a time' (see p. 158) dwells on the paradox that connections have been reopened by his enlistment – and by poetry: 'hammered out a melody' seems proleptic:

> … except sometimes in a frosty air
> When my heels hammered out a melody
> From pavements of a city left behind,
> I never would acknowledge my own glee
> Because it was less mighty than my mind
> Had dreamed of. Since I could not boast of strength
> Great as I wished, weakness was all my boast.
> I sought yet hated pity till at length
> I earned it … (128)

Once again, epistolary psychotherapy – boasting 'weakness', seeking 'pity' – is placed in the past. In having seen 'weakness' as the only alternative to exceptional (literary and psychological) 'strength', Thomas parallels Larkin's tendency to represent his condition in binary terms: 'devaluing dichotomies:/ Nothing, and paradise'. The source of the parallel may again be aesthetic desire: a destabilising reluctance to settle for anything less than full intensity and perfect beauty.

Thomas's autobiographical prose and his critical writings suggest that some inner evolution began before 1914: the key year of his friendship with Frost. Perhaps he was entering the chrysalis stage of his metamorphosis into a poet. He wrote to Bottomley in August 1913, two months after the bad period signalled in his letter to Farjeon: 'I will not be such a nuisance again just yet, as I am at last realising I had better fight my battles instead of sending out lists of the opposing forces'.[50] Here recovery figures as becoming less dependent on letters, written or received. Writing poetry certainly appears to have been a conclusive therapy or to have concluded the need for therapy. Thomas's most important 'literary' letters, from 1914 to his death, are his letters to Frost. Despite one or two depressive relapses into 'black talk',[51] and some neediness when Frost fails to write, this correspondence, if shadowed by war, pivots on poetry, not on psychological distress. It comes within the orbit of 'poets' letters'.

In Larkin's case, poetry could not come to the rescue since it had been there, or should have been there, all along. Indeed, his letters register its diminishing returns in a double sense. In 1975 he tells Barbara Pym that 'the notion of expressing sentiments in short lines having similar sounds at their ends seems as remote as mangoes on the moon'. Two epistolary poems from the early 1980s, which address fellow-poets on public occasions, allude to the difficulty of writing poetry as you grow older. Larkin represents himself to Gavin Ewart as: 'attic'd with all-too-familiar/ Teachers of truth-sodden grief' and as scrapping bad poems. He begins his epistle to Charles Causley: 'Dear CHARLES, My Muse, asleep or dead,/ Offers this doggerel instead'. Presumably, a verse-letter is no lyric: the worst of both worlds, perhaps. In the last few years before Larkin's death in 1985, he and Monica settled into something like married life in Hull because Monica had been ill. This cannot really be called a choice. Monica then barely left the house until her own death in 2001. Such an ending, which also involved much alcohol, was the disastrous outcome that Larkin's letters to her had foreboded. He wrote in 1962: 'I fear we are to turn slowly into living reproaches of the way I have dallied and lingered with you, neither one thing or the other.'[52] This image of frozen lives points to a difference between Thomas and Larkin: Thomas's psychic health fluctuates, whereas Larkin's letters record some irrevocable stalemate, rigidity, paralysis: 'My nature, perhaps, is rather like a spring – it can be stretched out straight, but when released leaps back into a coil.' It seems axiomatic that there can be no middle way, no 'grist', between 'Nothing, and paradise'. Larkin says: 'Every now & then I open the little trap door in my head & look in to see if the hideous roaring panic & misery has died down.

It hasn't, & I don't see why it should'. Larkin's letters never speak of 'fighting battles'. Therapy seems to stop at 'verbiage' or diagnosis: 'Ends in themselves, my letters plot no change'. Perhaps that distinguishes them from poems: the ending of 'The Trees' plots change as rhythm, not just as exhortation. Even if the speaker accepts that trees' 'yearly trick of looking new/ Is written down in rings of grain', rhythm tugs against fatalistic fact: 'Begin afresh, afresh, afresh'. Since Larkin lets no doctor invade the shell of his ego, self-diagnosis morphs into addictive self-medication. This includes writing letters that 'make life livable' rather than lived. Thomas's epistolary self-images are less determinedly deterministic. They have something in common with the complex weather of his poetry. Perhaps contingency played a larger part in his illness; whereas Larkin refers to 'violence/ A long way back'. Similarly, while Thomas's letters repeat themselves, they are not the loop-tape that *Letters to Monica* becomes – sometimes consciously so: 'I suppose one shouldn't be writing letters like this at 44'.[53] Perhaps Larkin needed a war.

Larkin also wrote diaries – burnt, at his request, after his death. He panics when he is ill in hospital and thinks that Monica may discover material written 'partly to relieve my feelings'.[54] The burnt diaries provide a vista in which all Larkin's textual self-expression or self-relief becomes a murky receding palimpsest. But – even if every written text is in some sense an 'address' – diaries, letters and lyrics (as 'letters to the world') should logically fall into some kind of sequence *vis à vis* an implied audience: oneself, Self and Other, whatever readers are out there, Thomas's 'understanding spirit'. Yet some writers' diaries and letters wink at posterity, and poems can be destined for drawers. Larkin's diaries certainly seem to have been for his eyes only, although he was less worried about his (in some ways, posterity-conscious) letters when a Larkin archive was mooted for Hull. We may be on firmer ground if we assume a progression as regards complexity of 'talk' or voice. If poetry has a distinctive psychotherapeutic function, which circulates between poet and reader, this must depend on 'formal shape'.

3. LYRIC CLARIFICATION

Thomas's poem 'Beauty' concentrates motifs that recur in his letters: exhaustion, irritability and depression; unkind behaviour towards his wife and children; suicidal thoughts. The poem has links with his 'east wind' letter ('I have no idea what it means'), and with an earlier letter to Bottomley in which he regrets that he cannot respond to 'a beautiful still evening', and says: 'So I am writing to you, which … simply clarifies my introspection a little but will not – I know well – lead it anywhere.' Jean Moorcroft Wilson has found a notebook-jotting from 1910 in which, sitting with two of his children, Thomas feels 'Tired, angry ill at ease', but glimpses 'beauty in dim-lit quiet vale' towards which 'some little thing' in him wants 'to fly'.[55] The poem not only 'clarifies … introspection', but also 'leads it' somewhere. It may also distinguish between epistolary psychotherapy and poetry:

> What does it mean? Tired, angry, and ill at ease,
> No man, woman, or child alive could please
> Me now. And yet I almost dare to laugh
> Because I sit and frame an epitaph –
> 'Here lies all that no one loved of him
> And that loved no one.' Then in a trice that whim
> Has wearied. But, though I am like a river
> At fall of evening while it seems that never
> Has the sun lighted it or warmed it, while
> Cross breezes cut the surface to a file,
> This heart, some fraction of me, happily
> Floats through the window even now to a tree
> Down in the misting, dim-lit, quiet vale,
> Not like a pewit that returns to wail
> For something it has lost, but like a dove
> That slants unswerving to its home and love.
> There I find my rest, and through the dusk air
> Flies what yet lives in me. Beauty is there. (58)

The difference between Thomas's letters and this poem parallels that between pewit and dove. 'Wailing/ For something ... lost', like pity-seeking in 'There was a time', marks melancholic lament from which there is no outlet. The dove, which paradoxically 'slants unswerving' (compare Dickinson's 'tell it slant'), suggests complex emotion achieving precise expression. Here 'home' may be poetry. The first part of the poem, where exaggerated speech-rhythms dramatise a series of moods, is a composite, epitomised by the 'epitaph', of how Thomas's letters have 'framed' his alienation from self and world. Imagery tightens the frame: cold river, serrated file. In *Feminine Influence on the Poets* Thomas quotes a depressed letter from Shelley to Mary Godwin in which Shelley says: 'My mind, without yours, is dead and cold as the dark midnight river when the moon is down.'[56] Yet recourse to imagery may itself mark the change from notebook-mode, or letter-mode, to poetry. And the intricate syntax at this point presents self-division in more positive terms, when the sentence's subject is eventually introduced as 'This heart, some fraction of me'. The still more positive 'what yet lives in me' seems to be the aesthetic impulse. 'There', the reiterated locus of 'rest', which encloses the last couplet, is both tree and poem. 'Beauty is there' signals that 'desire of beauty' has been satisfied. But that satisfaction is not necessarily confined to speaker or poet. This poem's ending (*a* poem's ending) addresses the reader too. It reflexively conflates what the poet has achieved with what we have absorbed.

Robert Frost encompasses poet and reader, psychology and metaphysics, when he proposes that a poem

> ends in a clarification of life – not necessarily a great clarification, such as sects and cults are founded on, but in a momentary stay against confusion ... No tears in the writer, no tears in the reader. No surprise for the writer, no surprise for the reader ... It must be a revelation, or a series of revelations, as much for the poet as for the reader.[57]

The poet forms ('stay') a unique cognitive complex to which form gives the reader access. A lyric has more resources than a letter for 'clarifying … introspection'. Clarification is not identical with reassurance ('tears'). As the poet experiences aesthetic pleasure by writing even the darkest lyric – pleasure bound up with the synaptic connections brought into play – so the reader's aesthetic pleasure involves joining up the same dots. To quote Louis MacNeice, another lyric poet given to gloom: 'the work of art itself is always *positive*. A poem in praise of suicide is an act of homage to life.'[58] 'Beauty', which comes back from the brink of suicide, and arrives at 'rest', might seem more directly reassuring. But this is partly because the poem identifies recovery with discovering poetry; because it suggests how poetic 'beauty' works – not only here. Rhythm, in which metre and syntax co-operate, is crucial to any positive or therapeutic outcome. As the last twelve lines of 'Beauty' move from depression to remission, rhythm takes on richer sensory life. These lines are strongly assonantal. 'Cross breezes'/'surface'/'file' reinforces the cold auditory and kinetic impression; while, by adding 'misting' to his notebook-jotting, Thomas deepens the harmonies that run from 'Floats' to 'vale'. 'Misting' is later picked up by 'rest' and 'dusk', which furthers the effect of twilight mystery. The three distinctly voiced adjectives – 'misting, dim-lit, quiet' – slow the pace, constituting and compelling a reflective pause. This prolonged sentence is followed by a briefer sentence, ordered to create maximum mutual impact between its co-subject ('what yet lives in me') and the final three-word sentence. 'Beauty' is another poem in which Thomas makes sonnet and couplet integral to psychodrama. With 'But', a truncated 'octet' gives way to an extended 'sestet' that matches the gradual return to life. In the last four lines, with their contracting syntax, their sense of homing in on a target, the couplet becomes more emphatic and end-stopped.

Form 'embodies' in a more than metaphorical sense. The rhythms of poetry engage our bodily as well as interior being: how the body moves, how it senses the world, how it inhabits the earth. Thomas even thought that 'the music of words' secretes 'an enduring echo of we know not what in the past and in the abyss'.[59] The movement of 'Beauty' seems to bring mind and body together according to Thomas's Keatsian model (see p. 101). In *Keats* Thomas quotes from Keats's notes on *Paradise Lost*: 'There is a cool pleasure in the very sound of vale'.[60] Lyric, as a clarifying space, has something in common with the practice or therapy of 'mindfulness'. 'Myriad-mindedness' dwells in the body. This is so, even when mind and body seem to 'dissolve' at the dark ending of 'Rain', which inverts the ending of 'Beauty': 'If love it be towards what is perfect and/ Cannot, the tempest tells me, disappoint' (105). 'Rain' may be (almost) a poem 'in praise of suicide', but form keeps it in touch with life. The mimesis of 'wild rain' does not surrender to 'wild rain'. The tone, rhythm and assonances of the last line ('Cannot', 'tempest', 'disappoint') complete a psychodrama, which, not just explicitly, clarifies the symptoms it presents. An anatomy of confusion is a stay against confusion.

Larkin's 'Wants' is another 'death-wish' poem:

Beyond all this, the wish to be alone:
However the sky grows dark with invitation-cards
However we follow the printed directions of sex
However the family is photographed under the flagstaff –
Beyond all this, the wish to be alone.

Beneath it all, desire of oblivion runs:
Despite the artful tensions of the calendar,
The life insurance, the tabled fertility rites,
The costly aversion of the eyes from death –
Beneath it all, desire of oblivion runs.[61]

Like 'Beauty', 'Wants' concentrates motifs from letters: 'the wish to be alone', sex and marriage, death-fear, death-desire. The poem also alludes to other texts and media: Larkin figures society's demands (its unwanted 'address') as 'invitation-cards', 'printed directions'. 'The artful tensions of the calendar' implies that poetry's more 'artful' tensions can see 'beyond' and 'beneath' such inscriptions or prescriptions. Thus rhythm conspires with the first-person plural to draw the reader in. The repeated structures of phrase and clause reinforce the enclosing refrain-lines, with their key-change both within and between the stanzas. The overall movement is disturbingly seductive. It proves, as prose cannot do, the psychological point. 'Wants' (which has something in common with Thomas's 'Melancholy' as well as 'Rain') exposes the nexus between solipsism and suicide by dramatising desire's nihilistic mode. The poem's rhythmic vibration also parallels Yeats's 'Nor know that what disturbs our blood/ Is but its longing for the tomb'.[62] Poetic rhythm derives from (and hence clarifies) all our bio-rhythms. Larkin's later poem, 'The Life with a Hole in it', proves the point negatively. Here 'life' is represented as paralysis: 'locked' and 'Blocked' by a 'Three-handed struggle between/ Your wants, the world's for you', and death.[63] The 'wants' of 'Wants', less narrowly Larkin's own, symbolise dark psychic tides in existential rather than theoretical terms. 'The Life with a Hole in it' is a poem with a rhythmic hole in it. For a poet to lose rhythm is to lose poetry, and hence any 'stay against confusion'. 'Wants' is a stay; 'The Life with a Hole in it', only confusion. Larkin's development might be said to reverse Thomas's. As his lyric 'impulse' recedes, psychoanalytical language, epistolary language, resurfaces and weakens the poetry.

Thomas and Larkin raise the stakes for lyric as psychology. Larkin calls a poem: 'the crossroads of my thoughts, my feelings, my imaginings, my wishes, & my verbal sense', all of which 'normally … run parallel'.[64] Synapses again: a rare intensity. Perhaps comparing poems with letters as psychological events tells us something about the difference between the poetic crossroads and the two-way – or sometimes one-way – epistolary street. But psychodrama does not have to be centre-stage for lyric to be doing psychological or mindful or myriad-mindful work. 'Beauty', rhythm, has incalculable effects.

To take one of Thomas's more explicitly 'positive' poems: 'Tall Nettles' is an epiphany with, it would seem, minimal subjective content. The 'I'-speaker simply 'likes' something twice. Yet 'This corner of the farmyard' attains an interior, possibly therapeutic, presence:

> Tall nettles cover up, as they have done
> These many springs, the rusty harrow, the plough
> Long worn out, and the roller made of stone:
> Only the elm butt tops the nettles now.
>
> This corner of the farmyard I like most:
> As well as any bloom upon a flower
> I like the dust on the nettles, never lost
> Except to prove the sweetness of a shower. (119)

'Tall Nettles' inscribes a movement that runs between past and present, obsolescence and freshness; and in which Nature prevails over human tools (of which the elm has been victim). There may also be a sense in which the nettles figure protection or renewal for some 'corner' of the unconscious mind. The second quatrain begins by dropping down a rhetorical key from the first. But the inversion of object and verb throws weight onto 'This corner', and the quatrain's sentence-structure, in a further inversion, starts, rather than ends, with a simple one-line statement, then swells into rhetorical crescendo. This mirror-image syntax is one means of enclosing the poem's corner-universe. The quatrains are also linked by rhyme-patterns. 'Flower' and 'shower' are full rhymes, as are 'plough' and 'now'. The first and third rhyme-words of each quatrain also match in being off-rhymes: 'done'/'stone'; 'most'/'lost'. But rhyme-words are only part of a larger orchestration of sound. Indeed, the full rhymes partly rhyme with one other: the finality of 'flower' and 'shower' increased by how they extend 'plough' and 'now'. There is also an assonantal pattern whereby the sounds in 'nettles' pervade the poem: rusty, elm butt, stone, tops, most, the internal off-rhyme dust/lost, except, sweetness. Rhythm, perhaps a rhythm of recovery from something unnamed, turns the sensory into the subjective. As it reverberates in mind and body, as the poem moves to its cathartic climax, the reader shares in the speaker's salutary feeling of organic kinship with the nettles. Here, as elsewhere, Thomas intertwines the psychology and ecology of being 'an inhabitant of the earth'. Perhaps when 'poems' deny or dismantle all poetry's 'traditional' structures, they cut their ties to deep psycho-ecology. By disconnecting mind and body, this may heap confusion upon confusion.

Edward Thomas's poetry faces into an 'unknown' that spans metaphysics and history. But the unknown starts with, and from, the self. The ultimate symbolic forest of 'Lights Out', 'shelf above shelf', may not only secrete war and death. It may also return Thomas to the original forest – the hidden self, the 'dumb source', the mystery – from which his lyric emerged: 'Its silence I hear and obey/ That I may lose my way/ And myself'. The unknown is poetry too. The lyric as psychology compels and impels Edward Thomas's poetic journey.

Archipelagic Thomas

The story of 'Edward Thomas and the English lyric' continues. Thirty years ago, speaking for poets, Ted Hughes called Thomas 'the father of us all' (although he failed to specify 'us').[1] Today, poets are still paying enthusiastic tribute. But this Afterword will be less concerned with Thomas's 'influence' than with his broader presence in British and Irish poetry, and some reasons for it. Thomas stays on the radar of poets and readers from different quarters of the 'Anglo-Celtic archipelago' (as the Australian poet Les Murray calls it), partly because he was exceptionally alert to the 'Celtic' as well as 'Anglo' strands in poetry of his own day: to Yeats as well as Hardy. That alertness informed his reading of earlier poetry and his response to Frost.

1. 'KINDRED POINTS'

Thomas grew up in London. His father was Welsh, his mother from a Welsh and English family. Thomas wrote in 1900:

> After all, Wales is good for me. In spite of my accidentally Cockney nativity, the air here seems to hold in it some virtue essential to my well-being, and I always feel, in the profoundest sense, at home.[2]

But he later called the English region which he evokes (creates) in *The South Country* (1909) 'a kind of home … to those modern people who belong nowhere',[3] and 'home' would prove an elusive locus in his poetry: 'That land,/ My home, I have never seen' (64). Thomas's 'at-homeness' or nationality, as between Wales and England, has been variously construed by biographers and critics – and, indeed, by Thomas himself. Jean Moorcroft Wilson flatly states: 'Thomas saw no contradiction in his dual allegiance.'⁴ If so, a factor in the appeal of Doughty's *Dawn in Britain* may have been that Celtic Britain erases borders from 'this home of my race' (see p. 132). Guy Cuthbertson and Lucy Newlyn find *some* contradiction in the 'puzzle of Thomas's hybrid national identity', his 'marginal, displaced identity'. Yet they also argue that the war changed matters: that 'becoming a conscious Englishman clearly involved a weakening of [Thomas's] Welsh consciousness'. His wartime tendency to 'include Wales in "England"' can be seen either as a symptomatic 'weakening' or as dissolving a possible dualism.⁵ Welsh mountains are on the horizon of 'This England', and in 'Words' the English language encompasses 'some sweetness/ From Wales'. Andrew Webb, in *Edward Thomas and World Literary Studies*, moves Thomas (and sees him as tacitly moving) in the opposite direction. He aims to reposition Thomas 'as a Welsh writer'; to 'recover him for an English-language Welsh tradition that is currently … emerging from the shadows of its Anglicisation'. For Webb, the English-Welsh literary relationship – and hence Thomas – is a site of colonial/economic inequality where a 'dominant' nation has occluded an 'emergent' nation.⁶

Whatever we think of this proposition, Webb is right to stress Thomas's attention to Welsh literature, mythology and folklore; his attachment to Welsh mentors like the bard Gwili and the historian O. M. Edwards. Welsh material appears throughout Thomas's prose, but his chief 'Welsh' works are *Beautiful Wales* (1905); *Celtic Stories* (1911), a re-telling of Welsh and Irish legends; and, most importantly, his autobiographical novel *The Happy-Go-Lucky Morgans* (1913). This novel, which concerns a London-Welsh family, prepares for poetry; as does Thomas's more direct autobiography, *The Childhood of Edward Thomas*, where Wales has a less central but significant role. Thomas was dissatisfied with *Beautiful Wales*, written hurriedly and (owing to his ignorance of north Wales) padded with covertly English scenes.[7] He gradually got to know mountainy and urban-industrial Wales, and developed a love-hate relationship with Swansea. Thomas wanted to write *The Heart of Wales* as a follow-up to *The Heart of England* (1906), although probably for a smaller market.[8] There were financial reasons why he lived in Steep, Hampshire, not too far from London, and wrote more about England than about Wales. Webb comments: 'the fact that most of Thomas's journalistic work was carried out for London-based institutions should not be read as a straightforward statement of his national allegiance'.[9]

But even if Thomas were given to straightforward statements, neither London nor its journalistic and literary milieu was (is) 'England'. Roy Foster dubs nineteenth-century Irish emigrants to London 'Micks on the Make', and London's attractions included its status as the print-culture metropolis.[10] Yeats 'made it' in London. There were Jocks and Taffs on the literary make too. In the 1890s Irish, Scottish and Welsh poets belonged to the effectively 'Anglo-Celtic' Rhymers' Club. As Yeats in 1890, so Thomas in 1900 began a London career as a literary journalist and freelance writer. He also resembles Yeats, whose family moved between London and Ireland, in possessing the hinterland of a childhood London, spliced or spiced with somewhere else. Or two somewheres: Thomas's Welsh paternal grandparents lived in Wiltshire and, as a child, he spent more time there than in Wales. To confuse matters further, he said in 1910: 'Wiltshire is almost my native county'.[11] Art may depend on formative encounters between 'familiar' and 'strange', but the custodians of national literatures do not always embrace writers who have multiple affiliations. If England appropriates 'Celtic' writers, Irish or Scottish or Welsh cultural nationalism can find literary migration to England problematic. This is one basis on which Yeats's 'Irishness' has been questioned, as has Thomas's 'Welshness'.

But does latterday willingness to repatriate Yeats or Thomas resolve the question? Although the family in *The Happy-Go-Lucky*

Morgans is called 'more Welsh than Balhamitish',[12] the novel itself is
as London as it is Welsh. It might also be called 'archipelagic': John
Kerrigan's term for a way of reading the map of literary relations in
these mixed-up islands.[13] One chapter is certainly 'archipelagic' *avant
la lettre*: 'Mr Stodham Speaks for England – Fog Supervenes'.[14] Here
a London clerk makes a patriotic speech. The speech prefigures
Thomas's wartime essays, and invokes three of his poetic touch-
stones: Coleridge's 'Fears in Solitude'; Wordsworth's 'True to the
kindred points of Heaven and Home' and lines about this world/
earth being 'where we have our happiness or not at all'. Mr Stodham
places England as 'home' in a series of necessarily defining 'boundar-
ies', and says: 'He is a bold man who hopes to do without earth,
England, family, and self'. Having spoken, Mr Stodham shyly 'runs
away'; a jingoistic character (Higgs) misinterprets him by singing
'Rule Britannia'; the youthful narrator (Arthur) shouts 'Home Rule
for Ireland'; and there is tension until everyone, except Higgs, sings
the pacific 'Land of my Fathers' (see p. 126). Webb calls Mr Stodham's
speech 'confused'. He sees him as unable to give 'England' a
locally-based meaning it has irrevocably lost; and Thomas's poetry
as a form of critique which confirms that loss.[15] Webb overlooks
Thomas's 'kindred points' and serio-comic tone – which includes
someone asking whether 'London fog' can be viewed patriotically.
Fog or confusion seems part of the point: the gap between political
rhetorics and genuine feeling for different locales. It's relevant that
Arthur and his friend Philip Morgan think of a woodland wilderness
outside London as 'Our Country'. 'Loss', indeed, might potentially
Celticise and romanticise England. But perhaps, rather, this chapter
suggests ways of finding England: finding it in terms that draw
on Welsh and Irish terms. Scotland makes an appearance at the
chapter's end, where Arthur, who desires to live 'in a state of poetic
pain', thrills to Walter Scott's 'And, Saxon, I am Roderick Dhu' from
The Lady of the Lake. Through the fog we may at least glimpse an
archipelagic ground for poetry.

2. 'CELTIC' POETICS

Thomas's friend W. H. Hudson wrote of *The Happy-Go-Lucky Morgans*: 'I believe he has taken the wrong path and is wandering lost in the vast wilderness … He is essentially a poet, one would say of the Celtic variety, and this book shows it, I think, more than any of the others.'[16] What is a poet 'of the Celtic variety'? Thomas's criticism has much to say on this topic, and *Beautiful Wales* contains a satirical attack on 'lovers of the Celt':

> Their aim and ideal is to go about the world in a state of self-satisfied dejection, interrupted, and perhaps sustained, by days when they consume strange mixed liquors to the tune of all the fine old Celtic songs which are fashionable. If you can discover a possible Celtic great-grandmother, you are at once among the chosen. I cannot avoid the opinion that to boast of the Celtic spirit is to confess you have it not … I should be inclined to call these lovers of the Celt a class of 'decadents', not unrelated to Mallarmé, and of aesthetes … They are sophisticated, neurotic – the fine flower of sounding cities … But it is probably true that when one has said that the typical Celt is seldom an Imperialist, a great landowner, a brewer, a cabinet minister … one has exhausted the list of his weaknesses …[17]

Thomas satirises 'Celticism' both as a literary package and as a politicised construct of nineteenth-century race-theory. It might be argued that the potency of the former compensated for the perpetual worldly defeat attributed by the latter. Literary Celticism did indeed reach its apogee in the 1890s: mainly thanks to Yeats's early poetry, founded on 'aestheticism' together with the Irish sources opened up by his ambition to create a literary movement. Yeats's 'The Wanderings of Oisin' reinvented James Macpherson's *Ossian* for a post-Romantic (Symbolist) rather than proto-Romantic ethos. Thomas traces 'much of the writing' of his Celt-loving decadents back to 'the vague, unobservant things in Ossian'. Here he does not mean Yeats, although he is again satirical when he refers to Yeats 'giving drugs [laudanum] to all the Irish heroes in turn'.[18] The Celtic vogue extended beyond the 1890s and beyond poetry. Thomas noted in 1910:

> This is the day of the Irish. They are – if not altogether to their own liking or advantage – the pet Kelts of the English. The Scotch are too triumphantly established, the Welsh and Cornish too little known, to count.[19]

Compare Louis MacNeice in *Autumn Journal*: 'Why do we like being Irish? Partly because/ It gives us a hold on the sentimental English/ As members of a world that never was,/ Baptised with fairy water …'.[20] Thomas and MacNeice are well-placed to spot English misreadings of 'Celts' and 'Celtic' poetry, as to understand Anglo-Celtic interactions. By the same token, Thomas resists any tendency to raise spurious barriers between poetry in English and in the Celtic languages. Thus he rejects the claim that Celtic poetry observes Nature with a precision and passion absent from English poetry before Wordsworth: a claim, he says, 'controverted by half the Elizabethans'.[21]

Thomas praised Ezra Pound's *Personae* for containing 'no apostrophe, no rhetoric, nothing "Celtic"'.[22] Although Pound actually owed some Celtic debts to Yeats, he and Eliot can obscure the fact that early twentieth-century poetry was as prolific in imitations of Yeats as 1930s poetry in imitations of Auden. As his aesthetic changed, Yeats rejected his Irish 'imitators': 'was there ever dog that praised his fleas?'[23] But not every flea or wannabe 'Celtic' poet was Irish. Thomas writes of *Ossian*: 'The figure … dimly seen through mountain mists and waveringly mirrored in wild lakes, which was mistaken for a refined and ancient Caledonian, was really the ghost of a long-haired, wan, romantic Englishman of the end of the nineteenth century' (this may be partly a joke against himself). Alfred Noyes's collection *The Loom of Years* (1902) fits the bill: 'His "Love-Song of Morna" is pretty and Celtic and all that; but the words "faint" and "dim" and "drear" and "desolate" have become jaded during their gay life in the last ten years, and are no longer able to make a poem by their presence.'[24] (It must be admitted that 'dim' and 'drear' occur in poems by Thomas.)[25] Thomas is aware that Yeats – 'in some ways the most influential artist of today', 'that most dangerous of masters' – has a peculiarly infectious style. His reviews often measure the degree to which lesser Irish poets (such as Katharine Tynan, Padraic Colum, Seumas O'Sullivan and James Stephens) manage to assert their individuality. He congratulates Colum because: 'His style is, wonderful to relate, his own, and free even from the best influences of his contemporaries in Ireland.' At a lower level, Thomas attacks all 'purveyors of a flimsy jargon, neither English nor Irish, which is … well suited to the half-thoughts and invented emotions of a set of mountebanks'.[26] But he is toughest on the 'loud-mouthed Celticity' (a nice oxymoron) of the Scottish William Sharp, further costumed as 'Fiona Macleod'. He indicts Sharp's posthumous *The Dominion of Dreams* for falsity that is the enemy of poetry:

> Sharp was a clever man and we are not going to be so bold as to pronounce that he was fundamentally insincere … [But he] was no discoverer, though that need not have prevented him from being sincere, any more than it compelled him to make a recipe by which Celtic studies might be cooked *ad infinitum* … Such is the fault of the journalist from Macpherson down to William Sharp, the fault of the journalist pretending to be something else, using other men's ideas, which is his right, but with an assumed ardour, which is his condemnation.[27]

Sometimes Thomas even perceives Yeats himself as a 'victim of the Irish literary movement'. This phrase occurs in a review of *Plays for an Irish Theatre*; and by 'victim' Thomas means that Yeats's plays are too exclusively focused on 'Irish subjects' to have activated all his 'qualities of … mind'. He thinks that 'On Baile's Strand' is 'so much occupied with the rich, heavy fabric of Irish heroic life' that Yeats 'has lost some of the more inward beauties in the gleam of their raiment'. Elsewhere, he maintains that 'old mythological terms' do not have an intrinsic poetic value; that Yeats is at his best when his 'symbols are natural, ancient, instinctive, not invented'. This book has already suggested that symbolic intensity, a belief in the primacy of 'inward beauties', aligns Thomas with Yeats. It's also the case that Yeats preceded (and influenced) Frost in re-affirming the nexus between speech and poetry and varying the blank-verse line (see p. 29). In 1907 Thomas wrote that Yeats 'proves as much as Wordsworth's preface that the speech of poetry can be that of life'.[28] For Thomas, the Irish literary movement, powered by Yeats and Synge, was about poetry, about speech, about rhythm. He calls 'Irish rhythm' 'a cause of renewal of youth in modern verse': a renewal he connects with folksong, with 'Irish fidelity to their native music'. Thomas does more than follow Yeats book by book. Uncannily, he almost seems to urge and anticipate Yeats's later development. What some of the plays lack are: 'especially the intellectual qualities, which I have … recognised in his printed and spoken utterances'. Thomas admires Yeats's prose for containing 'a body of critical ideas which it would be impossible to equal in England today', while seeing that not every idea has yet been poetically realised. And, just as Thomas discusses textual variants in new editions of Keats or Shelley, so he tracks the many revisions in the *Collected Works* that Yeats was then issuing. This brings Thomas up against the grain of speech and poetry. He usually finds that Yeats's revisions make his language more colloquial and concentrated; sometimes condemns changes as made for change's sake; always regrets that Yeats has not 'thrown all this energy of heart and head into new work'. As far as we know, Thomas never read Yeats's watershed collection *Responsibilities* (1914, 1916). But it's fresh 'creation' he desires when, in his last Yeats review, he loses patience with still more revision: 'He seems to have been revising in cold blood what was written in a mood now inaccessible.'[29]

Yet that 'mood' had helped to align Thomas's post-Romantic aesthetic bearings with Yeats's. Further, for all his resistance, Celticism percolated into Thomas's Wales. In *Beautiful Wales* his attack on 'lovers of the Celt' is followed by a rhapsodic roll-call of Welsh rivers. Here Thomas invokes Arthurian legend, calls some rivers the 'old, deserted … pathways of the early gods', and refers to 'Ebbw and Usk, that cut across my childhood with silver bars'. *The Childhood of Edward Thomas*, a conscious portrait of the emergent artist, traces how Wales became a romantic (Romantic) complex: the 'abiding memory' of several scenes; 'the street in Caerleon, the river and the Round Table'; 'phrases and images from *The Adventures of the Knights of the Round Table*, and a curious illusion of a knight with a shield kneeling at the foot of a pillar in the photograph at home of Tintern Abbey'. In *The Happy-Go-Lucky Morgans*, Arthur (whose name is no coincidence) visits the Morgans' Welsh home-place, and recognises the gap between the actual 'Abercorran' and the 'beautiful fantastic geography' in his head.[30] This weirdly atmospheric fiction – an unconscious portrait of the emergent artist or a portrait of the artist's unconscious self – essentially concerns Thomas's own fantastic imaginative geography and 'desire of beauty'. First, the characters are all aspects of Thomas as embryonic lyric protagonist. They are mostly depressed or alienated, far from 'happy', and two of them die: Philip (see p. 70) and his elder brother David, who goes mad in a Welsh tower because he is 'too poetical'. When calling Thomas a poet 'of the Celtic variety', Hudson may have had the 'melancholy Celt' stereotype in mind (a possible factor in Thomas's anatomy of melancholy). Second, everyone in *The Happy-Go-Lucky Morgans* is fixated on places and houses. Some of these are explicitly symbolic: 'the Castle of Leaves', 'the house of the days of the year'. As chronicler of the Morgan milieu, Arthur bears witness to the mind's endeavour to connect physical and metaphysical worlds; immediate worlds and lost or distant worlds. Abercorran, which shadows the Morgans' 'Abercorran House' in London, figures something lost – spiritually rather than territorially – is it poetry? Similarly, for Mr Torrance, a character who represents Thomas's life as a 'doomed hack', 'the valley of the river Uther … make[s] the one real thing that I know and cannot forget'. (There is no 'real' River Uther.) Again, 'Our Country' is 'supernaturally beautiful' precisely because it has 'London for a foil and background'. Guy Cuthbertson points out that Thomas is also recreating and mourning lost landscapes from his London childhood; but Romantic nostalgia, the novel's dominant 'mood', centres on Wales.[31] A shrewd reviewer noted that Thomas's recollected 'boyish' subjectivity had 'imported into the Celtic twilight of Abercorran House a twilight of its own'.[32] Perhaps writing *The Happy-Go-Lucky Morgans* also took Thomas back to his first reading of Yeats: to a poetic source.

Did Yeats inject some 'natural magic' into Thomas's approach to Nature? In his essay 'The Celtic Element in Literature' Yeats corrects Matthew Arnold's use of the term: 'I do not think he understood that our "natural magic" is but the ancient religion of the world, the ancient worship of nature and that troubled ecstasy before her, that certainty of all beautiful places being haunted, which it brought into men's minds'. For Thomas, Yeats's 'natural magic' consists in his ability to 'plunge us, as few other poets writing in English can, into a world where all the values are changed and the parochialism of humanity is forgotten, or rather it is inconceivable that it should ever have existed'. To illustrate this, he quotes from 'Into the Twilight': 'Come, heart, where hill is heaped upon hill:/ For there the mystical brotherhood/ Of sun and moon and hollow and wood/ And river and stream work out their will …'. Thomas (who has clearly read 'The Celtic Element') is less positive when he connects Yeats's over-reliance on 'old mythological terms' with his ascribing natural magic to 'a survival of a religious attitude'.[33] Yet, if we strip religion out of the Yeats-Thomas equation, it's possible to

AFTERWORD: ARCHIPELAGIC THOMAS

see Yeats as leaving his mark on Thomas's prose landscapes: helping the Romantic poets and Richard Jefferies to make them soul-landscapes:

> This is not the South Country which measures about two hundred miles from east to west and fifty from north to south. In some ways it is incomparably larger than any country that was ever mapped, since upon nothing less than the infinite can the spirit disport itself. In other ways it is far smaller – as when a mountain with tracts of sky and cloud and the full moon glass themselves in a pond, a little pond.[34]

Back in *Beautiful Wales* 'Morgan Rhys', the alter ego who personifies Thomas's youthful discovery of poetry, is allowed to be 'something of a Celt in the bad, fashionable sense of that strange word'. For Rhys, poetry reveals 'the possibility of a state of mind and spirit in which alone all things could be fully known at their highest power'. He has mystical moments during which he steps 'over the edge of the world and [sees] the gods leaning from the stars among the clouds'. Unsurprisingly, Rhys admires Yeats. In 1902 Thomas cited Yeats, together with 'Keats … *The Opium Eater & Religio Medici*', when listing 'a few books or passages in books … which quite overcome my intelligence, because (I think) I am so much in sympathy with them that they seem to belong to my own experience'.[35]

3. SYMBOLIC TOPOGRAPHIES

Thomas, like Yeats, moved on from twilight. And *The Childhood of Edward Thomas* is a much earthier portrait of the proto-poet or almost-poet than is the doubly retro (perhaps necessarily so) *Happy-Go-Lucky Morgans*. Thomas also had the robust antidote of Robert Frost. Yet his poetry's central mystery – that of being 'An old inhabit-ant of earth' – has not entirely lost contact with Yeats's 'mystical brotherhood' and haunted places: 'And star and I and wind and deer/

Are in the dark together …' (138). Their different reactions to Darwin, different means of getting beyond 'the parochialism of humanity', intersect.

In Thomas's poetry 'beautiful fantastic geography' becomes a symbolic topography for all his journeys. Twilight lingers here and there, especially when a poem has a Welsh connection or represents a Muse-place or both. 'The Unknown Bird', in which the bird's song 'wandering beyond my shore' figures an otherworldly summons to poetry, has links with the 'Uther valley' chapter of *The Happy-Go-Lucky Morgans*. The poet-speaker says: 'I told/ The naturalists; but neither had they heard/ Anything like the notes that did so haunt me' (55). Perhaps this finds literary 'naturalism' as wanting as science. 'The Ash Grove', another haunted poem, mingles Welsh hills with a Welsh song. Here Thomas's revision of the Wordsworthian epiphany (see p. 89) includes giving it a 'ghostly' and nostalgic tilt:

… And now an ash grove far from those hills can bring
The same tranquillity in which I wander a ghost
With a ghostly gladness, as if I heard a girl sing

The song of the Ash Grove soft as love uncrossed,
And then in a crowd or in distance it were lost,
But the moment unveiled something unwilling to die
And I had what most I desired, without search or desert or cost.
(108)

Such recession invites Thomas's own comment on the Ossianic trope of wallowing in loss: 'The reader feels that it is a baseness to exist.'[36] Nonetheless, like the twilight zone of 'An Old Song II', this is a place where poetry exists or comes into being. 'An Old Song II' has a partly Welsh origin: Thomas draws on a walk 'to the Mumbles up to Oystermouth Castle and back chiefly by the sands'.[37] But his vocational epiphany has multifarious sources, and it's the 'roving' sea-shanty 'Amsterdam' that crystallises them (see p. 21). The moon-lit 'footbridge' was a symbol for the lyric poem before it appeared (if it did) on the Welsh coast. It's also worth noting what doesn't survive into Thomas's poetry from Romantic Wales or the mood of *The Happy-Go-Lucky Morgans*. The Arthurian quest turns into something else. Legendary fancies, like 'the Castle of Leaves', become complex symbolism: the mental 'cloud castle' of 'Wind and Mist', aspens 'shaking their leaves'. In 'Roads', the gods' pathways are absorbed into the road to France. Here the Welsh goddess 'Helen of the roads,/ The mountain ways of Wales/ And the Mabinogion tales' mainly reinforces the mythic status of the road itself. She also gives twilight ghostliness a new edge in a poem haunted by the omnipresent 'dead/ Returning' from France (107).

Two early poems, 'The Mountain Chapel' and 'The Manor Farm', lay out an aesthetic (also psychological) antinomy, which implicates Wales and England as 'home'. Thomas's Welsh mountain-scenario has elements of 'Celtic' desolation and residuality: 'Chapel and grave-stones, old and few,/ Are shrouded by a mountain fold/ From sound and view/ Of life …' (43). Yet, paradoxically, 'a man could/ Be happy here'. There is again a link with *The Happy-Go-Lucky Morgans*, where David Morgan is 'said to have worshipped a god who never entered chapel or church' and 'to pray for the end of man or of the world'.[38] But the poem deflects both Christian and pagan 'worship', and moves Celticist melancholia onto the harder Darwinian ground of 'When gods were young/ This wind was old'. The same wind blows through Thomas's derelict 'English' landscapes (hence obliquely Celticised). In almost exaggerated contrast, 'The Manor Farm', a sunlit rather than 'shrouded' poem, evokes Priors Dean down the road in Hampshire. This different denominational/communal/ pastoral scenario – 'church and yew/ And farmhouse' – figures continuous tradition 'for ages since/ This England, Old already, was called Merry' (45). Here 'oldness' is more positive. Thomas then wrote his 'old songs', which touch both English and Welsh bases (the first being a version of 'The Lincolnshire Poacher'). His next poem,

'The Combe', its locus 'ancient and dark', brings historic England and Wales together in war, in the dead badger: 'That most ancient Briton of English beasts' (48). 'Ancient' is a favourite Yeats-adjective, with which Thomas's more usual 'old' shares some resonances. Yeats's poetry both reflects and exploits a process whereby Ireland has become exotic to itself – 'auto-exotic' – for ancientness, among other qualities. Joep Leerssen calls Irish cultural nationalism 'a form of internalised exoticism'.[39] Perhaps Thomas's shifting insider/outsider status works auto-exotically too. Perhaps 'England' and 'Wales' are subsumed into dialectics that keep his symbolic topographies at once 'familiar' and 'strange'. 'Our Country' needs its London backdrop. In *The South Country* Thomas refers to 'days and places which send us in search of another kind of felicity than that which dwells under the Downs', and continues: 'Then, or at home looking at a map of Britain, the West calls, out of Wiltshire and out of Cornwall and Devon beyond, out of Monmouth and Glamorgan and Gower and Caermarthen, with a voice of dead Townsends, Eastaways, Thomases, Philipses, Treharnes, Marendaz, sea men and mountain men.'[40] Here 'the West', both English and Welsh, 'calls' in a way more often associated with Irish or Scottish literature.

Thomas's map-making is ancestral, spiritual, psychological and aesthetic. It might also project an 'archipelagic' reading of his poems. Yet such a reading would necessarily focus on poetic structure rather than panoramic vista. Further, there are many gradations between the Downs and the West as symbolic topography. Thomas's auto-exotic relation to England and Wales renders them as poetically flexible as Yeats rendered Ireland. He notes how London street-names constitute 'a puzzle map of England', and something similar applies to his poetry. Just as Thomas always deplores guides to 'Hardy's Wessex' ('no better than offering pig's bones as relics of saints'),[41] so there may be no 'Edward Thomas country'. For instance, the passage quoted above – another of Thomas's cumulative prose roll-calls – invokes counties. As a 'neighbouring point' on Thomas's poetic compass (see p. 127), the county suggests some ways in which that compass works. When reviewing country books, Thomas had noticed a trend towards 'county patriotism'.[42] In 'Words' counties contribute individual accents to 'English words'. The speaker desires not only 'some sweetness/ From Wales', but also

From Wiltshire and Kent
And Herefordshire,
And the villages there, –
From the names, and the things
No less. (92)

But in '"Home"' counties 'divide' soldiers (see p. 131). Again, counties can contribute to a lyrical rather than national unit. 'Adlestrop' ends:

And for that minute a blackbird sang
Close by, and round him, mistier,
Farther and farther, all the birds
Of Oxfordshire and Gloucestershire. (51)

The blackbird marks a lyric centre; counties – both thing and name – mark its shifting circumference. These county-names suggest how, in Thomas's poetry, 'names' anchor and intensify 'words'. Perhaps poetry turns word into name. Lob's special 'care' is to name places, birds and plants (77). In 'Adlestrop' assonantal rhyme – 'mistier' – prepares for the county-names being absorbed into poetic music. 'Mistier' is at once visual and aural, and its echo in the names indeed seems to take this microcosm 'Farther and farther'. Besides being stitched into the verse-fabric, counties contribute to symbolic clusters. Thomas's poems name Wiltshire more often than any other county. 'Hampshire' (as opposed to local Hampshire names) never appears: probably because often an invisible vantage-point. Wiltshire may mediate between Hampshire and Wales. Thomas's 'Wiltshire' is western, mysterious and mythic: it's where English myth and history meet (in 'Lob'); where myth and Thomas's psychic history meet (in 'The Other'). Indeed, Wiltshire broadly takes the 'quintessential' place that Thomas had once proposed for Hampshire: 'Its people, place names, forests, churches, cities, villages, old camps and boundaries, if studied aright, would give up the quintessence and spirit of England and English history.'[43] But, as between all Thomas's poetic loci, there are intricate road-networks rather than 'boundaries'. 'Forest' seems to be everywhere. Even so, Hampshire and Wiltshire complement one another as sources of symbolic topography. Hampshire is, up to a point, home ground: its history, introduced by 'Up in the Wind', is more closely meshed with locality; and its 'spirit of wildness', also introduced by 'Up in the Wind', colours much of Thomas's psychological weather. Rain, wind and mist converge on the hangers (tree-covered slopes) around Steep.

In *Maurice Maeterlinck* Thomas says that a poem must 'create about itself a world of its own'.[44] His poetry is a model for other poets because its worlds are seamlessly interior and exterior, because they are multi-dimensional in time and space and mind. Witness the infinite minute of 'Adlestrop', the precise co-ordinates of 'Thaw':

Over the land freckled with snow half-thawed
The speculating rooks at their nests cawed
And saw from elm-tops, delicate as flower of grass,
What we below could not see, Winter pass. (114)

Like the end of 'Adlestrop', this brief quatrain/sentence covers spatial and temporal distance. Syntax is integral to perspective: from the prepositional phrase that occupies the first line, to the subordinated 'we below' in the last. The triangulation of 'we', 'land' and 'rooks' involves cross-overs ('freckled', 'speculating' and their assonance), as well as different vantage-points. The syntactical and rhythmic resolution 'Winter pass' ultimately allies 'us' with the birds. If 'Adlestrop' is about 'song', 'Thaw' might represent the 'speculative' aspect of Thomas's lyric: its enquiry into relations between humanity and earth. Poetry has long explored those relations. But Thomas pondered them at a moment when they were being recast by modernity, when a new consciousness was in formation. That may give his symbolic topographies, his lyric microcosms, his lyric ecology a special (and archipelagic) appeal. His poetry is also the 'quintessence' of a unique intimacy with country books. Here he should be considered a significant theorist. Besides transmuting his actual and literary hinterlands, Thomas's poems condense complex ideas (derived from those hinterlands) about the mediation of Nature and landscape. The following passage, already quoted in Chapter 2, seems to reach for poetry:

> We are not merely twentieth-century Londoners or Kentish men or Welshmen … And of these many folds in our nature the face of the earth reminds us, and perhaps, even where there are no more marks visible upon the land than there were in Eden, we are aware of the passing of time in ways too difficult and strange for the explanation of historian and zoologist and philosopher. It is this manifold nature that responds with such indescribable depth and variety to the appeals of many landscapes.[45]

Of the 'many folds in our nature' Edward Thomas's poetry reminds us.

* * *

A last word about poets, Thomas's lyric and the archipelago. There are many reasons, whether to do with sensibility or aesthetics, why Thomas might attract poets from all quarters; why they might 'remix' his poems. But I want to stick with symbolic topography, and cite two examples of how, having taken something from Yeats, Thomas gave something back to Irish poetry. For instance, Seamus Heaney was not the first poet to write a poem called 'Digging': Edward Thomas wrote two. Heaney's Belfast mentor Michael

McLaverty introduced him to Thomas's poetry in the early 1960s, and Heaney's 'Digging' contains evidence that the introduction mattered. In Thomas's first 'Digging' poem, the speaker 'think[s]/ Only with scents' and savours 'Odours that rise/ When the spade wounds the root of tree' (79). This parallels Heaney's 'The cold smell of potato mould … the curt cuts of an edge/ Through living roots awaken in my head'.[46] Since Heaney's 'Digging' has been read as an early manifesto, it's interesting that immersion in sense-experience, figured by digging, seems common aesthetic ground. In both poems, synaesthesia is transmitted by strongly stressed assonance. Thomas's second 'Digging' poem connects (as do his place-name poems) with the poems in Heaney's *Wintering Out* (1972), where landscape becomes historicised, archaeological and inscribed by war. Thomas asks: 'What matter makes my spade for tears or mirth,/ Letting down two clay pipes into the earth?/ The one I smoked, the other a soldier/ Of Blenheim, Ramillies, and Malplaquet/ Perhaps …' (99). This vista extends to 'bones of ancients'. Heaney's poem 'Toome' conjures up 'a hundred centuries'// loam, flints, musket-balls'.[47] Heaney later wrote two poems that directly invoke 'As the team's head-brass' (which he calls 'Homeric'): 'Edward Thomas on the Lagans Road' and 'In a field'.[48] But, as regards symbolic topography and 'war pastoral', Heaney's links with Thomas go further back.

Thomas's model of war pastoral also enters poems written by Michael Longley during the Northern Ireland Troubles and after. 'Edward Thomas's War Diary' arranges passages from the diary so that they juxtapose home and violence in a way that covers civil war too: 'One night in the trenches/ You dreamed you were at home/ And couldn't stay for tea …'. Thomas is then said to wake 'where shell holes/ Filled with bloodstained water'. In 'Edward Thomas's Poem' Longley symbolises the mystery of Thomas's life, death and poetry by evoking the indecipherable notebook found in his pocket when he was killed: 'I couldn't read the poem'. The next stanza conflates the landscape of Thomas's death with 'Adlestrop'. In so doing, it suggests how his lyric has re-echoed since 1917:

From where he lay he could hear the skylark's
Skyward exultation, a chaffinch to his left
Fidgeting among the fallen branches,
Then all the birds of the Western Front.[49]

ABBREVIATIONS

Note: Bracketed numbers in the text are the page numbers of poems in Edward Thomas, *The Annotated Collected Poems*, ed. Edna Longley (Tarset: Bloodaxe Books, 2008).

B: The Bookman

DC: The Daily Chronicle

EF: Eleanor Farjeon, *Edward Thomas: The Last Four Years* (1958; Stroud: Sutton Publishing, 1997)

ER: The English Review

ETPW I: Edward Thomas Prose Writings, Vol. I: Autobiographies, ed. Guy Cuthbertson (Oxford: Oxford University Press, 2011)

ETPW II: Edward Thomas Prose Writings, Vol. II: England and Wales, ed. Guy Cuthbertson and Lucy Newlyn (Oxford: Oxford University Press, 2011)

FCPPP: Robert Frost, *Collected Poems, Prose, and Plays* (New York: The Library of America, 1995)

JMW: Jean Moorcroft Wilson, *Edward Thomas: From Adlestrop to Arras: A Biography* (London: Bloomsbury, 2015)

K: Edward Thomas, *Keats* (London: T. C. and E. C. Jack, 1916)

LCP: Philip Larkin, *Collected Poems*, ed. Anthony Thwaite (London: Marvell Press & Faber, 1988)

LGB: Letters from Edward Thomas to Gordon Bottomley, ed. R. George Thomas (London: Oxford University Press, 1968)

LM: Philip Larkin, *Letters to Monica*, ed. Anthony Thwaite (London: Faber, 2010)

LNB: A Language Not to be Betrayed: Selected Prose of Edward Thomas, ed. Edna Longley (Manchester: Carcanet, 1981)

LRF I: The Letters of Robert Frost, Vol. I: 1886-1920 (Cambridge, Mass: Harvard University Press, 2014)

LSL: Selected Letters of Philip Larkin, ed. Anthony Thwaite (London: Faber, 1992)

MM: Edward Thomas, *Maurice Maeterlinck* (London: Methuen, 1911)

MP: The Morning Post

RFET: Elected Friends: Robert Frost and Edward Thomas to One Another, ed. Matthew Spencer (New York: Handsel Books, 2003)

RJ: Edward Thomas, *Richard Jefferies: His Life and Work* (1909; repr. London: Faber, 1978)

RW: Philip Larkin, *Required Writing: Miscellaneous Pieces 1955-1982* (London: Faber, 1983)

SC: Edward Thomas, *The South Country* (London: J.M. Dent, 1909)

SR: The Saturday Review

TSL: Edward Thomas, *Selected Letters*, ed. R. George Thomas (Oxford: Oxford University Press, 1995)

NOTES

Preface

1 Note to Edward Thomas (ed.), *This England: An Anthology from her Writers* (Oxford: Oxford University Press, 1915); *DC*: 27 August 1901; *LNB*, 62-4.
2 *MM*, 28.
3 Published by Oxford University Press, 2011-.
4 See Guy Cuthbertson & Lucy Newlyn (eds), *Branch-Lines: Edward Thomas and Contemporary Poetry* (London: Enitharmon Press, 2007), 142, 124, 167, 150, 162.
5 Seamus Heaney, 'The Ministry of Fear', *North* (London: Faber, 1975), 65.
6 Andrew Webb, *Edward Thomas and World Literary Studies* (Cardiff: University of Wales Press, 2013), 1.
7 Review of Paul Elmer More, *Shelburne Essays: Second Series*, *Academy*: 19 August 1905; *LNB*, 8-9.
8 Cuthbertson & Newlyn, *Branch-Lines*, 99.
9 *LGB*, 251.

Chapter 1: 'The myriad-minded lyric'

1 *DC*: 27 August 1901; *LNB*, 62-4.
2 Review of Felix E. Schelling, *The English Lyric*, ?April 1913, Edward Thomas Collection, Cardiff University Library.
3 Virginia Jackson & Yopie Prins (eds), *The Lyric Theory Reader* (Baltimore: Johns Hopkins University Press, 2014), 452.
4 'Ecstasy', unpublished essay, Berg Collection, New York Public Library.
5 Jackson & Prins, *Lyric Theory Reader*, 451, 452, 457.
6 Charles Altieri, quoted *Lyric Theory Reader*, 255.
7 Ralph Cohen, 'History and Genre' (1986), reprinted *Lyric Theory Reader*, 58.
8 W. B. Yeats, *Collected Works*, Vol. V: Later Essays (New York: Scribner, 1994), 92; *Collected Works*, Vol. IV: Early Essays (New York: Scribner, 2007), 114, 116.
9 Review of Schelling, *The English Lyric*, see note 2; review of J. M. Synge, *Poems and Translations*, *DC*: 20 July 1909; *LNB*, 87.
10 Review of Arthur Symons, *The Romantic Movement in English Poetry*, *MP*: 20 January 1910; *LNB*, 17-19.
11 Review of George Leveson-Gower, *Poems*, *DC*: 21 February 1903.
12 *RW*, 49.
13 Review of John Masefield, *The Street of Today*, *SR*: 10 June 1911; *LGB*, 80, 171.
14 Thomas Pfau, *Romantic Moods: Paranoia, Trauma, and Melancholy, 1790-1840* (Baltimore: Johns Hopkins University Press, 2005), 70.
15 Mutlu Konuk Blasing, *Lyric Poetry: The Pain and Pleasure of Words* (Princeton & Oxford: Princeton University Press, 2007), 4.
16 *EF*, 46.
17 Theodor Adorno, *Aesthetic Theory*, tr. & ed. Robert Hulot-Kentor (Minneapolis: University of Minnesota Press, 1997), 167.
18 Louis MacNeice, *Collected Poems*, ed. Peter McDonald (London: Faber, 2007), 791, 162.
19 *RFET*, 38-9.
20 *SC*, 241.
21 See Jonathan Bate, *Romantic Ecology: Wordsworth and the Environmental Tradition* (London: Routledge, 1991).
22 *ETPW II*, 135.
23 Review of Walter Jerrold, ed., *The Book of Living Poets*, *DC*: 13 January 1908; *LNB*, 66.
24 *DC*: 27 August 1901; *LNB*, 62.
25 *DC*: 5 February 1907.
26 *LGB*, 187.
27 *B*: February 1914.
28 Review of Rudyard Kipling, *Actions and Reactions*, *SR*: 16 October 1909; review of John Davidson, *The Triumph of Mammon*, *DC*: 30 April 1907; *LNB*, 78-9.
29 Review of new verse, *DC*: 30 October 1905; *LNB*, 201-2; review of Laurence Housman and W. Somerset Maugham (eds), *The Venture: An Annual of Art and Literature*, *DC*: 28 November 1903.
30 Review of John Davidson, *Fleet Street and Other Poems*, *MP*: 17 June 1909.
31 Review of S. T. Coleridge, *Biographia Literaria*, ed. J. Shawcross, *DC*: 8 June 1908.
32 Review of A. C. Bradley, *Poetry for Poetry's Sake*, *DC*: 12 July 1902; review of A. C. Bradley, *Oxford Lectures on Poetry*, *MP*: 10 June, 1909; *LNB*, 12-14.

33 *LGB*, 181.

34 Review of T. S. Omond, *English Metrists in the Eighteenth and Nineteenth Centuries*, DC: 24 June 1907; review of Liddell, *Introduction*, DC: 18 September 1902; *LNB*, 12.

35 Review of W. H. Davies, *New Poems*, MP: 3 January 1907; *LNB*, 89-90; review of Walter de la Mare, *Songs of Childhood* and *Poems*, ER: December 1910; *LNB*, 98-100.

36 Reviews of Thomas Sturge Moore, *The Gazelles and Other Poems* DC: 21 April 1904; *Pan's Prophecy* DC: 14 August 1904; *Toleda and Other Odes*, DC: 27 November 1904. Review of Lascelles Abercrombie, *Emblems of Love*, DC: 28 December 1911.

37 Review of Robert Bridges, *Poetical Works*, Vol. VI, *Academy*: 14 October 1905.

38 See Note 23.

39 Edward Thomas, *Walter Pater* (London, Martin Secker, 1913), 220, 210; Thomas, *Algernon Charles Swinburne* (London: Martin Secker, 1912), 23, 171.

40 Review of W. B. Yeats, *Plays for an Irish Theatre*, Vols II and III, *Week's Survey*: 18 June 1904; *LNB*, 80-1.

41 Review of D. H. Lawrence, *Love Poems and Others*, DC: ?early 1913; *LNB*, 105-6.

42 Reviews of Ezra Pound, *Personae*, DC: 7 June, 1909; ER: June 1909, B: July 1909; review of Ezra Pound, *Exultations*, DC: 23 November 1909; see *LNB*, 116-123.

43 Review of Robert Frost, *North of Boston*, *Daily News*: 22 July, 1914; *LNB*, 126.

44 *FCPPP*, 677.

45 Review of Ezra Pound, *The Spirit of Romance*, MP: 1 August 1910; *LNB*, 121-3.

46 *MM*, 27-8.

47 Peter McDonald, *Sound Intentions: The Workings of Rhyme in Nineteenth-Century Poetry* (Oxford: Oxford University Press, 2012), 55.

48 See Note 2.

49 *MM*, 27.

50 *ETPW II*, 575-6.

51 Review of Eden Phillpotts, *Up Along, Down Along*, DC: 26 December 1905. He made similar comments on poetry collections by Israel Zangwill and Maurice Hewlett.

52 Keith Douglas, *Collected Poems* (London: Faber, 1966), 148; *LGB*, 245.

53 *FCPPP*, 665.

54 *JMW*, 94.

55 'The Frontiers of English Prose', *Literature*: 23 September 1899; *LNB*, 136-9.

56 *LGB*, 57.

57 Review of Mark H. Liddell, *An Introduction to the Scientific Study of English Poetry*, *Week's Survey*: 20 September 1902; *LNB*, 10-12.

58 Review of J. M. Synge, *The Playboy of the Western World*, B: August 1907; *LNB*, 143-4.

59 Review of *Poems in Prose from Charles Baudelaire*, tr. Arthur Symons, DC: 25 January 1906; *LNB*, 141-3.

60 Review of D. H. Lawrence, *Love Poems and Others*, DC: ?early 1913; *LNB*, 105-6.

61 Review of C. J. W. Farwell, *Poems* etc, DC: 2 July 1901.

62 *RFET*, 10.

63 Review of Robert Louis Stevenson, *The Letters*, ed, Sidney Colvin, *SR*: I July 1911.

64 *TSL*, 106.

65 Arthur Symons, 'The Decadent Movement in Literature', *Harper's New Monthly Magazine* 87 (November 1893), 858-67; Walter Pater, *The Renaissance*, ed. Donald L. Hill (Berkeley: University of California Press, 1980), 118.

66 Reviews of Robert Frost, *North of Boston*, *Daily News*: 12 July 1914; *New Weekly*: 8 August 1914; *LNB*, 125-30.

67 *EF*, 51.

68 'A Third-Class Carriage', Thomas, *The Last Sheaf* (London: Jonathan Cape, 1928), 49.

69 Review of William T. Palmer, *In Lakeland Dells and Fells*, DC: 26 November 1903.

70 *JMW*, 85.

71 *RJ*, 298.

72 *SC*, 168-9, 148.

73 Review of Robert Frost, *North of Boston*, *New Weekly*: 8 August 1914; *LNB*, 128-30.

74 Review of Robert Frost, *North of Boston*, ER: August 1914; *LNB*, 130-1.

75 Review of Laurence Binyon, *London Visions*, SR: 14 November 1908.

76 *RFET*, 39.

77 *TSL*, 106.

78 See Louis MacNeice, *Varieties of Parable* (London: Cambridge University Press, 1965).

Chapter 2:
Remixing the Romantics

1 Review of W. J. Courthope, *A History of English Poetry*, *DC*: 23 February 1910.

2 *DC*: 27 August 1901; *LNB*, 62.

3 Review of W. B. Yeats, *Collected Works*, *DC*: 5 March 1909; *LNB*, 86-7.

4 Jerome J. McGann, *The Romantic Ideology: A Critical Investigation* (Chicago and London: University of Chicago Press, 1983), 1.

5 Nicholas Roe, Introduction to Roe (ed.), *Romanticism* (Oxford: Oxford University Press, 2005), 10.

6 Gene W. Ruoff, *Wordsworth and Coleridge: The Making of the Major Lyrics, 1802–1804* (New Brunswick: Rutgers University Press, 1989), 3.

7 Michael Löwy and Robert Sayre, *Romanticism Against the Tide of Modernity* (Durham/ London: Duke University Press, 2001), 234; see Anne Janowitz, *Lyric and Labour in the Romantic Tradition* (Cambridge: Cambridge University Press, 1998).

8 McGann, *Romantic Ideology*, 13.

9 Richard Eldridge, *The Persistence of Romanticism* (Cambridge: Cambridge University Press, 2001), 11, 103.

10 Review of John Davidson, *The Triumph of Mammon*, *DC*: 30 April 1907; *LNB*, 78.

11 *Collected Letters of Samuel Taylor Coleridge*, ed. Earl Leslie Griggs (Oxford: Clarendon Press, 1956–1971), 2: 814.

12 Seamus Perry, 'Romanticism: The Brief History of a Concept', in Duncan Wu (ed.), *A Companion to Romanticism* (Oxford: Blackwell, 1998), 6.

13 Review of *Poetical Works of William Blake*, ed. Edwin J. Ellis, *MP*: 29 October, 1906; review of Arthur Symons, *The Fool of the World and Other Poems*, *DC*: 20 November 1906; review of AE, *The Divine Vision*, *Week's Survey*: 7 May 1904.

14 Review of William Watson, *New Poems*, *DC*: 22 October 1909.

15 *ETPW II*, 243.

16 Review of Stopford A. Brooke, *Studies in Poetry*, *MP*: 28 December 1907.

17 Reviews of W. J. Courthope, *A History of English Poetry*, Vol. 6, *DC*: 23 February 1910; *MP*: 28 February 1910.

18 *K*, 55-6.

19 Review of Irving Babbitt, *The New Laokoon*, *DC*: 5 October, 1910.

20 Review of Arthur Symons, *The Romantic Movement in English Poetry*, *MP*: 20 January 1910; *LNB*, 17-19.

21 Review of George Crabbe, *Poems*, ed. Adolphus William Ward, *DC*: 4 July 1906; review of Algernon Charles Swinburne, *A Channel Passage and Other Poems*, *World*: 6 September 1904.

22 Review of Lord Byron, *Poetical Works*, ed. E. H. Coleridge, *DC*: 13 February 1906.

23 Review of *William Blake*, Vol. 1, Illustrations on the Book of Job, *MP*: 17 December 1906.

24 *Collected Works of W. B. Yeats*, Vol. V, Later Essays (New York: Scribner, 1994), 121-2; *Collected Works*, Vol. IV: Early Essays (New York: Scribner, 2007), 51; Thomas, review of Francis Thompson, *Shelley*, *DC*: 5 April 1909.

25 Review of *Poetical Works of Percy Bysshe Shelley*, ed. Thomas Hutchinso 1, *DC*: 29 August 190; *LNB*, 23-4.

26 See *ETPW 1*, 165-8.

27 Review of John Keats, *The Poems*, ed. E. de Sélincourt, *DC*: 3 May 1905.

28 Review of *Confessions of Lord Byron*, ed. W. A. Lewis Bettany, *DC*: 18 July 1905.

29 Review of *Blake's Poetry* and *The Lyrical Poems of Blake*, ed. John Sampson, *DC*: 31 March 1906; review of *The Prophetic Books of William Blake: Jerusalem*, ed. E. R. D. Maclagan & A. G. B. Russell, *DC*: 11 January 1904; *LNB*, 20-1.

30 Review of Sir Alfred Lyall, *Tennyson*, *DC*: 7 October 1902; *LNB*, 35; *MM*, 28; review of W. H. Davies, *The Soul's Destroyer and Other Poems*, *DC*: 21 October 1905; *LNB*, 89.

31 Reviews of *North of Boston*, *New Weekly*: 8 August 1914; *ER*: August 1914; *LNB*, 128, 130.

32 Reviews of Percy Bysshe Shelley, *The Complete Poetical Works*, ed. Thomas Hutchinson, *DC*: 27 December 1904; Shelley, *Letters*, ed. Roger Ingpen, *MP*: 9 September 1909.

33 Reviews of Samuel Taylor Coleridge, *The Poems*, ed. Ernest Hartley Coleridge, *DC*: 26 March 1908; Coleridge, *The Complete Poetical Works*, ed. Ernest Hartley

Coleridge, *Orpheus* (April 1913), 46.

34 *K*, 57.

35 Review of Coleridge, *The Complete Poetical Works*, ed. Ernest Hartley Coleridge, *Orpheus* (April 1913), 48; *K*, 14; review of John Keats, *The Poems*, ed. E. de Sélincourt, *DC*: 3 May 1905.

36 Review of *The Prophetic Books of William Blake: Jerusalem*, ed. E. R. D. Maclagan & A. G. B. Russell, *DC*: 11 January 1904; *LNB*, 20.

37 M. H. Abrams, *Natural Supernaturalism: Tradition and Revolution in Romantic Literature* (London: Oxford University Press, 1971), 375.

38 Review of Arthur Symons, *William Blake*, *SR*: 19 October 1907; *RJ*, 44; Jefferies, *The Story of My Heart*, quoted *RJ*, 169.

39 *ETPW I*, 73, 67.

40 McGann, *Romantic Ideology*, 2.

41 See 'War Poetry', *Poetry and Drama* 2 (8 December 1914), 341-5; repr. *LNB*, 131-5.

42 Michael Kirkham, *The Imagination of Edward Thomas* (Cambridge: Cambridge University Press, 1986), 41-2.

43 Angela Leighton, *Shelley and the Sublime: An Interpretation of the Major Poems* (Cambridge: Cambridge University Press, 1984), 24.

44 *The Letters of John Keats*, Vol I, ed. Hyder Edward Rollins (Cambridge: Cambridge University Press, 1958), 387.

45 Review of Lord Byron, *Poetical Works*, ed. E. H. Coleridge, *DC*: 13 February 1906: Thomas reprints some of this review in *The South Country*; *RJ*, 189.

46 Keats, *Letters*, Vol. I, 193, 186.

47 Review of Ernest A. Baker and Francis E. Ross (eds), *The Voice of the Mountains*, *DC*: 3 November 1905.

48 Leighton, *Shelley and the Sublime*, 48-9.

49 E.g., 'The Other', 'Liberty', 'Beauty', 'Home' ('Not the end, but there's nothing more'), 'Over the Hills'.

50 Samuel Taylor Coleridge, *Biographia Literaria*, Chapter XIV.

51 Thomas, *The Heart of England* (London: J.M. Dent, 1906), 161; *K*, 39.

52 Review of T. F. Husband & M. F. A. Husband, *Punctuation*, *Academy*: 23 September 1905.

53 See Peter Simonsen, 'Reading

Wordsworth after McGann: Moments of Negativity in "Tintern Abbey" and the Immortality Ode', https://www.researchgate.net.

54 *RJ*, 298.

55 *SC*, 150-2.

56 See Edna Longley (ed.), *Edward Thomas: The Annotated Collected Poems* (Tarset: Bloodaxe Books, 2008), 172.

57 *TSL*, 51.

58 Review of *Poems of Anne, Countess of Winchilsea*, ed. Myra Reynolds, *DC*: 24 June 1902.

59 Review of George Bourne, *The Bettesworth Book*, *DC*: 25 November 1901; *LNB*, 181.

60 *K*, 57.

61 See John Burrow, 'Keats and Edward Thomas', *Essays in Criticism* 7, 4 (October 1957), 404-15.

62 *K*, 56, 53.

63 Thomas, Introduction to William Cobbett, *Rural Rides* (London: J.M. Dent, 1912), xi.

64 Coleridge, *Biographia Literaria*, Chapter XIV.

65 Anthony Berridge (ed.), *The Letters of Edward Thomas to Jesse Berridge* (London: Enitharmon, 1983), 36.

66 Peter McDonald, *Sound Intentions: The Workings of Rhyme in Nineteenth-Century Poetry* (Oxford: Oxford University Press, 2012), 160-1.

67 *FCPPP*, 31.

68 *K*, 41-2, 45.

69 *FCPPP*, 26.

70 See Abrams, *Natural Supernaturalism*, 255-324.

71 Berg Collection, New York Public Library.

72 *K*, 54-5.

73 Review of Robert Burton, *The Anatomy of Melancholy*, new edn, *DC*: 3 March 1906.

74 Jennifer Radden (ed.), *The Nature of Melancholy: From Aristotle to Kristeva* (New York: Oxford University Press, 2000), 1.

75 Emily Brady and Arto Harpaalo, 'Melancholy as an Aesthetic Emotion', *Contemporary Aesthetics* 1 (2003), 12.

76 Ibid., 30.

77 See Thomas Pfau, *Romantic Moods: Paranoia, Trauma and Melancholy, 1790–1848* (Baltimore: Johns Hopkins University

Press, 2005); Löwy & Sayre, *Romanticism*, 18-21.

78 Turgenev's novella, *The Diary of a Superfluous Man*, was published in 1850.

79 *ETPW* I, 39; review of *The Poems of Ernest Dowson*, *DC*: 26 May 1905; *LNB*, 60-1.

80 Pfau, *Romantic Moods*, 331.

81 Yeats, *Collected Works*, IV: *Early Essays*, 143.

82 *K*, 53-4.

83 See Note 75.

84 *K*, 50.

85 *K*, 51.

86 McDonald, *Sound Intentions*, 163.

87 Guy Cuthbertson, 'The Literary Geography in Edward Thomas's Work', unpublished thesis, Oxford University, 2004.

Chapter 3:
'The compact essential real truth': Thomas and Great War Poetry

1 Entry in field notebook dated 'from October-December 1914'; see R. George Thomas (ed.), *The Collected Poems of Edward Thomas* (Oxford: Clarendon Press, 1978), 406 (a slightly different transcription).

2 'War Poetry', *Poetry and Drama* 2, 8 (December 1914), 341-5; *LNB*, 131-5.

3 *The Poems of Wilfred Owen*, ed. Jon Stallworthy (London: The Hogarth Press, 1985), 192; John Bell (ed.), *Wilfred Owen: Selected Letters* (Oxford: Oxford University Press, 1985, 1998), 269, 273.

4 *The Letters of W. B. Yeats*, ed. Allan Wade (London: Rupert Hart-Davis, 1954), 922.

5 Quotations from: Charles Hamilton Sorley, 'A hundred thousand million mites we go'; Siegfried Sassoon, 'The Dug-Out'; Isaac Rosenberg, 'August 1914'; Wilfred Owen, 'Insensibility'; Edward Thomas, 'Digging'; Ivor Gurney, 'War Books'; W. B. Yeats, 'The Second Coming'.

6 William Cooke, *Edward Thomas: A Critical Biography* (London: Faber, 1970), 209.

7 Letter to Edward Garnett, 29 April 1917, *LRF* I, 552.

8 Santanu Das, 'Reframing First World War Poetry', in Das (ed.), *The Cambridge Companion to the Poetry of the First World War* (Cambridge: Cambridge University Press, 2013), 6-8.

9 Martin Stephen (ed.), *Poems of the First World War* (London: J. M. Dent, 1991, 1993), xiv.

10 Kenneth Baker, *The Faber Book of War Poetry* (London: Faber, 1996), 121.

11 Tim Kendall (ed.), *Poetry of the First World War* (Oxford: Oxford University Press, 2013), xxviii.

12 Section-headings in I. M. Parsons (ed.), *Men Who March Away: Poems of the First World War* (London: Chatto & Windus, 1965).

13 *Poems of Owen*, 167.

14 *LGB*, 253.

15 *SC*, 71; Diary, 29 September 1901, National Library of Wales; *ETPW* I, 130.

16 *Edward Thomas's Letters to Jesse Berridge*, ed. Anthony Berridge (London: Enitharmon, 1983), 74.

17 For 'England', see *ETPW* II, 526-38.

18 Andrew Webb, *Edward Thomas and World Literary Studies* (Cardiff: University of Wales Press, 2013), 169-71.

19 Review of John Cooke (ed.), *The Dublin Book of Irish Verse*, *MP*: 6 January 1910.

20 Rupert Brooke, *The Complete Poems* (London: Sidgwick & Jackson, 1932), 146-50.

21 *RFET*, 61.

22 See *JMW*, 291-4.

23 *ETPW* II, 576; see *JMW*, 82.

24 Ivor Gurney, *Collected Poems* (Manchester: Carcanet, 2004), 263, 3; Ivor Gurney, *War Letters*, ed. R. K. R. Thornton (Mid Northumberland Arts Group & Manchester: Carcanet, 1983), 130.

25 Ivor Gurney, *Severn and Somme and War's Embers*, ed. R. K. R. Thornton (Mid Northumberland Arts Group & Manchester: Carcanet, 1987), 49; Gurney: *War Letters*, 178.

26 Gurney, *Severn & Somme*, 51.

27 Gurney, *War Letters*, 137; *Collected Poems*, 39.

28 *Poems of Owen*, 162.

29 Thomas, review of Charles M. Doughty, *The Dawn in Britain*, V & VI, *DC*: 7 February 1907; review of Doughty, *The Cliffs*, *MP*: 22 July 1909; see *LNB*, 75-7; *LGB*, 118-19, 135; review of Doughty, *The Dawn in Britain* I & II, *DC*: 30 March 1906.

30 *This England: An Anthology from her Writers* (Oxford: Oxford University Press, 1915),

Note; review of Ernest Pertwee (ed.), *Lyra Britannica*, DC: 10 August 1906.

31 'Reprints and Anthologies', *Poetry and Drama* 2, 7 (September 1914), 300; 'Reprints and Anthologies', *Poetry and Drama* 2, 8 December 1914), 384.

32 Owen, *Letters*, 130.

33 Review of A. B. Paterson, *Rio Grande's Last Race, and Other Poems*, DC: 8 February 1904.

34 Review of Harold Begbie, *The Handy-Man, and Other Verses*, DC: 23 November 1900.

35 Review of R. C. Lehmann, *Crumbs of Pity and Other Verses*, DC: 19 June 1903.

36 See Dominic Hibberd and John Onions (eds), *The Winter of the World: Poems of the Great War* (London: Constable, 2007), 94, 98, 126.

37 Owen, *Letters*, 282.

38 Siegfried Sassoon, *War Poems* (London: Heinemann, 1919), 61; Sarah Cole, 'Siegfried Sassoon', in Das (ed.), *Cambridge Companion to the Poetry of the First World War*, 95; see entry for Sassoon in *Oxford Dictionary of National Biography* (Oxford: Oxford University Press, 2004).

39 Siegfried Sassoon, *Collected Poems 1908-1956* (London: Faber, 1961), 69, 124, 102.

40 Santanu Das, *Touch and Intimacy in First World War Literature* (Cambridge: Cambridge University Press, 2005), 155-6.

41 *Poems of Owen*, 117.

42 Sassoon was influenced by the pioneer reportage in Henri Barbusse's novel *Le Feu* (1916).

43 Jahan Ramazani, *Poetry and Its Others: News, Prayer, Song, and the Dialogue of Genres* (Chicago: University of Chicago Press, 2014), 7, 103.

44 Owen, *Letters*, 287.

45 Owen, *Letters*, 216; *Poems of Owen*, 162.

46 Ramazani, *Poetry and Its Others*, 90.

47 Owen, *Letters*, 304.

48 Jay Winter, *Sites of Memory, Sites of Mourning* (Cambridge: Cambridge University Press, 1995), 3.

49 Randall Stevenson, *Literature & the Great War* (Oxford: Oxford University Press, 2013), 182, 174, 177; Peter Howarth, 'Poetic Form and the First World War', in Das (ed.), *Cambridge Companion to the Poetry of the First World War*, 53.

50 Ibid.

51 Samuel Taylor Coleridge, *Poems* (London: Oxford University Press, 1912), 259.

52 *Poems of Owen*, 156.

53 *The Collected Works of Isaac Rosenberg*, ed. Ian Parsons (London: Chatto & Windus, 1979), 188; Gurney, *War Letters*, 196.

54 *Poems of Owen*, 93, 122.

55 Das (ed.), *Cambridge Companion to the Poetry of the First World War*, 8.

56 Thomas, review of *Georgian Poetry, 1911-1912*, DC: 14 January 1913; *LNB*, 112-13; Stephen, *Poems of the First World War*, 2; Kendall, *Poetry of the First World War*, xvii.

57 Gurney, *War Letters*, 160.

58 *Poems of Owen*, 125, 192; Gurney, *War Letters*, 34; *Collected Works of Rosenberg*, 237.

59 *Poems of Owen*, 135, 101.

60 Christopher Clark, *The Sleepwalkers: How Europe Went to War in 1914* (London: Penguin, 2012, 2013), 561.

61 *Collected Works of Rosenberg*, 110.

62 Winter, *Rites of Memory*, 221.

63 *RJ*, 298.

64 Owen, *Letters*, 276.

65 MacNeice, 'Broken Windows or Thinking Aloud', in Alan Heuser (ed.), *Selected Prose of Louis MacNeice* (Oxford: Oxford University Press, 1990), 142.

66 Robert Graves, *The Complete Poems in one volume* (Manchester: Carcanet, 2000), 414.

67 Kendall, *Poetry of the First World War*, 177.

68 Gurney, *Collected Poems*, 258.

69 *Poems of Owen*, 146, 117.

70 In Wiles Lectures series, 'Imagining War in the Twentieth Century and Beyond', Queen's University Belfast, 18-21 May 2016.

71 *Poems of Owen*, 133.

72 *Gurney: War Letters*, 234.

73 Gurney, *Collected Poems*, 197, 144, 140, 127.

74 Michael Hurd, *The Ordeal of Ivor Gurney* (Oxford: Oxford University Press, 1978), 53, 70.

75 *TSL*, 156; Gurney, *War Letters*, 75, 113-14.

76 Gurney, *Collected Poems*, 141, 203.

77 Graves, *Complete Poems*, 232.

78 Clark, *Sleepwalkers*, xxi; Jay Winter and Antoine Prost, *The Great War in History: Debates and Controversies, 1914 to the Present* (Cambridge: Cambridge University Press, 2005), 172, 187-8.

79 *SC*, 5.
80 Winter and Prost, *Great War in History*, 210.
81 'Insensibility', *Poems of Owen*, 123.
82 *Poems of Owen*, 149.
83 *K*, 72.
84 Ibid.

Chapter 4:
An Atlantic Chasm? Thomas and Frost again

1   Ricks's Anthony Hecht Lectures bear the title: *True Friendship: Geoffrey Hill, Anthony Hecht, and Robert Lowell Under the Sign of Eliot and Pound* (New Haven & London: Yale University Press, 2010).
2   *FCPPP*, 802-3.
3   Letter to John Freeman, 14 August 1914. See *Edward Thomas Fellowship Newsletter* 38 (January 1998), 7.
4   Helen Vendler, ed., *The Faber Book of Contemporary American Poetry* (Cambridge: Harvard University Press, 1985; London, Faber, 1986), 1.
5   Dana Gioia, *Barrier of a Common Language: An American Looks at Contemporary British Poetry* (Ann Arbor: University of Michigan Press, 2003), ix-x.
6   *FCPPP*, 665, 671, 677.
7   See Edna Longley, *Yeats and Modern Poetry* (Cambridge: Cambridge University Press, 2013), 93-101.
8   *RFET*, xxxiii-iv, xxxviii.
9   Dana Gioia, 'Frost and the Modern Narrative Poem', in Mark Richardson (ed.), *Robert Frost in Context* (Cambridge: Cambridge University Press, 2014), 72-84 (73).
10 Richardson, *Frost in Context*, xxi-ii.
11 Letter to Grace Walcott Conkling, 28 June 1921.
12 *FCPPP*, 103.
13 *RFET*, 86, 49; and see *JMW*, 290-1.
14 *RFET*, 62-3.
15 *RFET*, 63-4, 70.
16 *RFET*, 78; Tim Kendall, *The Art of Robert Frost* (New Haven and London: Yale University Press, 2012), 181-2.
17 David Orr, *The Road Not Taken: Finding America in the Poem Everyone Loves and Almost Everyone Gets Wrong* (New York: Penguin, 2015), 67, 159, 84.
18 Ibid., 12.

19 Ibid., 9.
20 *LRF I*, 552.
21 Ibid., 60.
22 *FCPPP*, 288.
23 Review of Edward Heath Crouch, *A Treasury of South African Poetry and Verse*, *MP*: 30 August 1909.
24 Reviews of Alice Marble, *Heralds of American Literature*, *MP*: 27 April 1908; Madison Cawein, *The Shadow Garden and Other Plays*, *MP*: 7 July 1910; Stewart Edward White, *The Forest*, *DC*: 2 February 1904.
25 Review of Stewart Edward White, *The Cabin*, *DC*: 28 August 1912.
26 Review of Edward Carpenter, *Days with Walt Whitman*, *DC*: 7 June 1906.
27 Also, Frost quarrelled with Helen Thomas because he disliked her memoirs, *As It Was* (1926) and *World Without End* (1931). He removed her name from the dedication to his *Selected Poems*.
28 E.g. *The Norton Anthology of Poetry*; *The Norton Anthology of Modern and Contemporary Poetry*.
29 'After moving his family to the country in 1913, Thomas began to write fiction'; '[He would see] none of [his poems] published', *LRF I*, 752.
30 *LRF I*, 552.
31 Quoted by Richard Poirier, in *Robert Frost: The Work of Knowing* (New York: Oxford University Press, 1977), 45.
32 *RFET*, 43.
33 Quoted, Richardson, *Frost in Context*, 126.
34 William Pritchard, 'Frost Biography and *A Witness Tree*', in Robert Faggen (ed.), *The Cambridge Companion to Robert Frost* (Cambridge: Cambridge University Press, 2001), 38.
35 Thomas, review of John Burroughs, *Literary Values and Other Papers*, *DC*: 14 July 1903, *LNB*, 7; *LRF I*, 240.
36 *FCPPP*, 341.
37 Frank Lentricchia, *Robert Frost* (Durham: Duke University Press, 1975), 119; Blanford Parker, 'Frost and the Meditative Lyric', in Faggen, *Companion to Frost*, 194; *FCPPP*, 777.
38 Orr, *Road Not Taken*, 95.
39 Kendall, *Art of Frost*, 381-2; *FCPPP*, 806.
40 *FCPPP*, 777-8.
41 *FCPPP*, 118, 212.

42 See *ETPW I*, 253.

43 Robert Faggen, *Robert Frost and the
    Challenge of Darwin* (Ann Arbor:
    University of Michigan Press, 1997), 1, 317.

44 *FCPPP*, 753-4.

45 *FCPPP*, 70, 208.

46 Faggen, *Frost and Darwin*, 317.

47 *FCPPP*, 275; Faggen, *Frost and Darwin*, 89.

48 *FCPPP*, 307; *SC*, 26.

49 *FCPPP*, 106.

50 *FCPPP*, 307, 210, 317; *ETPW II*, 244;
    Thomas, review of *Collected Works of W. B.
    Yeats*, *MP*: 17 December 1908, *LNB*, 85;
    SC, 144; *TSL*, 51.

51 *FCPPP*, 116.

52 *FCPPP*, 221.

53 *TSL*, 106; *RFET*, 124.

54 Review of Felix E, Schelling, *The English
    Lyric*: ?April 1913; Edward Thomas
    Collection, Cardiff University Library;
    review of *North of Boston*, *New Weekly*: 8
    August 1915; *LNB*, 128.

55 Review of John Masefield, *The Street of
    Today*, *SR*: 10 June 1911.

56 *FCPPP*, 66.

57 *RFET*, 43.

58 *FCPPP*, 48.

59 *FCPPP*, 269.

60 Jay Parini, *Robert Frost: A Life* (New York:
    Henry Holt, 1999), 286.

61 Poirier, *Frost*, x, 27, 10.

62 *FCPPP*, 39, 120, 116, 117.

63 *FCPPP*, 215.

64 Poirier, *Frost*, xi.

65 Guy Cuthbertson & Lucy Newlyn (eds),
    *Branch-Lines: Edward Thomas and
    Contemporary Poetry* (London: Enitharmon,
    2007), 202.

66 Quoted by Kendall, *Art of Frost*, 380.

67 *FCPPP*, 39.

68 *FCPPP*, 117, 341.

69 *FCPPP*, 224.

70 *LRF I*, 213.

71 *LRF I*, 552; and see Kendall, 'Robert Frost
    and the First World War', in Richardson,
    Robert Frost in Context, 190-7.

72 *LRF I*, 218; *RFET*, 72; *JMW*, 333.

73 *RFET*, 167.

74 *LRF I*, 334-5.

75 Ibid., 550, 494.

76 *FCPPP*, 240.

77 *FCPPP*, 125-7, 101.

78 *FCPPP*, 134.

79 *FCPPP*, 205.

80 Kendall, *Art of Frost*, 316.

81 See Parini, *Frost*, 200-2.

82 *FCPPP*, 206, 203.

83 *FCPPP*, 209.

84 See Parini, *Frost*, 224.

85 *FCPPP*, 207.

86 *LRF I*, 551.

Chapter 5:
Epistolary Psychotherapy:
The Letters and Lyrics of
Thomas and Larkin

1   *Collected Works of W. B. Yeats*, Vol. V: Later
    Essays (New York: Scribner, 1994), 204;
    Thomas, review of Felix E. Schelling, *The
    English Lyric*, ?April 1913, Edward Thomas
    Collection, Cardiff University Library.

2   See *RW*, 188-90.

3   *LCP*, 89, 152.

4   *RW*, 188.

5   *LCP*, 41.

6   *Sunday Times*, 17 October 2010; *Guardian*, 4
    August 2011.

7   *LCP*, 180, 170.

8   Jonathan Ellis, Introduction, in Ellis (ed.),
    *Letter Writing Among Poets from William
    Wordsworth to Elizabeth Bishop* (Edinburgh:
    Edinburgh University Press, 2015), 10.

9   *RW*, 84.

10 See Mutlu Konuk Blasing, *Lyric Poetry: The
    Pain and the Pleasure of Words* (Princeton
    and Oxford: Princeton University Press,
    2007), 1-13.

11 Donald Hall, *Essays After Eighty* (Boston,
    New York: Houghton, Mifflin, Harcourt,
    2015), 12.

12 Review of Schelling, *The English Lyric*, see
    note 1.

13 *EF*, 13.

14 *LGB*, 163.

15 *LCP*, 41.

16 W. B. Yeats, *Autobiographies* (London:
    Macmillan, 1955), 300.

17 *LM*, 368.

18 *LGB*, 84-5, 57.

19 Walter Pater, Conclusion to *The
    Renaissance*, ed. Donald L. Hill (Berkeley:
    University of California Press, 1980), 190.

20 Review of John Sampson (ed.), *The Lyrical
    Poems of Blake*, etc., *DC*: 31 March 1906.

21 Thomas, *Feminine Influence on the Poets* (London: Martin Secker, 1910), 91; *LNB*, 23.

22 *LSL*, 106; *LM*, 109.

23 Review of *The Correspondence of William Cowper*, ed. Thomas Wright, *DC*: 5 April 1904; review of C. M. Masterman, *Folia Dispersa*, etc. *DC*: 27 December 1902.

24 See William Waters, *Poetry's Touch: On Lyric Address* (Ithaca and London: Cornell University Press, 2003), 1-2, 5.

25 Thomas, *Walter Pater* (London: Martin Secker, 1913), 215; Thomas, *Feminine Influence*, 76; *LNB*, 22.

26 Review of John Ruskin, *Works* (Letters), ed. E. T. Cook & Alexander Wedderburn, *SR*: 6 March 1909; review of Percy Bysshe Shelley, *Letters to Elizabeth Hitchener*, ed. Bertram Dobell, *MP*: 30 March 1908.

27 *LGB*, 251; *LRF I*, 173.

28 *LGB*, 160.

29 Hugh Haughton, 'Just Letters: Corresponding Poets', in Ellis (ed.), *Letter Writing Among Poets*, 59.

30 Ibid., 13-14.

31 Bruce Redford, *The Converse of the Pen: Acts of Intimacy in the Eighteenth-Century Familiar Letter* (Chicago and London: Chicago University Press, 1986), 49, 91.

32 Review of *The Correspondence of William Cowper*, ed. Thomas Wright, *DC*: 5 April 1904; review of William Cowper, *The Poems*, ed. J.C. Bailey, *DC*: 21 March 1906.

33 Judy Kendall, ed., *Poet to Poet, Edward Thomas's Letters to Walter de la Mare* (Bridgend: Seren, 2012), 133.

34 *LGB*, 226, 218, 123.

35 *LGB*, 91.

36 *LM*, 154-5, 305-6.

37 *LCP*, 129.

38 *LM*, 306, 389.

39 *LM*, 63-4, 168, 162.

40 *LCP*, 69. *LSL*, xi; *LCP*, 209.

41 A. T. Tolley (ed.), *Philip Larkin: Early Poems and Juvenilia* (London: Faber, 2005), 58, 54, 134.

42 *LSL*, 165; *LCP*, 69; Tolley (ed.), *Early Poems and Juvenilia*, 74.

43 *LGB*, 221.

44 *LSL*, 52, 144, 19.

45 *LM*, 23, 58, 107.

46 *LCP*, 25.

47 *LGB*, 148, 129; *LSL*, 152, 159.

48 *LSL*, 159; *LM*, 107.

49 *EF*, 13.

50 *LGB*, 230.

51 *RFET*, 150.

52 *LSL*, 521; *LCP*, 216, 217; *LM*, 305.

53 *LM*, 41, 317; *LCP*, 69, 166, 215; *LM*, 365.

54 *LM*, 279.

55 *LGB*, 139; *JMW*, 85.

56 *Feminine Influence on the Poets*, 43.

57 *FCPPP*, 777.

58 Alan Heuser (ed.), *Selected Prose of Louis MacNeice* (Oxford: Oxford University Press, 1990), 138.

59 Thomas, *Walter Pater* (London: Martin Secker 1913), 219.

60 *K*, 15.

61 *LCP*, 42.

62 'The Wheel', *Collected Works of W. B. Yeats*, Vol. I: The Poems (New York: Scribner, 1997), 214.

63 *LCP*, 202.

64 *LSL*, 173.

Afterword: Archipelagic Thomas

1 Hughes used this phrase when unveiling the War Poets' memorial at Westminster Abbey in November 1985.

2 *TSL*, 16.

3 *SC*, 7.

4 *JMW*, 13.

5 *ETPW II*, xix, xx, xliv.

6 Andrew Webb, *Edward Thomas and World Literary Studies* (Cardiff: University of Wales Press, 2013), 3, 188, 24.

7 See Sally Roberts Jones, 'Edward Thomas and Wales', in Jonathan Barker (ed.), *The Art of Edward Thomas* (Bridgend: Poetry Wales Press, 1987), 79.

8 This was in 1913; *TSL*, 89.

9 Webb, *Edward Thomas*, 106-7.

10 See R. F. Foster, 'Marginal Men and Micks on the Make', in *Paddy & Mr Punch: Connections in Irish and English History* (London: Allen Lane, 1993), 281-305.

11 Letter to W. H. Hudson, 23 October 1910, quoted *ETPW I*, 207n.

12 *ETPW I*, 13.

13 See John Kerrigan, *Archipelagic English* (Oxford: Oxford University Press, 2008).

14 See *ETPW I*, 127-34.

15 Webb, *Edward Thomas*, 186.

16 *Letters from W. H. Hudson to Edward Garnett* (London: J.M. Dent, 1925), 134.

17 *ETPW II*, 98-100.

18 *LGB*, 151.

19 Review of Frank Frankfort Moore, *The Life of Oliver Goldsmith*, SR: 10 December 1910.

20 Louis MacNeice, *Collected Poems*, ed. Peter McDonald (London: Faber, 2007), 139.

21 Review of Magnus Maclean, *The Literature of the Celts*, DC: 21 October, 1903.

22 Review of Ezra Pound, *Personae*, DC: 7 June 1909; *LNB*, 117.

23 'To a Poet, who would have me Praise certain Bad Poets, Imitators of His and Mine', W. B. Yeats, *Collected Works*, Vol. I: The Poems, ed. Richard J. Finneran (New York: Scribner, 1997), 93.

24 Review of J. S. Smart, *James Macpherson: An Episode in Literature*, DC: 8 September 1905; review of Alfred Noyes, *The Loom of Years*, DC: 5 December 1902.

25 'Dim' occurs in 'The Signpost', 'Beauty' and 'House and Man'; 'drear' in 'Out in the dark'.

26 Review of F. H. Trench, *Deirdre Wed, and Other Poems*, MP: 11 June 1908; review of Alfred Perceval Graves, *The Irish Poems*, B: September 1908; review of Padraic Colum, *Wild Earth*, MP: 13 April 1908.

27 Review of Fiona Macleod, *Where the Forest Murmurs*, DC: 1 November 1906; review of Macleod, *The Dominion of Dreams*, MP: 24 June 1909.

28 Review of W. B. Yeats, *Plays for an Irish Theatre*, Vols II and III, *Week's Survey*: 18 June 1904; *LNB*, 80-1; review of *Collected Works of W. B. Yeats*, MP: 17 December 1908; *LNB*, 84-5; review of W. B. Yeats, *Poems, 1899-1905*, DC: 1 January 1907; *LNB*, 81-2.

29 Review of Alfred Perceval Graves, *Irish Literary and Musical Studies*, *Broad Sheet Ballads*, introduced by Padraic Colum, etc, *Saturday Westminster Gazette*: 21 March 1914; review of *Collected Works of W. B. Yeats*, DC: 5 March 1909; *LNB*, 85-7; review of Yeats, *Poems, 1899-1905*, DC: 1 January 1907; *LNB*,

81-2; review of W. B. Yeats, *Poems*, New Edition entirely Revised, *Poetry and Drama* 1, 1 (March 1913), 56.

30 *ETPW II*, 102; *ETPW I*, 213, 63.

31 *ETPW I*, 67, 121, 135, 81, 50, xxxviii-ix.

32 Quoted, ibid., 6.

33 *The Collected Works of W. B. Yeats*, Vol. IV: Early Essays, ed. George Bornstein & Richard J. Finneran (New York: Scribner, 2007), 130; Thomas, review of *The Collected Works of W. B. Yeats*, MP: 17 December 1908; *LNB*, 84-5.

34 *SC*, 11.

35 *ETPW II*, 134-7; *LGB*, 40.

36 *ETPW II*, 99.

37 Letter to Helen Thomas from Swansea, 10 October 1914, National Library of Wales.

38 *ETPW I*, 64.

39 See Joep Leerssen, *Remembrance and Imagination*: Patterns in the Historical and Literary Representation of Ireland in the Nineteenth Century (Cork: Cork University Press, 1996), 35-8, 67.

40 *SC*, 8-9.

41 Thomas, *In Pursuit of Spring* (London: Thomas Nelson, 1914), 39; review of Bertram C. A. Windle, *The Wessex of Thomas Hardy*, DC: 6 December 1901.

42 'County patriotism' occurs, for example in Thomas's review of W. H. Hudson, *Hampshire Days*, DC: 5 June 1903.

43 Review of D. H. Moutray Read, *Highways and Byways in Hampshire*, DC: 1 May 1908.

44 *MM*, 28.

45 *SC*, 152.

46 Seamus Heaney, *Death of a Naturalist* (London: Faber, 1966), 14.

47 Seamus Heaney, *Wintering Out* (London: Faber, 1972), 26.

48 Guy Cuthbertson & Lucy Newlyn (eds), *Branch-Lines: Edward Thomas and Contemporary Poetry* (London: Enitharmon, 2007), 134-6; Carol Ann Duffy (ed.), *1914: Poetry Remembers* (London: Faber, 1914), 94.

49 Michael Longley, *Collected Poems* (London: Cape, 2006), 103, 307.

INDEX

Liddell, Mark H.: *An Introduction to the Scientific Study of English Poetry*, 28, 39
'Lincolnshire Poacher, The' (folk song), 22, 56, 275
Lloyd George, David, 220
London, Jack, 188
Longley, Edna: *Yeats and Modern Poetry*, 11
Longley, Michael: 'Edward Thomas's Poem'; 'Edward Thomas's War Diary', 280
Löwy, Michael and Robert Sayre, 64, 110
lyric
    Blasing on, 231–2
    and clarification, 258–9
    and eclogue, 206
    ET's commitment to, 9, 16, 238
    ET's view of, 34–5, 61, 63, 202, 232, 237
    in Great War poetry, 153, 154–66
    in literary theory, 17–20
    and 'mood', 111
    as psychology, 229, 231–2, 260, 262

McDonald, Peter, 34, 104, 115–16
McGann, Jerome J.: *The Romantic Ideology*, 64–5, 74
McLaverty, Michael, 279–80
Macleod, Fiona *see* Sharp, William
MacNeice, Louis, 59, 154, 190, 258
    Autumn Journal, 20, 143, 268
Macpherson, James: *Ossian*, 267–8
Maeterlinck, Maurice
    ET writes on, 10, 12, 26, 31, 34–5, 278
    'Serres Chaudes' (poem), 31
Mansfield, Katherine, 248
Marble, Annie Russell: *Heralds of American Literature*, 187
Marsh, Sir Edward, 149
Masefield, John, 10, 203
    The Street of Today (novel), 19
melancholy, 107–20, 124, 176
memory
    in ET's poems, 34, 43–6, 85, 88, 95, 131, 164, 168, 205, 216, 224, 232
    and expectation, 91
    Frost and, 214
    and Great War, 38, 145, 147, 153
    historical and personal, 50, 91
    MacNeice and, 143
    Owen and, 144

and poetry, 152–3, 162
and romantic Wales, 271
and smell, 35, 48, 100
Wordsworth and, 88, 90
Meredith, George: *Modern Love*, 40
Mill, John Stuart, 240
Milton, John, 249
mindfulness, 259
modernism, 11, 145, 150, 179, 190, 195
modernity, 26–7
Monro, Harold, 121
moon
    in ET's poems, 14, 16
    as symbol for poetry, 14–15, 185–6
Moore, Thomas Sturge: *The Gazelles and Other Poems*, 28
Morning Post: ET writes for, 12
Motion, Andrew, 230
Murray, Les, 263
Murry, John Middleton, 248

Napoleonic Wars, 121, 147
Nation (journal), 36
natural magic, 272
Nature
    ET and, 199, 279
    Romantics and, 149
    Wordsworth on, 111
Neo-Romanticism, 65–6, 149
Nerval, Gérard de, 110
Newbolt, Henry, 135
Newlyn, Lucy, 264
Nietzsche, Friedrich, 78
Noakes, Vivien: *Alternative Book of First World War Poetry*, 125
Noyes, Alfred: *The Loom of Years*, 269

Orr, David: *The Road Not Taken*, 183–4, 194
O'Sullivan, Seumas, 269
Owen, Wilfred
    admires Yeats, 150
    believes revolutionising English poetry, 144
    letters, 142, 151
    and mental disturbance, 156
    posterity, 166
    reads ET's *Keats*, 149
    rhythms, 152
    as war poet, 121–3, 141–3, 166